TEST YOURSELF MCSE

Designing Windows 2000 Directory Services

(Exam 70-219)

MICROSOFT CERTIFIED SYSTEMS ENGINEER

TEST YOURSELF MCSE

Designing Windows® 2000 Directory Services

(Exam 70-219)

Syngress Media, Inc.

Osborne/McGraw-Hill

Berkeley New York St. Louis San Francisco Auckland Bogotá
Hamburg London Madrid Mexico City Milan Montreal New Delhi
Panama City Paris São Paulo Singapore Sydney Tokyo Toronto

Osborne/**McGraw-Hill**
2600 Tenth Street
Berkeley, California 94710
U.S.A.

For information on translations or book distributors outside the U.S.A., or to arrange bulk purchase discounts for sales promotions, premiums, or fund-raisers, please contact Osborne/**McGraw-Hill** at the above address.

Test Yourself MCSE Designing Windows 2000 Directory Services (Exam 70-219)

1234567890 DOC DOC 01987654321

ISBN 0-07-212929-8

KEY	SERIAL NUMBER
001	XY6MN3EM9F
002	23781YTD4N
003	CRNOPQZMPE
004	KONC9UFZQM
005	Q2BF6YUXI3

Publisher
Brandon A. Nordin

Vice President and Associate Publisher
Scott Rogers

Editorial Director
Gareth Hancock

Associate Acquisitions Editor
Timothy Green

Editorial Management
Syngress Media, Inc.

Project Editor
Maribeth A. Corona

Project Manager
Laurie Stewart

Acquisitions Coordinator
Jessica Wilson

Technical Editor
Paul Smith

Proofreaders
Andrea Fox,
Sachi Guzman,
Dann McDorman

Copy Editor
Julianna Smith

Computer Designer
Maureen Forys,
Happenstance Type-O-Rama

Illustrator
Jeff Wilson

Series Design
Maureen Forys,
Happenstance Type-O-Rama

Cover Design
Greg Scott

Cover Image
imagebank

This book was composed with QuarkXPress 4.11 on a Macintosh G4.

About Syngress Media

Syngress Media creates books and software for Information Technology professionals seeking skill enhancement and career advancement. Its products are designed to comply with vendor and industry standard course curricula and are optimized for certification exam preparation. Visit the Syngress Web site at www.syngress.com.

Author

Michael Cross (MCSE, MCPS, MCP+I, and CNA) is a Microsoft Certified System Engineer, Microsoft Certified Product Specialist, Microsoft Certified Professional + Internet, and a Certified Novell Administrator.

Michael is the Network Administrator, Internet Specialist, and a Programmer for the Niagara Regional Police Service. He is responsible for network security and administration, and programming applications, and he is Webmaster of their Web site at www.nrps.com. He has consulted and assisted in computer-related/Internet criminal cases, and is part of an Information Technology team that provides support to a user base of over 800 civilian and uniform users.

Michael also owns KnightWare, a company that provides consulting, programming, networking, Web page design, computer training, and various other services. He has served as an instructor for private colleges and technical schools in London, Ontario Canada. He has been a freelance writer for several years, and has been published over two dozen times in numerous books and anthologies. He currently resides in St. Catharines, Ontario Canada with his lovely fiancée Jennifer, and two slightly neurotic cats.

For Jennifer Carruthers who believed in me when no one else did, pushed me when I didn't want to go on, and carried me when I could go no further. This book would not have been possible without her.

Technical Editor

Paul Smith (MCSE, MCT, and PMP) is Program Manager for a major computer manufacturer in Austin, Texas. He manages large-scale implementations, specializing primarily in Microsoft operating systems and Microsoft BackOffice products. He has over ten years of program management and computer consulting experience. During his career, Paul has worked on many extensive and diverse projects, including client/server solutions, application development, training, Web development, and Windows NT and 2000 project rollout planning and implementations.

Paul lives with his wife Susan and their two dogs, Ernie and Kellie, in Austin, Texas, and can be reached at psmith99@cox-internet.com.

Technical Reviewer

James Truscott (MCSE, MCP+I, and Network+) is an instructor in the MCSE program at Eastfield College and the Dallas County Community College District. He is also Senior Instructor for the Cowell Corporation and, is teaching the Windows 2000 track for CLC Corporation in Dallas, Texas. He is also working with DigitalThink of California, developing online training courses for Windows 2000.

He is the Webmaster for Cowell Corporation in Richardson, Texas, and provides consulting services for several Dallas-based businesses. His passion for computers started back in the 1960s when he was a programmer for Bell Telephone. One of his current projects includes developing Web sites for his students.

ACKNOWLEDGMENTS

We would like to thank the following people:

- All the incredibly hard-working folks at Osborne/McGraw-Hill: Brandon Nordin, Scott Rogers, Gareth Hancock, Tim Green, and Jessica Wilson for their help in launching a great series and being solid team players.
- Monica Kilwine at Microsoft Corp., for being patient and diligent in answering all our questions.
- Laurie Stewart and Maureen Forys for their help in fine-tuning the project.

CONTENTS

This book's primary objective is to help you prepare for the MCSE Designing a Microsoft Windows 2000 Directory Services Infrastructure exam under the new Windows 2000 certification track. As the Microsoft program transitions from Windows NT 4.0, it will become increasingly important that current and aspiring IT professionals have multiple resources available to assist them in increasing their knowledge and building their skills.

At the time of publication, all the exam objectives have been posted on the Microsoft Web site and the beta exam process has been completed. Microsoft has announced its commitment to measuring real-world skills. This book is designed with that premise in mind; its authors have practical experience in the field, using the Windows 2000 operating systems in hands-on situations and have followed the development of the product since early beta versions.

In This Book

This book is organized in such a way as to serve as a review for the MCSE Designing a Microsoft Windows 2000 Directory Services Infrastructure exam for both experienced Windows NT professionals and newcomers to Microsoft networking technologies. Each chapter covers a major aspect of the exam, with an emphasis on the "why" as well as the "how to" of working with and supporting Windows 2000 as a network administrator or engineer.

In Every Chapter

We've created a set of chapter components that call your attention to important items, reinforce important points, and provide helpful exam-taking hints. Take a look at what you'll find in every chapter.

Test Yourself Objectives

Every chapter begins with a list of Test Yourself Objectives—what you need to know in order to pass the section on the exam dealing with the chapter topic. Each objective in this list will be discussed in the chapter and can be easily identified by the clear headings that give the name and corresponding number of the objective, so you'll always know an objective when you see it! Objectives are drilled down to the most important details—essentially what you need to know about the objectives and what to expect from the exam in relation to them. Should you find you need further review on any particular objective, you will find that the objective headings correspond to the chapters of Osborne/McGraw-Hill's *MCSE Designing a Windows 2000 Directory Study Guide*.

Exam Watch Notes

Exam Watch notes call attention to information about, and potential pitfalls in, the exam. These helpful hints are written by authors who have taken the exams and received their certification; who better to tell you what to worry about? They know what you're about to go through!

Practice Questions and Answers

In each chapter you will find detailed practice questions for the exam, followed by a Quick Answer Key where you can quickly check your answers. The In-Depth Answers section contains full explanations of both the correct and incorrect choices.

The Practice Exam

If you have had your fill of explanations, review questions, and answers, the time has come to test your knowledge. Turn toward the end of this book to the Practice Exam where you'll find a simulation exam. Lock yourself in your office or clear the kitchen table, set a timer, and jump in.

About the Web Site

Syngress Media and Osborne/McGraw-Hill invite you to download one free practice exam for the MCSE Designing a Microsoft Windows 2000 Directory Services Infrastructure exam. Please visit www.syngress.com or www.certificationpress.com for details.

MCSE CERTIFICATION

This book is designed to help you prepare for the MCSE Designing a Microsoft Windows 2000 Directory Services Infrastructure exam. This book was written to give you an opportunity to review all the important topics that are targeted for the exam.

The nature of the Information Technology industry is changing rapidly, and the requirements and specifications for certification can change just as quickly without notice. Table 1 shows you the different certification tracks you can take. Please note that they accurately reflect the requirements at the time of this book's publication. You should regularly visit Microsoft's Web site at http://www.microsoft.com/mcp/certstep/mcse.htm to get the most up to date information on the entire MCSE program.

TABLE 1	Core Exams
Windows 2000 Certification Track	**Track 1: Candidates Who Have *Not* Already Passed Windows NT 4.0 Exams**
	All four of the following core exams are required:
	Exam 70-210: Installing, Configuring, and Administering Microsoft Windows 2000 Professional
	Exam 70-215: Installing, Configuring, and Administering Microsoft Windows 2000 Server
	Exam 70-216: Implementing and Administering a Microsoft Windows 2000 Network Infrastructure
	Exam 70-217: Implementing and Administering a Microsoft Windows 2000 Directory Services Infrastructure

TABLE 1 (cont.) Windows 2000 Certification Track	**Track 2: Candidates Who Have Passed Three Windows NT 4.0 Exams (Exams 70-067, 70-068, and 70-073)**

Instead of the four core exams above, you may take the following:

> **Exam 70-240:** Microsoft Windows 2000 Accelerated Exam for MCPs Certified on Microsoft Windows NT 4.0.

> The accelerated exam will be available until December 31, 2001. It covers the core competencies of exams 70-210, 70-215, 70-216, and 70-217.

PLUS—All Candidates

One of the following core exams are required:

> *Exam 70-219:** Designing a Microsoft Windows 2000 Directory Services Infrastructure

> *Exam 70-220:** Designing Security for a Microsoft Windows 2000 Network

> *Exam 70-221:** Designing a Microsoft Windows 2000 Network Infrastructure

Two elective exams are required:

> **Any current MCSE electives** when the Windows 2000 exams listed above are released in their live versions. **Electives scheduled for retirement will not be considered current.** Selected third-party certifications that focus on interoperability will be accepted as an alternative to one elective exam.

> *Exam 70-219:** Designing a Microsoft Windows 2000 Directory Services Infrastructure

> *Exam 70-220:** Designing Security for a Microsoft Windows 2000 Network

> *Exam 70-221:** Designing a Microsoft Windows 2000 Network Infrastructure

> **Exam 70-222:** Upgrading from Microsoft Windows NT 4.0 to Microsoft Windows 2000

> * Note that some of the Windows 2000 core exams can be used as elective exams as well. An exam that is used to meet the design requirement cannot also count as an elective. Each exam can only be counted once in the Windows 2000 Certification.

Let's look at two scenarios in Table 1. The first applies to the person who has already taken the Windows NT 4.0 Server (70-067), Windows NT 4.0 Workstation (70-073), and Windows NT 4.0 Server in the Enterprise (70-068) exams. The second scenario covers the situation of the person who has not completed those Windows NT 4.0 exams and would like to concentrate ONLY on Windows 2000.

In the first scenario, you have the option of taking all four Windows 2000 core exams, or you can take the Windows 2000 Accelerated Exam for MCPs if you have already passed exams 70-067, 70-068, and 70-073. (Note that you must have passed those specific exams to qualify for the Accelerated Exam; if you have fulfilled your NT 4.0 MCSE requirements by passing the Windows 95 or Windows 98 exam as your client operating system option, and did not take the NT Workstation Exam, you don't qualify.)

After completing the core requirements, either by passing the four core exams or the one Accelerated exam, you must pass a "design" exam. The design exams include Designing a Microsoft Windows 2000 Directory Services Infrastructure (70-219), Designing Security for Microsoft Windows 2000 Network (70-220), and Designing a Microsoft Windows 2000 Network Infrastructure (70-221). One design exam is REQUIRED.

You also must pass two exams from the list of electives. However, you cannot use the design exam that you took as an elective. Each exam can only count once toward certification. This includes any of the MCSE electives that are current when the Windows 2000 exams are released. In summary, you would take a total of at least two more exams, the upgrade exam and the design exam. Any additional exams would be dependent on which electives the candidate may have already completed.

In the second scenario, if you have not completed, and do not plan to complete the Core Windows NT 4.0 exams, you must pass the four core Windows 2000 exams, one design exam, and two elective exams. Again, no exam can be counted twice. In this case, you must pass a total of seven exams to obtain the Windows 2000 MCSE certification.

HOW TO TAKE A MICROSOFT CERTIFICATION EXAM

If you have taken a Microsoft Certification exam before, we have some good news and some bad news. The good news is that the new testing formats will be a true measure of your ability and knowledge. Microsoft has "raised the bar" for its Windows 2000 certification exams. If you are an expert in the Windows 2000 operating system and can troubleshoot and engineer efficient, cost effective solutions using Windows 2000, you will have no difficulty with the new exams.

The bad news is that if you have used resources such as "brain-dumps," boot camps, or exam-specific practice tests as your only method of test preparation, you will undoubtedly fail your Windows 2000 exams. The new Windows 2000 MCSE exams will test your knowledge and your ability to apply that knowledge in more sophisticated and accurate ways than was expected for the MCSE exams for Windows NT 4.0.

In the Windows 2000 exams, Microsoft will use a variety of testing formats that include product simulations, adaptive testing, drag-and-drop matching, and possibly even "fill-in-the-blank" questions (also called "free response" questions). The test-taking process will measure the examinee's fundamental knowledge of the Windows 2000 operating system rather than the ability to memorize a few facts and then answer a few simple multiple-choice questions.

In addition, the "pool" of questions for each exam will significantly increase. The greater number of questions combined with the adaptive testing techniques will enhance the validity and security of the certification process.

We will begin by looking at the purpose, focus, and structure of Microsoft certification tests and examining the affect that these factors have on the kinds of questions you will face on your certification exams. We will define the structure of exam questions and investigate some common formats. Next, we will present a strategy for answering these questions. Finally, we will give some specific guidelines on what you should do on the day of your test.

Why Vendor Certification?

The Microsoft Certified Professional program, like the certification programs from Cisco, Novell, Oracle, and other software vendors, is maintained for the ultimate purpose of increasing the corporation's profits. A successful vendor certification program accomplishes this goal by helping to create a pool of experts in a company's software and by "branding" these experts so companies using the software can identify them.

We know that vendor certification has become increasingly popular in the last few years because it helps employers find qualified workers and because it helps software vendors like Microsoft sell their products. But why vendor certification rather than a more traditional approach like a college degree in computer science? A college education is a broadening and enriching experience, but a degree in computer science does not prepare students for most jobs in the IT industry.

A common truism in our business states, "If you are out of the IT industry for three years and want to return, you have to start over." The problem, of course, is *timeliness*; if a first-year student learns about a specific computer program, it probably will no longer be in wide use when he or she graduates. Although some colleges are trying to integrate Microsoft certification into their curriculum, the problem is not really a flaw in higher education, but a characteristic of the IT industry. Computer software is changing so rapidly that a four-year college just can't keep up.

A marked characteristic of the Microsoft certification program is an emphasis on performing specific job tasks rather than merely gathering knowledge. It may come as a shock, but most potential employers do not care how much you know about the theory of operating systems, networking, or database design. As one IT manager put it, "I don't really care what my employees know about the theory of our network. We don't need someone to sit at a desk and think about it. We need people who can actually do something to make it work better."

You should not think that this attitude is some kind of anti-intellectual revolt against "book learning." Knowledge is a necessary prerequisite, but it is not enough. More than one company has hired a computer science graduate as a network administrator, only to learn that the new employee has no idea how to add users, assign permissions, or perform the other day-to-day tasks necessary to maintain a network. This brings us to the second major characteristic of Microsoft certification that affects the questions you must be prepared to answer. In addition to timeliness, Microsoft certification is also job-task oriented.

The timeliness of Microsoft's certification program is obvious and is inherent in the fact that you will be tested on current versions of software in wide use today. The job-task orientation of Microsoft certification is almost as obvious, but testing real-world job skills using a computer-based test is not easy.

Computerized Testing

Considering the popularity of Microsoft certification, and the fact that certification candidates are spread around the world, the only practical way to administer tests for the certification program is through Sylvan Prometric or Vue testing centers, which operate internationally. Sylvan Prometric and Vue provide proctor testing services for Microsoft, Oracle, Novell, Lotus, and the A+ computer technician certification. Although the IT industry accounts for much of Sylvan's revenue, the company provides services for a number of other businesses and organizations, such as FAA pre-flight pilot tests. Historically, several hundred questions were developed for a new Microsoft certification exam. The Windows 2000 MCSE exam pool is expected to contain hundreds of new questions. Microsoft is aware that many new MCSE candidates have been able to access information on test questions via the Internet or other resources. The company is very concerned about maintaining the MCSE as a "premium" certification. The significant increase in the number of test questions, together with stronger enforcement of the NDA (Non-disclosure agreement) will ensure that a higher standard for certification is attained.

Microsoft treats the test-building process very seriously. Test questions are first reviewed by a number of subject matter experts for technical accuracy and then are presented in a beta test. Taking the beta test may require several hours, due to the large number of questions. After a few weeks, Microsoft Certification uses the statistical feedback from Sylvan to check the performance of the beta questions. The beta test group for the Windows 2000 certification series included MCTs, MCSEs, and members of Microsoft's rapid deployment partners groups. Because the exams will be normalized based on this population, you can be sure that the passing scores will be difficult to achieve without detailed product knowledge.

Questions are discarded if most test takers get them right (too easy) or wrong (too difficult), and a number of other statistical measures are taken of each question. Although the scope of our discussion precludes a rigorous treatment of question analysis, you should be aware that Microsoft and other vendors spend a great deal of time and effort making sure their exam questions are valid.

The questions that survive statistical analysis form the pool of questions for the final certification exam.

Test Structure

The questions in a Microsoft form test will not be equally weighted. From what we can tell at the present time, different questions are given a value based on the level of difficulty. You will get more credit for getting a difficult question correct than if you got an easy one correct. Because the questions are weighted differently, and because the exams will likely use the adapter method of testing, your score will not bear any relationship to how many questions you answered correctly.

Microsoft has implemented *adaptive* testing. When an adaptive test begins, the candidate is first given a level three question. If it is answered correctly, a question from the next higher level is presented, and an incorrect response results in a question from the next lower level. When 15 to 20 questions have been answered in this manner, the scoring algorithm is able to predict, with a high degree of statistical certainty, whether the candidate would pass or fail if all the questions in the form were answered. When the required degree of certainty is attained, the test ends and the candidate receives a pass/fail grade.

Adaptive testing has some definite advantages for everyone involved in the certification process. Adaptive tests allow Sylvan Prometric or Vue to deliver more tests with the same resources, as certification candidates often are in and out in 30 minutes or less. For candidates, the "fatigue factor" is reduced due to the shortened testing time. For Microsoft, adaptive testing means that fewer test questions are exposed to each candidate, and this can enhance the security, and therefore the overall validity, of certification tests.

One possible problem you may have with adaptive testing is that you are not allowed to mark and revisit questions. Since the adaptive algorithm is interactive, and all questions but the first are selected on the basis of your response to the previous question, it is not possible to skip a particular question or change an answer.

Question Types

Computerized test questions can be presented in a number of ways. Some of the possible formats are used on Microsoft certification exams and some are not.

True/False Questions

We are all familiar with True/False questions, but because of the inherent 50 percent chance of guessing the correct answer, you will not see questions of this type on Microsoft certification exams.

Multiple-Choice Questions

The majority of Microsoft certification questions are in the multiple-choice format, with either a single correct answer or multiple correct answers. One interesting variation on multiple-choice questions with multiple correct answers is whether or not the candidate is told how many answers are correct.

> **EXAMPLE:**
>
> Which two files can be altered to configure the MS-DOS environment? (Choose two.)
>
> or
>
> Which files can be altered to configure the MS-DOS environment? (Choose all that apply.)

You may see both variations on Microsoft certification exams, but the trend seems to be toward the first type, where candidates are told explicitly how many answers are correct. Questions of the "choose all that apply" variety are more difficult and can be merely confusing.

Graphical Questions

One or more graphical elements are sometimes used as exhibits to help present or clarify an exam question. These elements may take the form of a network diagram, pictures of networking components, or screen shots from the software on which you are being tested. It is often easier to present the concepts required for a complex performance-based scenario with a graphic than with words.

Test questions known as *hotspots* actually incorporate graphics as part of the answer. These questions ask the certification candidate to click on a location or graphical element to answer the question. For example, you might be shown the diagram of a network and asked to click on an appropriate location for a router. The answer is correct if the candidate clicks within the *hotspot* that defines the correct location.

Free Response Questions

Another kind of question you sometimes see on Microsoft certification exams requires a *free response* or type-in answer. An example of this type of question might present a TCP/IP network scenario and ask the candidate to calculate and enter the correct subnet mask in dotted decimal notation.

Simulation Questions

Simulation questions provide a method for Microsoft to test how familiar the test taker is with the actual product interface and the candidate's ability to quickly implement a task using the interface. These questions will present an actual Windows 2000 interface that you must work with to solve a problem or implement a solution. If you are familiar with the product, you will be able to answer these questions quickly, and they will be the easiest questions on the exam. However, if you are not accustomed to working with Windows 2000, these questions will be difficult for you to answer. This is why actual hands-on practice with Windows 2000 is so important!

Knowledge-Based and Performance-Based Questions

Microsoft Certification develops a blueprint for each Microsoft certification exam with input from subject matter experts. This blueprint defines the content areas and objectives for each test, and each test question is created to test a specific objective. The basic information from the examination blueprint can be found on Microsoft's Web site in the Exam Prep Guide for each test.

Psychometricians (psychologists who specialize in designing and analyzing tests) categorize test questions as knowledge-based or performance-based. As the names imply, knowledge-based questions are designed to test knowledge, while performance-based questions are designed to test performance.

Some objectives demand a knowledge-based question. For example, objectives that use verbs like *list* and *identify* tend to test only what you know, not what you can do.

EXAMPLE:

Objective: Identify the MS-DOS configuration files.

Which two files can be altered to configure the MS-DOS environment? (Choose two.)

A. COMMAND.COM

B. AUTOEXEC.BAT

C. IO.SYS

D. CONFIG.SYS

Correct answers: B, D

Other objectives use action verbs like *install*, *configure*, and *troubleshoot* to define job tasks. These objectives can often be tested with either a knowledge-based question or a performance-based question.

EXAMPLE:

Objective: Configure an MS-DOS installation appropriately using the PATH statement in AUTOEXEC.BAT.

Knowledge-based question:

What is the correct syntax to set a path to the D: directory in AUTOEXEC.BAT?

A. SET PATH EQUAL TO D:

B. PATH D:

C. SETPATH D:

D. D:EQUALS PATH

Correct answer: B

Performance-based question:

Your company uses several DOS accounting applications that access a group of common utility programs. What is the best strategy for configuring the computers in the accounting department so that the accounting applications will always be able to access the utility programs?

A. Store all the utilities on a single floppy disk and make a copy of the disk for each computer in the accounting department.

B. Copy all the utilities to a directory on the C drive of each computer in the accounting department and add a PATH statement pointing to this directory in the AUTOEXEC.BAT files.

C. Copy all the utilities to all application directories on each computer in the accounting department.

D. Place all the utilities in the C directory on each computer, because the C directory is automatically included in the PATH statement when AUTOEXEC.BAT is executed.

Correct answer: B

Even in this simple example, the superiority of the performance-based question is obvious. Whereas the knowledge-based question asks for a single fact, the performance-based question presents a real-life situation and requires that you make a decision based on this scenario. Thus, performance-based questions give more bang (validity) for the test author's buck (individual question).

Testing Job Performance

We have said that Microsoft certification focuses on timeliness and the ability to perform job tasks. We have also introduced the concept of performance-based questions, but even performance-based multiple-choice questions do not really measure performance. Another strategy is needed to test job skills.

Given unlimited resources, it is not difficult to test job skills. In an ideal world, Microsoft would fly MCP candidates to Redmond, place them in a controlled environment with a team of experts, and ask them to plan, install, maintain, and troubleshoot a Windows network. In a few days at most, the experts could reach a valid decision as to whether each candidate should or should not be granted MCDBA or MCSE status. Needless to say, this is not likely to happen.

Closer to reality, another way to test performance is by using the actual software and creating a testing program to present tasks and automatically grade a candidate's performance when the tasks are completed. This *cooperative* approach would be practical in some testing situations, but the same test that is presented to MCP candidates in Boston must also be available in Bahrain and Botswana. The most workable solution for measuring performance in today's testing environment is a *simulation* program. When the program is launched during a test, the candidate sees a simulation of the actual software that looks, and behaves, just like the real thing. When the testing software presents a task, the simulation program is launched and the candidate performs the required task. The testing software then grades the candidate's performance on the required task and moves to the next question. Microsoft has introduced simulation questions on the certification exam for Internet Information Server 4.0. Simulation questions provide many advantages over other testing methodologies, and simulations are expected to become increasingly important in the Microsoft certification program. For example, studies have shown that there is a very high correlation between the ability to perform simulated tasks on a computer-based test and the ability to perform the actual job tasks. Thus, simulations enhance the validity of the certification process.

Another truly wonderful benefit of simulations is in the area of test security. It is just not possible to cheat on a simulation question. In fact, you will be told exactly what tasks you are expected to perform on the test. How can a certification candidate cheat? By learning to perform the tasks? What a concept!

Study Strategies

There are appropriate ways to study for the different types of questions you will see on a Microsoft certification exam.

Knowledge-Based Questions

Knowledge-based questions require that you memorize facts. There are hundreds of facts inherent in every content area of every Microsoft certification exam. There are several keys to memorizing facts:

Repetition   The more times your brain is exposed to a fact, the more likely you are to remember it.

Association   Connecting facts within a logical framework makes them easier to remember.

Motor Association   It is often easier to remember something if you write it down or perform some other physical act, like clicking on a practice test answer.

We have said that the emphasis of Microsoft certification is job performance and that there are very few knowledge-based questions on Microsoft certification exams. Why should you waste a lot of time learning filenames, IP address formulas, and other minutiae? Read on.

Performance-Based Questions

Most of the questions you will face on a Microsoft certification exam are performance-based scenario questions. We have discussed the superiority of these questions over simple knowledge-based questions, but you should remember that the job-task orientation of Microsoft certification extends the knowledge you need to pass the exams; it does not replace this knowledge. Therefore, the first step in preparing for scenario questions is to absorb as many facts relating to the exam content areas as you can. In other words, go back to the previous section and follow the steps to prepare for an exam composed of knowledge-based questions.

The second step is to familiarize yourself with the format of the questions you are likely to see on the exam. You can do this by answering the questions in this book, or by using Microsoft assessment tests. The day of your test is not the time to be surprised by the construction of Microsoft exam questions.

At best, performance-based scenario questions really do test certification candidates at a higher cognitive level than knowledge-based questions. At worst, these questions can test your reading comprehension and test-taking ability rather than your ability to use Microsoft products. Be sure to get in the habit of reading the question carefully to determine what is being asked.

The third step in preparing for Microsoft scenario questions is to adopt the following attitude: Multiple-choice questions aren't really performance-based. It is all a cruel lie.

These scenario questions are just knowledge-based questions with a story wrapped around them.

To answer a scenario question, you have to sift through the story to the underlying facts of the situation and apply your knowledge to determine the correct answer. This may sound silly at first, but the process we go through in solving real-life problems is quite similar. The key concept is that every scenario question (and every real-life problem) has a fact at its center, and if we can identify that fact, we can answer the question.

Simulations

Simulation questions really do measure your ability to perform job tasks. You must be able to perform the specified tasks. One of the ways to prepare for simulation questions is to get experience with the actual software. If you have the resources, this is a great way to prepare for simulation questions.

SIGNING UP

Signing up to take a Microsoft certification exam is easy. Sylvan Prometric or Vue operators in each country can schedule tests at any testing center. There are, however, a few things you should know:

- If you call Sylvan Prometric or Vue during a busy time, get a cup of coffee first because you may be in for a long wait. The exam providers do an excellent job, but everyone in the world seems to want to sign up for a test on Monday morning.

- You will need your social security number or some other unique identifier to sign up for a test, so have it at hand.

- Pay for your test by credit card if at all possible. This makes things easier, and you can even schedule tests for the same day you call, if space is available at your local testing center.

- Know the number and title of the test you want to take before you call. This is not essential, and the Sylvan operators will help you if they can. Having this information in advance, however, speeds up and improves the accuracy of the registration process.

TAKING THE TEST

Teachers have always told you not to try to cram for exams because it does no good. If you are faced with a knowledge-based test requiring only that you regurgitate facts, cramming can mean the difference between passing and failing. This is not the case, however, with Microsoft certification exams. If you don't know it the night before, don't bother to stay up and cram.

Instead, create a schedule and stick to it. Plan your study time carefully, and do not schedule your test until you think you are ready to succeed. Follow these guidelines on the day of your exam:

- Get a good night's sleep. The scenario questions you will face on a Microsoft certification exam require a clear head.

- Remember to take two forms of identification—at least one with a picture. A driver's license with your picture and social security or credit card is acceptable.

- Leave home in time to arrive at your testing center a few minutes early. It is not a good idea to feel rushed as you begin your exam.

- Do not spend too much time on any one question. You cannot mark and revisit questions on an adaptive test, so you must do your best on each question as you go.

- If you do not know the answer to a question, try to eliminate the obviously wrong answers and guess from the rest. If you can eliminate two out of four options, you have a 50 percent chance of guessing the correct answer.

- For scenario questions, follow the steps we outlined earlier. Read the question carefully and try to identify the facts at the center of the story.

Finally, we would advise anyone attempting to earn Microsoft MCDBA and MCSE certification to adopt a philosophical attitude. The Windows 2000 MCSE will be the most difficult MCSE ever to be offered. The questions will be at a higher cognitive level than seen on all previous MCSE exams. Therefore, even if you are the kind of person who never fails a test, you are likely to fail at least one Windows 2000 certification test somewhere along the way. Do not get discouraged. Microsoft wants to ensure the value of your certification. Moreover, it will attempt to so by keeping the standard as high as possible. If Microsoft certification were easy to obtain, more people would have it, and it would not be so respected and so valuable to your future in the IT industry.

MICROSOFT CERTIFIED SYSTEMS ENGINEER

1

Analyzing the Existing Business and IT

B efore you can decide how to design Windows 2000 Active Directory Services, you need to identify characteristics of the business. Active Directory (AD) supports domain and site structures, as well as organizational units (OUs) that map closely to business models. Because of this, an Active Directory implementation requires that you look at the business, entities that make up that business, and current business practices. The AD implementation also presents an opportunity to restructure business practices, as well as organizational and IT structures.

In addition to providing summary information on analyzing existing business models, this chapter will also look at the need to identify a company's tolerance for risk, cost of operations, and relevant laws and regulations that will impact the business. Risk is the possibility of suffering loss, while risk management is a process involving continuous assessment of potential risks, as well as a series of decisions to define and implement strategies to counter those risks. Cost of operations determines how much is spent on a project, and is used to calculate the return on investment. Finally, identifying relevant laws and regulations is important to ensure the project doesn't expose the business to criminal or civil litigation. These topics are important elements of analysis because they can affect the success of a project.

TEST YOURSELF OBJECTIVE 1.01

Analyzing the Existing Business Models

When analyzing existing business models, it is important to analyze both IT management and business management. In terms of Active Directory, a business model can be divided into two basic components—the part that implements, maintains, and supports it, and the part that uses it and depends on it. Each of these areas will impact the design of your Active Directory.

Before you begin to plan for a company's Active Directory design, you should gather as much information as possible about organizational and geographical structure, and the way information flows through the company. You should also gather information on IT structure (how sites are connected, technical information, and so on), and the business's relationships with suppliers, customers, partnerships, and so forth. These will play a significant role in the composition of your Active Directory.

When preparing to analyze the existing business models, it is important to remember the following points:

- Most business models will either be hierarchical, with a pyramidal command structure cascading from the point at the top down to the base, or a flat structure where different branches enjoy a high degree of autonomy. Project-based companies often utilize both models, with the project staff having two reporting structures.

- Take any existing Windows NT domain models into account when examining a business structure, but don't be unduly influenced by them. Remember that limitations in the Windows NT domain model may have forced structural decisions on the company.

- Keep it simple when planning the Active Directory structure around the business model. If you can accommodate the organizational structure by OUs rather than domains, then do it. It will be easier to administer in the future.

- Examine the IT infrastructure and the business organization separately. Remember that apparently independent branches and sites might need to be brought under central control, and you may have to design both the Active Directory and the network around that business requirement.

exam
Ⓦatch

It is important to remember that Microsoft stresses simplicity as the key element in domain and OU design. A good design will affect the ease of administering your Windows 2000 network, as well as its performance. Remember that an OU hierarchy within a single domain structure is easier to build and administer than a multiple domain structure. Generally, a single domain is the preferred structure, and should be the choice in organizations where users often move (geographically or organizationally) between areas of the business. It is much easier to move an object (such as a user account) between OUs in Active Directory than it is to move it between domains, but you'll need to remember that Active Directory performance degrades with every nested layer. Because of this, you should try to limit OU layers wherever you can. If you find it difficult to accommodate all the existing OUs in one single domain, you may find that an existing structure will work better if you create two domains, each with a simpler OU hierarchy.

QUESTIONS

1.01: Analyzing the Existing Business Models

1. A local computer college has hired you to design their Windows 2000 Active Directory network. When analyzing their requirements, you sit down with school faculty to create an organizational chart, which will be used for your Active Directory design. The chart you create is shown in the following illustration:

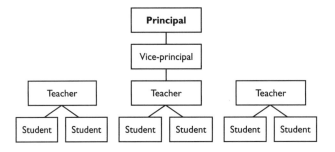

   What type of business model is shown in the organizational chart?

   A. Hierarchical

   B. Flat

   C. Neither

   D. Both

2. You are gathering information used for analyzing business models. You decide to look at how much data is shared between sites, how sites are connected, and whether each site currently has its own servers in place. What type of structure are you analyzing?

   A. Geographic structure

   B. Organizational structure

C. IT structure

D. Information flow

3. **Current Situation:** Asimov Robotics and Housekeeping has hired you to design their new network and Windows 2000 Active Directory. This company consists of a head office, with several smaller branch offices located in several cities. It takes on projects for other companies and creates solutions for them. Because of this, employees of the company commonly move from one project to another and from one corporate office to another. Currently, there are multiple Windows NT domains, but administrators have complained of difficulties managing these domains.

   Required Result: Active Directory needs to reflect the structure of the business, but also needs to make administration as easy as possible.

   Optional Desired Results:

   1. Change the domain structure so that the current problems arising from the old Windows NT design are resolved.

   2. IT management should have a centralized structure to avoid conflicting policies on security, user rights, and other access issues.

   Proposed Solution: Design the Active Directory to use organizational units rather than multiple domains. Have network administrators located at each site to reduce the responsibilities of the IT staff at the head office.

   What results are produced from the proposed solution?

   A. The proposed solution produces the required result only.

   B. The proposed solution produces the required result and only one of the optional results.

   C. The proposed solution produces the required result and both of the optional results.

   D. The proposed solution does not produce the required result.

   Questions 4–6   The next three questions are based upon the scenario that follows. Read the following case study, and then answer the questions. You may refer to this scenario as often as needed.

   You are designing a Windows 2000 Active Directory for WidgetSoft Sprockets and Gadgets, a company that creates and sells computer games. This company has offices in Atlanta, Detroit, and Toronto. The Atlanta office has 60 people in top management and finance, including the owners of the company. However, each of the offices has its own management, and is largely autonomous. The Detroit office has a staff of 75 people who are skilled in programming and computer graphics. The Toronto office focuses on merchandising, and employs 90 people with expertise in advertising, graphic design, sales, marketing, and other related skills.

The IT staff in Atlanta has a Windows NT 4.0 network in place. Each city has its own domain in place, and the domains trust one another. In discussing this structure with IT staff and management, the IT Manager states he likes the current design of the network, and doesn't want to see his previous work altered. Business management in Atlanta would like to see their ownership role in the company reflected in the Active Directory design.

4. Which course will you follow in designing the Windows 2000 Active Directory for this company?

A. Disregard IT management, and design the Active Directory to reflect the wishes of Atlanta's business management. This will reflect their view of the organizational structure. Create child organizational units beneath the parent organizational unit of Atlanta's business management.

B. Disregard business management, and design the Active Directory so that it matches the current Windows NT structure.

C. Disregard business and IT management, and create the Active Directory the way you want it to be.

D. Consider business and IT management perspectives, and take any existing Windows NT domain models into account, but don't be unduly influenced by the models.

5. What type of business model does this company have? (Choose all that apply.)

A. Flat

B. Hierarchical

C. Decentralized

D. Centralized

6. Which of the following is the best model to create under the root domain of widgetsoft.net?

    A. Create child domains for each role the office plays in the organization. Have one child domain called main.widgetsoft.net, another called programming.widgetsoft.net, and another called graphics.widgetsoft.net.

    B. Create a single layer of OUs. Each office will have its own organizational unit so they are visible to one another, and ignore geographic structure.

    C. Create child domains for each city. Child domains would consist of atlanta.widgetsoft.net, detroit.widgetsoft.net, and toronto.widgetsoft.net. Within these domains, create additional child domains for each department

    D. Three organizational units named after the three cities, each containing other organizational units named for the departments within that city's office.

TEST YOURSELF OBJECTIVE 1.02

Identifying Tolerance for Risk

Risk isn't necessarily a problem that will harm the success of your project. Risk is the possibility of suffering loss, and managing risks is a trade-off between how much damage a problem will cause and how much you are willing to write off in order to guard against it. Risk to an Active Directory program can take two forms: risk to the implementation project or its schedule, and risk to its efficient running after implementation. As you can see, identifying and managing risks needs to be an ongoing process, and needs to be absorbed as part of your project plan.

When assessing a company's tolerance for risk and devising ways to deal with it, you should remember the following points:

The five steps in Microsoft's risk management process are as follows:

- Risk identification
- Risk analysis
- Risk action planning
- Risk tracking
- Risk control

The steps in identifying and evaluating a risk are as follows:

- Risk source

- Risk condition

- Possible consequence(s)

- Possible effect on implementation

- Risk probability refers to the probability that the risk will actually take place. Risk impact evaluates the effect that it will have on your implementation if it does happen. Risk exposure is calculated by balancing the probability of a risk becoming reality against the potential problems it will cause.

- A high probability of a low-problem risk and a low probability of a high-problem risk might both be a low risk exposure.

exam
Watch

Remember that risk is the probability of suffering some sort of loss, and is inherent to any project. Microsoft stresses that the management of risks should be proactive rather than reactive. To put it simply, you should prepare for risks before they happen, rather than dealing with them as they occur. Proactive risk management addresses risks before they result in loss. It involves formulating a plan to deal with risks before the project begins, and requires knowledge of all aspects of the implementation beforehand. Reactive risk management is used when, or waits until, the risk becomes an actual problem. When reactive risk management is used, the consequences or risks are dealt with as they occur.

QUESTIONS

1.02: Identifying Tolerance for Risk

7. The following graphic depicts a step in Microsoft's risk management process. Which step does this graphic illustrate?

A. Risk analysis

   B. Risk tracking

   C. Risk identification

   D. Risk control

8. You are designing the Active Directory of a Windows 2000 network for a manufacturing company. You have identified a risk to your project: the possibility that employees of this company may go on strike. You begin to analyze this risk, and determine that the consequences of the risk becoming real will have a financial impact and affect your project's schedule. Which of the following types of analysis have you done here?

   A. Risk probability

   B. Risk exposure

   C. Risk impact

   D. Risk condition

9. You are evaluating risks involved in upgrading a Windows NT environment to Windows 2000. A member of your team is concerned about a risk that has a risk probability of 100 percent. What does this mean?

   A. There is no risk or likelihood that the risk will occur.

   B. The risk has already become an actual problem.

   C. The success of the project is ensured.

   D. The failure of the project is ensured.

10. **Current Situation:** Positronic Robotics and Automotive is a manufacturing company that has hired you to design their Windows 2000 Active Directory. The employees' union of this company has been asking for better health insurance in the worker contract they are negotiating. You have researched the risk of a strike for your Risk Action Plan, and calculated a risk probability of 25 percent and a risk impact of four weeks.

Required Result: Deal with risks that have been researched for the Risk Action Plan.

Optional Desired Results:

   1. Calculate the risk exposure of a possible strike.

   2. Implement a method of tracking the risk.

Proposed Solution: After researching the risk for your Risk Action Plan, you choose to ignore the risk. You calculate the risk exposure to be one week, and assign the task of monitoring the negotiations of the union and company to a member of your team.

What results are produced from the proposed solution?

A.   The proposed solution produces the required result only.

B.   The proposed solution produces the required result and only one of the optional results.

C.   The proposed solution produces the required result and both of the optional results.

D.   The proposed solution does not produce the required result.

TEST YOURSELF OBJECTIVE 1.03

Identifying Cost of Operations

Implementing Windows 2000 Active Directory will always incur costs, and determining these costs is an important part of the design process. A TCO (total cost of ownership) analysis provides you with the actual amount spent in IT in terms of quantifiable objects, such as per user per year, or per desktop PC per year. Only by establishing TCO will you be able to predict return on investment (ROI) figures with any degree of accuracy, which is just what you will need to do in order to secure executive sponsorship.

The TCO model created by Microsoft and Interpose identifies seven categories of costs. Five of these are considered direct IT costs, while the other two are indirect costs. Direct cost areas include hardware and software, management costs, development costs, support costs, and communication costs. Indirect costs include end-user costs and downtime. Hardware and software costs include capital and lease costs and depreciation on new installations and upgrades. Management costs include network and system support, outsourcing, cost of management tasks, and management salaries. Development costs include application development, testing, and documentation. Support costs include maintenance and support contracts, training help desk staff, and travel expenses. Communication costs include leased lines and access charges. End-user costs include costs arising from unofficial self-support and peer-support efforts, as well as unnecessary workstation and desktop modification, while downtime costs include lost productivity and revenue.

There are many ways to reduce cost of operations. Assigning or publishing applications and upgrades can reduce the cost of software distribution. You can also implement standardization by using a single desktop operating system throughout your organization and restricting users from making changes on their desktops. This will reduce support calls to the help desk and reduce unbudgeted costs, reduce the range of potential problems, and allow help desk staff to focus their expertise and knowledge on fewer areas.

When identifying the total cost of operations, it is important to remember the following points:

- ■ Downtime costs depend on availability requirements; for example, a mission-critical server or application will incur costs almost immediately after going down.

- ■ TCO models show that indirect costs could add up to 50 percent of a corporate IT budget.

- ■ The Microsoft TCO model applies *only* to the client/server environment.

- ■ Group Policy can significantly reduce the cost of software distribution by assigning or publishing applications and upgrades.

exam
Ⓦatch

The cost of software distribution can be reduced by assigning or publishing applications and upgrades. While publishing an application and assigning it may appear to be the same, there are significant differences. Applications can also be published through Active Directory services. This method should be used if only a selection of users will need the application, and you want them to have the ability to uninstall. A published application will appear in the list of installable programs in the Add/Remove Programs applet in Control Panel. Through this applet, users can install and uninstall published applications. If you don't want users to be able to install or uninstall applications, Group Policy can be used to assign software. This allows the system to install or upgrade applications automatically. The application can install when the client connects, or if the application is to be run from an application server, by installing a connection to the application that cannot be deleted.

QUESTIONS

1.03: Identifying Cost of Operations

11. You are evaluating costs and assets related to your project of upgrading a Windows NT environment to Windows 2000. Which of the following is a metric used in creating a baseline?

    A. The true cost of each asset in an organization

    B. An industry average

    C. A comparison of industry averages to the cost of an asset in an organization

    D. The cost of the same asset in another single organization in the same industry as yours

12. You are determining TCO, and have been given a list of items that are budgeted costs. These will go into calculating the TCO. You know that it is also important to include unbudgeted costs. Which of the following are unbudgeted costs that must be included when calculating the TCO? (Choose all that apply.)

    A. Hardware costs

    B. Management costs

    C. Downtime costs

    D. End-user costs

13. As illustrated in the following graphic, the company for which you are designing a Windows 2000 Active Directory network is based in three cities. Servers and workstations at each of the cities, except San Diego, are currently running Windows NT 4.0. San Diego is running Windows 2000 Servers and Windows 2000 Professional workstations. Currently, each of the city's offices is on a separate network. The company would like these three cities connected with a WAN line, with a contingency plan for when this private network WAN is down. Which of the following would be costs associated with the

project, and which you would include in your calculations of TCO for this
network? (Choose all that apply.)

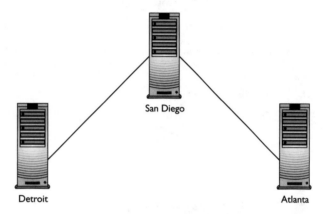

A. Cost of the WAN lines connecting the three cities

B. Cost of dial-up connections to connect these cities

C. Hardware and software costs

D. Baseline metrics

14. **Current Situation:** You are attempting to find ways to reduce the cost of
operations. At present, users of the network have computers running
Windows NT Workstation 4.0, Windows 2000 Professional, or Linux. In
identifying costs, you find that members of the IT staff are spending a
significant amount of time on help-desk duties or training. Often, users are
causing problems for themselves when they make changes to their computers.
You also find that when new software needs to be installed for certain groups to
use, a member of the IT staff must go around to each computer and install it.

Required Result: Reduce the cost of help-desk support and training in the
organization.

Optional Desired Results:

1. Reduce the cost of software distribution.

2. Prevent users from uninstalling applications deemed necessary for them to
use, or making changes to their desktop environment.

Proposed Solution: Publish applications through Active Directory. Restrict users from making changes on their desktops. Implement standardization by using a single desktop operating system throughout your organization.

What results are produced from the proposed solution?

A. The proposed solution produces the required result only.

B. The proposed solution produces the required result and only one of the optional results.

C. The proposed solution produces the required result and both of the optional results.

D. The proposed solution does not produce the required result.

TEST YOURSELF OBJECTIVE 1.04

Identifying Relevant Laws and Regulations

Identifying relevant laws and regulations is an important, albeit difficult, part of design. What may be legal in one state, province, or country may be illegal in another. A good example of this, and one that you will come across in international enterprises, is encryption. The United States and Canada allow strong encryption methods, but other countries have different data encryption laws. To comply with the laws and regulations dealing with these countries, you should learn about local legislation before implementing Active Directory in an international enterprise.

In addition to encryption, there may be laws or regulations regarding the type of information that is stored, how long it may be stored, and who may view it. It may be illegal to store certain types of personal information in a database, it may be necessary to have a security clearance in order to view certain data, and/or it may be necessary to purge or archive data after a certain period of time.

When networks have a presence on the Web, provide users with Internet access, or connect users across the Internet, the data that is accessed or displayed on the Net may be another concern. The Internet has blurred former legal boundaries, and companies conducting business internationally must comply with customs regulations, international laws, and treaties that they may not be aware of. As with other issues discussed here, what may be legal to access or post on the Internet in one country may not be in another.

When identifying relevant laws and regulations, it is important to keep the following points in mind:

- It is illegal to export strong encryption technology *out of* the United States (except to Canada or U.S.-dependent territories). This means that you cannot use such technologies as MPPE Strong (128-bit) security or IPSec 3DES (or triple-DES) outside of North America.

- Windows 2000 supports two security types, MPPE and IPSec, each of which has two standards. The weaker of these (40- or 56-bit) is usable in international implementations. (Windows 2000/SP1 also supports 128-bit.)

- Data-protection laws restrict the type of information that you can legally hold on private individuals in some countries.

exam
ⓦatch

In identifying relevant laws and regulations for your Windows 2000 Active Directory network, there are a number of issues to be aware of. The primary issues are encryption, data protection, and privacy; the rights of authorities to demand access to your data; and the jurisdiction over disputes involving your operations in another country or with its nationals. In terms of your Microsoft exam, be aware of the different encryption methods supported by Windows 2000. MPPE supports Standard (40- or 56-bit) security and Strong (128-bit) security. IPSec has two standards, 56-bit DES and 3DES (or triple-DES). 56-bit DES was designed for international use and adheres to U.S. export encryption legislation, whereas 3DES uses two 56-bit keys and is designed for high-security environments in North America only.

QUESTIONS

1.04: Identifying Relevant Laws and Regulations

15. **Current Situation:** Asimov Robotics and Housewares has a head office in Atlanta, with branch offices in Toronto, Canada, and Paris, France. Currently, this company runs Windows NT 4.0 servers and workstations, and uses MPPE

with Strong encryption security. The company has hired you to design their Windows 2000 network with Active Directory.

Required Result: Ensure that the network complies with any relevant laws and regulations.

Optional Desired Results:

1. Active Directory design should reflect the structure of the organization.

2. Multiple sites may be placed in the same domain, but the company would prefer not to use multiple domains.

Proposed Solution: By default, standard (40-bit and 56-bit) MPPE encryption is installed with Windows 2000. This will replace the Strong encryption used by the previous Windows NT network.

What results are produced from the proposed solution?

A. The proposed solution produces the required result only.

B. The proposed solution produces the required result and only one of the optional results.

C. The proposed solution produces the required result and both of the optional results.

D. The proposed solution does not produce the required result.

16. You are designing a Windows 2000 Active Directory network for a company with subsidiaries throughout North America and Europe. These two companies need to keep their networks separated, but occasionally share information using the Internet. You design the North American subsidiaries to use MPPE Strong encryption while the European networks will use MPPE Standard encryption. To share information over the Internet, each subsidiary will use Internet Explorer with 128-bit encryption. Which of the following is true?

A. Because the European subsidiaries will use MPPE Standard on the Windows 2000 network, your design fails to comply with the law.

B. Because the North American subsidiaries will use MPPE Strong on the Windows 2000 network, your design fails to comply with the law.

C. Because Internet Explorer is using 128-bit encryption on computers outside North America, your design fails to comply with the law.

D. Because Internet Explorer is using 128-bit encryption on computers inside North America, your design fails to comply with the law.

17. You are designing a Windows 2000 Active Directory network for a company with subsidiaries throughout North America and Europe. Which of the following encryptions can you use, and in what locations? (Choose all that apply.)

A. MPPE Standard or IPSec 56-bit DES in all locations

B. MPPE Strong or IPSec 3DES in European locations

C. MPPE Strong in North American locations, and IPSec 56-bit DES in European locations.

D. MPPE Standard in European locations, and IPSec 56-bit DES in North American locations.

18. As shown in the following illustration, a software company consists of a holding company and two separate subsidiaries. The government has broken up a monopoly so that it can't share information. Company 1 focuses on creating operating systems, while Company 2 creates applications. To protect data, they want to use strong encryption. Although they are subsidiaries of a main company, you need to design the Windows 2000 Active Directory network so that one company is separate from the other. How will you do this?

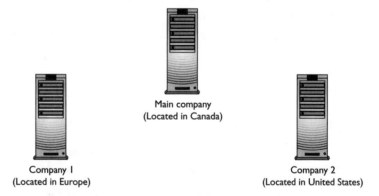

Main company
(Located in Canada)

Company 1
(Located in Europe)

Company 2
(Located in United States)

A. Split the domain in order to comply with different rule sets, and keep the two companies separated.

B. Place the two sites in the same domain, using strong encryption to protect data being transferred between sites.

C. Place the two sites in the same domain. Use encryption methods that will comply with laws in each country.

D. None of the above.

LAB QUESTION

Objectives 1.01–1.04

Uneeda Date is a rapidly growing cookie company, specializing in cookies made with dates and figs. The company has a head office, with smaller branch offices around the country. It also has two subsidiaries, in France and Germany, which answer to the head office, and have similar functions. In total, the company has slightly more than 100,000 employees. About three-quarters of these employees will use the network. Due to the need for security, you plan to use IPSec 56-bit DES at each site.

To help you with the analysis of business requirements, you receive information on costs—including capital and lease costs and depreciation on new installations and upgrades, network and system support, outsourcing, cost of management tasks, and management salaries.

Recently, a new vice-president has been hired, who has asked your team to fill out forms that outline everything each team member is doing to create the new network. There is some debate as to whether the new vice-president's decision will stand, as it will add an extra two weeks to the project. Therefore, this task has a risk probability of 50 percent.

1. What type of business model is this company?

2. Should you create a multidomain Active Directory or a series of OUs in a single domain?

3. What are the five steps of a risk management solution that can be applied to this project?

4. Calculate the risk exposure of the excessive paperwork.

5. What cost areas have you been given to calculate TCO, and what cost area information will you still need for the TCO?

6. Based on the information provided in the scenario, what laws are being violated by your initial plan for the Windows 2000 Active Directory network?

QUICK ANSWER KEY

Objective 1.01

1. **A**
2. **C**
3. **B**
4. **D**
5. **A** and **C**
6. **D**

Objective 1.02

7. **C**
8. **C**
9. **B**
10. **D**

Objective 1.03

11. **B**
12. **C** and **D**
13. **A**, **B**, and **C**
14. **B**

Objective 1.04

15. **D**
16. **C**
17. **A** and **D**
18. **A**

IN-DEPTH ANSWERS

1.01: Analyzing the Existing Business Models

1. ☑ **A.** Hierarchical. This organizational structure has a pyramidal command structure cascading from the point at the top down to the base. In this structure, students report to teachers, who report to a vice-principal, who reports to the principal.

    ☒ **B** is incorrect because a flat structure has different branches that enjoy a high degree of autonomy. At no point in this organizational chart is one unit autonomous from another. **C** is incorrect because business models always have either a flat or hierarchical structure. **D** is incorrect because there are no autonomous branches shown in the graphic, where each unit would be on its own. Despite this, it's important to realize that project-based companies often utilize both hierarchical and flat structures, with project staff having two separate reporting structures.

2. ☑ **C.** IT structure depicts how information is shared between sites, how these sites are connected, and the central data storage areas. It also looks at issues like what operating platforms and applications are in use at each site.

    ☒ **A** is incorrect because geographic structure looks at the physical locality of each site that comprises the business as a whole. Geographic structure provides information detailing how the company is spread out, and how administrative, regional, branch, and subsidiary offices play a part in the business. **B** is incorrect because organizational structure looks at how the business is organized. For example, who answers to whom, and are there clearly defined decision-makers? **D** is incorrect because information flow shows how information travels through a company.

3. ☑ **B.** Since employees of the company commonly move from one project team to another, and one branch to another, using organizational units will make administration easier. It is much easier to move an object (such as a user

account) between OUs in Active Directory than it is to move them between domains. Although the current network uses Windows NT domains, this should not influence your design, as using OUs will make administration easier and solve problems resulting from the old system's limitations.

☒   **A**, **C**, and **D** are incorrect, because the solution meets the required result, but does not meet both of the optional desired results. Because there are network administrators at each location, it is a decentralized IT structure. Decentralized structures are run by local IT management teams, and are more likely to have conflicting policies regarding security, user rights, and other access issues. This form of administration could impose rule changes on some users when you implement Active Directory.

4.   ☑   **D.** When examining a business structure, take any existing Windows NT domain models into account, but don't be unduly influenced by them. Business structure will not be accurate if you follow the Atlanta business management's view of the organization. IT management has a certain pride in the current design, but limitations in the Windows NT domain model may have forced structural decisions on the company.

☒   **A** is incorrect because its structure doesn't reflect the autonomous nature of the office in each city. The scenario states that each office enjoys autonomy, and the Active Directory design should reflect this. **B** is incorrect because the current Windows NT domain model may have forced structural decisions on the company. **C** is incorrect because when designing Active Directories, you should consider IT management and business management perspectives and structure, and take any existing Windows NT domain models into account. The models should not unduly influence your design, but you should consider them.

5.   ☑   **A** and **C** are correct. This business model has a flat structure and is decentralized. A flat-structured business model has different branches with high degrees of autonomy. Because decentralization refers to the shifting of control away from the center into the regions, autonomous divisions would indicate a decentralized model.

☒   **B** is incorrect because a hierarchical business model has a pyramidal command structure cascading from the point at the top down to the base. Most businesses have this type of structure. **D** is incorrect because a centralized business model shows no autonomy.

6. ☑ **D.** Remember that Microsoft stresses you should always use the simplest model. In this case, a single domain offers the easiest solution. Because each office has a minimal number of employees (less than 100), there is no need for separate domains. Since each office operates with a high degree of autonomy, local administrators may need to run their own offices, so you can delegate administrative permissions through the OU structure.

   ☒ **A** and **C** are incorrect because their design is more complicated than necessary. Child domains or multiple layers of child domains are used in these choices, when none are needed. **B** is incorrect because by making OUs for each office, ignoring their geographic structure, and making each unit visible to the others, you are also ignoring the autonomous nature of the individual offices.

1.02: Identifying Tolerance for Risk

7. ☑ **C.** Risk identification involves looking at what risks may arise and their effect on the success of a project. It consists of identifying the source of risk, the risk condition, its possible consequence, and the possible effect on implementation.

   ☒ **A** is incorrect because risk analysis consists of looking at a risk that's been identified, and determining the likelihood the risk will occur and how it will affect the project. It consists of analyzing risk probability, risk impact, and risk exposure. **B** is incorrect because risk tracking involves monitoring risks to determine if their likelihood or impact has changed. **D** is incorrect because risk control involves responding to the triggers that indicate a project plan is failing. In responding to these triggers, you deal with the risk by making corrections to the initial risk action plan.

8. ☑ **C.** Risk impact is an evaluation of the consequences of a risk becoming real. The impact of a risk can be measured in monetary terms for risks with a financial impact, in time increments (days, weeks, or months) for risks with a scheduling impact, or on a subjective scale for risks that don't fall into such obvious areas.

   ☒ **A** is incorrect because risk probability evaluates the probability that a risk will occur. **B** is incorrect because risk exposure is the overall threat to a project. It factors risk impact and risk probability together, and is used to balance the likelihood of an actual loss with the magnitude of a potential loss. **D** is incorrect because a risk condition is a condition that might lead to loss for a project.

9. ☑ **B.** When a risk has a risk probability of 100 percent, it means that the risk has already become an actual problem. When this occurs, the consequences of the risk need to be dealt with.

☒ **A** is incorrect because the risk has a risk probability of 100 percent, meaning the risk has become a problem. If a risk were to have a risk probability of 0 percent, there would be no chance that the risk will occur. **C** and **D** are incorrect because the risk probability doesn't necessarily guarantee the success or failure of the project itself. Risk management is used to deal with the risk, so that it doesn't adversely affect the project's success.

10. ☑ **D.** The proposed solution does not produce the required result. The four key areas of risk action planning are research, acceptance, management, and avoidance. There is no key area for ignoring the risk, as this would cause the risk to become an actual problem for the project. Since research has been done, you can accept the risk, manage the risk by putting any required steps into action, or avoid the risk by changing your plans accordingly.

☒ **A**, **B**, and **C** are incorrect because the proposed solution does not produce the required result, although the optional desired results are fulfilled. Risk tracking involves monitoring a known risk. Risk exposure is the overall threat to a project. It factors risk impact and risk probability together, and is used to balance the likelihood of an actual loss with the magnitude of a potential loss. It is calculated by using the following formula:

Risk Probability x Risk Impact = Risk Exposure

In this question, the size of loss for the risk impact was four weeks, the risk probability was 25 percent. Multiplying these gives you a risk exposure of one week.

1.03: Identifying Cost of Operations

11. ☑ **B.** A metric is an industry average. The cost of assets used in an organization is compared to averages called metrics, which allows the organization to make rough comparisons between the industry TCO figures and your organization's figures.

☒ **A** is incorrect because the cost of an asset isn't a metric. A metric is an industry average, not the cost of an asset in a single organization. **C** is incorrect because this describes the problem-recognition phase. During this phase, the data collected on assets may be compared to industry averages. Such an analysis may indicate issues that need to be addressed or further investigated. **D** is incorrect because a metric is a figure averaged from the cost of assets from numerous organizations. A metric is not derived from a single organization.

12. ☑ **C** and **D** are correct. Downtime and end-user costs. Downtime costs include lost productivity and revenue, while end-user costs include costs arising from unofficial self-support and peer-support efforts, as well as unnecessary workstation and desktop modification.

☒ **A** and **B** are incorrect because hardware and management costs are budgeted costs. Management costs including network and system support, outsourcing, cost of management tasks, and management salaries. Hardware costs include capital and lease costs and depreciation on new installations and upgrades.

13. ☑ **A**, **B**, and **C** are correct. The cost of WAN lines connecting offices in these cities is an obvious cost to include in your TCO. To keep these cities connected in the event that the WAN line goes down, you should also include the cost of dial-up connections. Because the current system uses Windows NT 4.0, the operating system will need to be upgraded to Windows 2000, and computer hardware may need to be upgraded to support Windows 2000.

☒ **D** is incorrect because baseline metrics are industry averages used to calculate TCO. These are averages used for comparison, not part of your company's assets.

14. ☑ **B.** The proposed solution produces the required result and only one of the optional results. By restricting users from making changes on their desktops, and implementing standardization using a single desktop operating system throughout your organization, costs can be reduced. This action will reduce support calls to the help desk and reduce unbudgeted costs, reduce the range of potential problems, and allow help desk staff to focus their expertise and knowledge on fewer areas.

☒ **A**, **C**, and **D** are incorrect, because the proposed solution produces the required result and only one of the optional results. If an application is published through Active Directory, a published application appears in the list of installable programs in the Add/Remove Programs applet in Control Panel. This gives users the ability to uninstall the program, and thereby fails to meet one of the optional desired results.

1.04: Identifying Relevant Laws and Regulations

15. ☑ **D.** The proposed solution does not produce the required result. MPPE supports Standard security (40- or 56-bit) and Strong (128-bit) security. The proposed solution is correct in saying that by default, standard (40-bit and 56-bit) MPPE encryption is installed with Windows 2000. However, if 128-bit MPPE security were being used on a Windows NT system, and upgraded to Windows 2000, then it would still be using 128-bit strong MPPE security. As the network would still be using Strong security, it doesn't comply with laws and regulations that stipulate strong encryption cannot be used outside of the United States and Canada.

    ☒ **A**, **B**, and **C** are incorrect, because the proposed solution does not produce the required result. This is because the proposed solution will not bring the network into compliance with laws and regulations dealing with encryption.

16. ☑ **C.** Although the Internet blurs jurisdiction, there are laws regarding encryption methods over the Internet. Internet Explorer with 128-bit encryption can only be used in North America, because this strong encryption cannot be used outside Canada and the United States.

    ☒ **A** is incorrect because MPPE Standard security can be used outside the United States and Canada. **B** is incorrect because MPPE Strong security can be used within North America. **D** is incorrect because 128-bit encryption for Internet Explorer can be used on computers in North America.

17. ☑ **A** and **D** are correct. IPSec 56-bit DES was designed for international use and adheres to U.S. export encryption legislation, while MPPE Standard security uses 40- or 56-bit encryption and also adheres to export legislation. As such, each of these can be used in any location. The United States and Canada allow Strong encryption, and can therefore use any of these methods. European locations can only use the MPPE Standard or IPSec 56-bit DES, which come with Windows 2000.

☒ **B** is incorrect because you can't use MPPE Strong or IPSec 3DES in European locations. IP Sec has two standards: 56-bit DES and 3DES (or triple-DES). 3DES uses two 56-bit keys. **C** is incorrect because MPPE Strong uses 128-bit security. Each of these is designed for high-security environments in North America only.

18. ☑ **A.** Because information cannot be shared between the companies, you are limited in how you can design Active Directory. As such, you need to split the domain in order to comply with different rule sets, and keep the two companies separated.

☒ **B** is incorrect because by placing two sites in the same domain, the domain as a whole will not comply with the law. Remember that by using strong encryption, you are violating laws prohibiting the use of strong encryption outside North America. **C** is incorrect because placing the two sites in one domain will make it possible for these companies to share data. These companies need to be separated, because they are two distinct entities. **D** is incorrect because you need to split the domain in order to comply with different rule sets, and keep the two companies separated.

LAB ANSWER

Objectives 1.01–1.04

1. Centralized. Each of the branch offices has similar functions, and answers to the head office. Decentralization refers to the shifting of control away from the center into the regions.

2. Multiple domains. Active Directory has been tested with object counts in the millions. However, you should consider two or more domains when Active Directory reaches 100,000 objects. The company has 100,000 employees, and about three-quarters of them will use the network. In addition, there will be groups and OUs, with the possibility that these requirements may increase as the company grows.

3. Risk identification, risk analysis, risk action planning, risk tracking, and risk control.

4. One week. Risk exposure is the overall threat to a project. It factors risk impact and risk probability together, and is used to balance the likelihood of an actual loss with the magnitude of a potential loss. It is calculated by using the following formula:

    Risk Probability x Risk Impact = Risk Exposure

    In this question, the size of loss for the risk impact was two weeks, the risk probability was 50 percent. Multiplying these gives you a risk exposure of one week.

5. You have been given information on hardware and software costs, and management costs. Budgeted or direct cost areas include hardware and software, management costs, development costs, support costs, and communication costs. Unbudgeted costs include end-user costs and downtime.

6. None. IPSec 56-bit DES was designed for international use and adheres to U.S. export encryption legislation.

MCSE
MICROSOFT CERTIFIED SYSTEMS ENGINEER

2

Analyzing the Planned Business Models

I n the previous chapter we discussed the importance of analyzing existing business models. A business model is a comprehensive description of business requirements, and it provides an overview of how the business works and what its requirements are. It provides insight into the needs of the business by looking at such factors as what the business does, how information flows, its organizational structure, and how decisions are made. Whereas it is vital to analyze existing business models, in this chapter we will summarize the importance of looking at planned business models and gaining an understanding of where a business is going.

Active Directory (AD) provides the ability to manage a large and complicated infrastructure, and its design will be affected by how the company's structure is organized. This does not mean that the infrastructure must match the organizational structure of the company, but Active Directory design will be influenced by it. Other influences will be the geographic scope of the company, company processes, and the growth strategy of the business. Similarly, your work on the AD design will expose limitations about the current business model as well as the local area network (LAN) or wide area network (WAN) architectures, and provide the opportunity to make changes. This gives the opportunity to make changes that will affect the business model, including the company's structure and processes.

TEST YOURSELF OBJECTIVE 2.01

Analyzing the Planned Business Models

How a company is organized will affect the network, and how the network is designed will affect the company. This symbiotic relationship is a key reason for analyzing planned business models in addition to current ones. During your analysis of current and planned business models, you should examine factors such as funding, decision-making, outsourcing, and change management. Funding is a risk factor, and it is important to determine how the project will be funded, what its budget is, and how any potential funding problems (such as going over budget) will be handled. Understanding who makes the decisions and what types of decisions they are responsible for will aid you in your analysis. Outsourcing is hiring other information technology professionals to perform information technology management functions. Such firms may be brought in to do specialized work such as programming large applications, analyzing a network and doing upgrades, or other tasks. Finally, change management will help users adapt to changes made in your project. This will aid you in implementing changes quickly, efficiently, and with minimal disruption to users.

In establishing the requirements of the business, you will need to set priorities with the company and IT staff. To do this, first establish goals for the project, and then determine the importance of certain goals over others. These are then integrated with the limitations defined by the IT department. In establishing priorities, it is important to remember that it is a process of trading off one element of a project for another. The three elements that will be affected by these tradeoffs are resources, schedule, and features. When one of these three elements is adjusted, it affects the other two. For example, if it is vital that features are in place, then the budget or schedule will adjust to ensure those features are part of the network infrastructure.

You will also need to look at how these goals, priorities, and limitations will affect relationships, and how relationships will affect your design. Some companies have temporary, long-term, or permanent relationships with other organizations or individuals. In some cases they will share an infrastructure, but in others, such as customer relationships , there may be a need for minimal access, such as to Web pages on an Internet site. By establishing the types of relationships a business has, you can better design Active Directory and your network to meet those needs.

When analyzing planned business models, it is important to pay close attention to the following points:

- To fully understand how the IT changes will affect the business model, you must analyze the contributing factors, such as funding, outsourcing, decision-making, and change management.

- Implement change quickly, efficiently, and with minimal disruption to users.

- Be sure to outline a set of goals for the project with senior management prior to developing priorities.

- Setting priorities is a process of trading off one element of a project for another. The three elements that will be affected by these tradeoffs are resources, schedule, and features. When one of these three elements is adjusted, it affects the other two.

- Try to match the current organizational structure and the planned organizational structure to either the vertical or horizontal organizational model.

- Your plan must be flexible for all types of changes. The analysis is to be certain you are aware of or prepared for most changes that will occur.

■ When planning your structure you must include policies in the discussions. Some examples of the types of policies are Control Panel, desktop settings, and Office settings.

exam **Ⓦatch**

Although some questions are straight to the point, be aware that the Microsoft exam goes beyond straightforward questions. It will require knowledge of Windows 2000 features, as well as knowledge on key exam topics. An example of this would be knowledge of differences between Mixed mode and Native mode when designing your Active Directory. Mixed mode allows you to have domain controllers running Windows 2000 and Windows NT in the same domain. In Mixed mode, some Windows 2000 features are disabled, but the domain features from previous versions of Windows NT Server are still enabled. In Native mode, all the domain controllers in a given domain are running Windows 2000 Server. Native mode allows organizations to take advantage of new Active Directory features such as universal groups, nested group membership, and interdomain group membership. In Mixed mode, one key element is that you cannot place one group within another, unless they are built-in groups. Such a limitation may have a significant impact in designing Active Directory, if you initially planned to nest groups.

QUESTIONS

2.01: Analyzing the Planned Business Models

1. **Current Situation:** Murky Motors is a car manufacturing company. They have a head office in New Jersey and factories located in several states. The network hasn't been upgraded in years, so users are still running Windows for Workgroups on 386 computers. As a member of the IT staff for Murky Motors, you are responsible for designing the Active Directory for the new Windows 2000 network and coming up with new ways to improve network performance. Unfortunately, your team doesn't have the equipment or experience to do a proper analysis and do upgrades to WAN technologies.

The top decision-makers of the company understand that Active Directory can be designed to reflect the organization of a company, and they want your design to show their importance in the company. They have also shown some concern over how users of the network will react to changes in the network, and a way to manage these changes needs to be imposed.

Required Result: Design an Active Directory that will improve management of the network and reflect company organization.

Optional Desired Results:

1. Improve performance of the WAN by determining its speed and designing and implementing new methods of speeding up the network.

2. Implement change management to lessen the impact of change and not adversely affect users.

Proposed Solution: Since company organization and a decision-maker's place in it should not dictate AD design, your team will identify decision-makers but not allow their place in the company to dictate design. Design of the AD will consider how the company itself is organized, such as hierarchical versus flat organization, departments and members, and other factors. Plan the Outsource analysis of WAN to a firm that specializes in network analysis. Implement change slowly and shut down areas while computers are upgraded to support Windows 2000 Professional.

What results are produced from the proposed solution?

A. The proposed solution produces the required result only.

B. The proposed solution produces the required result and only one of the optional results.

C. The proposed solution produces the required result and both of the optional results.

D. The proposed solution does not produce the required result.

2. Murky Motors is a large car manufacturer and has the following company structure. At the top level, a board of directors presides over administration and departmental directors, who oversee the work of a large number of staff members. In lower portions of the organizational chart, there is a significant amount of departmentalization. Within this level, groups of users are divided

by project-based strategy or by function and enjoy a high degree of autonomy. An example of this is Information Technology, a department which, as seen in the following illustration, is broken into smaller departments.

Which of the following structures does Information Technology have? (Choose all that apply.)

A. Horizontal

B. Vertical

C. Hierarchical

D. Flat

3. The management you work for is meeting with your team to set goals and priorities for upgrading the Windows NT network to a Windows 2000 Active Directory network. You are attempting to establish priorities for your project with decision-makers in the company. In setting these priorities, which of the following will be considered acceptable elements to trade off against each other? (Choose all that apply.)

A. Features of the project

B. Schedule

C. The business model

D. Resources

4. The company you work for is currently upgrading to a Windows 2000 Active Directory network. Since it is vital than upgrades occur as soon as possible, scheduling is more important than other elements of the project. The company currently uses ISDN connections to connect ten branch offices to the headquarters. Each office also has its own servers for storing data, but the headquarters has two servers from which applications at the branch offices obtain data. The data these applications access is used by two departments and is essential to their day-to-day duties. In addition to designing the Active Directory, the company decides to make upgrading the network to fiber optics

a priority. None of the IT staff has the experience or knowledge to do this. What will you do? (Choose the best answer.)

A. Increase the IT budget to train IT staff to install fiber optics and improve network performance.

B. Outsource the work to a firm that will install fiber optics and improve network performance.

C. Change the schedule so that the upgrades occur at a later date. This will give the project team more time to analyze the problem and come up with other options.

D. Nothing. Windows 2000 features will improve performance so that media upgrades won't be needed. Add users that use this data and application to the same organizational group when designing Active Directory.

TEST YOURSELF OBJECTIVE 2.02

Analyzing the Company Geographic Scope

How a business is structured geographically often controls the type of network it will require. Many of the factors that determine how you design your Windows 2000 network and Active Directory are determined by the size of your network, and how it is geographically distributed. Significant knowledge about how to design Active Directory and the network infrastructure can be acquired by analyzing the locations of business units.

When analyzing the geographic scope of a company, there are several models that may apply. Of the models discussed here, regional businesses are the smallest and generally the easiest to plan and manage. They may be spread across large cities, counties, or regions. National companies are spread across a country and provide greater challenges such as staffing and network management. International companies offer these same challenges, but on a greater scale. They also present issues such as differing languages, currencies, laws, and so on. A subsidiary is a company that has been purchased by another larger company, but is run as a separate business. It may have different requirements and needs from the main company. The operating systems, software, processes, and so forth may be different from the main company. A final type of company model is branch offices. These are not separate companies, but smaller units of the business as a whole. Users in the company are separated into smaller offices, which may or may not perform different tasks.

In looking at these models, it is important to remember that despite the physical location of units making up the company, the business may consider itself global in nature. This is particularly relevant when the company conducts business using the Internet and e-commerce. Each of these issues will need to be addressed when designing your Active Directory and Windows 2000 network.

When analyzing the geographic scale of a company, it is important to keep the following points in mind:

- Well-defined Group Policy Objects and well-positioned domain controllers are key to working over slow links. Be sure you have all the information about growth and expansion prior to your design.

- Across the nation we are seeing an ever-increasing demand for e-commerce, quick delivery of products, and easy purchases. Be sure your design can handle such changes.

exam
ⓦatch

An important part of Active Directory design is the placement of domain controllers, Administrators, Group Policy Objects (GPOs), and organizational units (OUs). A domain is a logical grouping of resources (for example, servers, organizational units, and so on) under a single domain name. AD organizes resources hierarchically in domains, and each domain requires one or more domain controllers. A domain controller is a server running Windows 2000 Server or Advanced Server, and it is responsible for managing user access to the network. This includes logons, authentication, security, and so forth. Because all domain controllers in a domain are considered as equals, you can administer your Active Directory network from a single point. This means that changes can be made to any domain controller, and these changes are replicated to other domain controllers. Performance problems occur when users must use a slow link to access information from the domain.

Geographic scope will have an impact on your Active Directory design, since how areas are connected will impact the placement of domain controllers, Administrators, Group Policy Objects, and OUs. Since you don't want users to have to connect to domain controllers over a slow link, it is important to properly position domain controllers and Group Policy Objects. You can also schedule replication to occur during nonpeak hours to improve performance. To determine where objects and domain controllers should be placed, it is important to gather information about growth and expansion prior to your design.

QUESTIONS

2.02: Analyzing the Company Geographic Scope

5. **Current Situation:** The company for whom you are designing a Windows 2000 Active Directory network has its headquarters in Atlanta and has just opened branch offices in London and Paris. These networks have servers in each location, and currently use routers and dial-up connections to connect these locations. There is also some concern that replication of Active Directory will affect performance of the network.

    Required Result: Determine which servers should be domain controllers so that the users will experience the best network performance.

    Optional Desired Results:

    1. Devise a replication scheme for Active Directory so that performance of the network will not be adversely affected.

    2. Determine the location of Group Policy Objects so that users will experience the best network performance.

    Proposed Solution: Make the server in Atlanta the domain controller for this network. Place all Group Policy Objects on the domain controller in Atlanta. Schedule replication to occur during nonpeak hours.

    What results are produced from the proposed solution?

    A. The proposed solution produces the required result only.

    B. The proposed solution produces the required result and only one of the optional results.

    C. The proposed solution produces the required result and both of the optional results.

    D. The proposed solution does not produce the required result.

6. Asimov Robotics is located in New York, Paris, and Toronto. It has a North American headquarters and a European headquarters. The North American

headquarters has one branch office in Toronto, Canada, which connects to its North American headquarters using a slow link. The European headquarters has two local branch offices connected to the headquarters with fiber optics. Based on this information and the following illustration, what company model does the geographic scope of this company reflect, and where should domain controllers be placed?

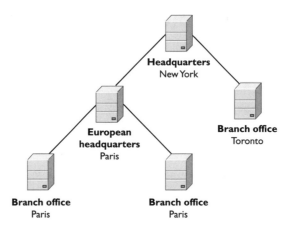

A. It follows the international model. Domain controllers should be placed in New York only.

B. It follows the regional model. Domain controllers should be placed at both headquarters only.

C. It follows the international model. Domain controllers should be placed at both headquarters and at the Toronto branch office.

D. It follows the international model. Domain controllers should be placed at both headquarters and at all branch offices.

7. You have been hired by a consulting firm that wants you to start researching business requirements and designing an easier Active Directory. Due to your experience, they do not want you to start on Windows 2000 networks with the most difficult geographic scope. Which of the following are generally the easiest to plan and manage when designing a Windows 2000 Active Directory network?

A. Regional

B. National

C. International

D. None of the above

Questions 8–10   The next three questions are based upon the scenario that follows. Read the following case study, and then answer the questions. You may refer to this case study as often as needed.

You are designing a Windows 2000 Active Directory for WidgetSoft Sprockets and Gadgets, a company that creates and sells computer games. This company has its headquarters in Atlanta and has opened new offices in Detroit and Toronto. These offices are run under WidgetSoft Sprockets and Gadgets, and they report to the headquarters in Atlanta. WidgetSoft has just purchased a Canadian company called Jennifer Carruthers Graphics, which will continue to run as a separate company. To increase sales, the main company is planning to implement e-commerce and has already provided Internet access to every department in the company.

The offices in Atlanta, Detroit, and Toronto are connected by a fast WAN. At present, the only IT staff is located in Atlanta. The new graphics company runs as a separate business and currently has its own network. It only occasionally connects to this network to upload graphics used in computer games. To deal with the size of these graphics, an ISDN line has been installed, connecting Jennifer Carruthers Graphics to the Toronto office.

8. Looking at the geographic scope of this corporation, which of the following is true?

A. WidgetSoft Sprockets and Gadgets is a national company with branch offices in Detroit and Toronto. Jennifer Carruthers Graphics is a new branch office.

B. WidgetSoft Sprockets and Gadgets is a national company with branch offices in Detroit and Toronto. Jennifer Carruthers Graphics is a subsidiary.

C. WidgetSoft Sprockets and Gadgets is an international company with subsidiaries in Detroit and Toronto. Jennifer Carruthers Graphics is a new subsidiary.

D. WidgetSoft Sprockets and Gadgets is an international company with branch offices in Detroit and Toronto. Jennifer Carruthers Graphics is a new subsidiary.

9. The decision-makers in WidgetSoft Sprockets and Gadgets want to limit the domain controllers to the number representing only the areas that especially require them. Where should domain controllers be placed in this company?

   A. Atlanta, Detroit, and the new graphics company

   B. Atlanta and Toronto

   C. Detroit and the new graphics company

   D. The new graphics company

10. Which of the following possible improvements may be implemented in the future and should be considered in your design?

   A. Atlanta, Detroit, and Toronto may change to ISDN lines.

   B. The graphics company may become a subsidiary and have diverse technologies.

   C. Departments have Internet access.

   D. E-commerce may become a method to increase sales.

TEST YOURSELF OBJECTIVE 2.03

Analyzing Company Processes

A company process is a function or procedure within the business that allows it to deliver its products and services. These processes are followed so that the business can function successfully. A business process relies on information being available to the people who need it. This means you need to analyze and document the flow of information and communication. Whereas information flow shows the availability of data and how it travels from person to person in an organization, communication flow shows how this information is conveyed and the method and frequency with which it is distributed. Windows 2000 provides a number of security and file system features to make information available. This includes such features as NTFS (New Technology

File System), distributed file system, LDAP (Lightweight Directory Access Protocol), IPSec, and Group Policy Objects. It also supports various methods of communication, which includes email, intranets, the Internet, video conferencing, and more.

In analyzing this information, you will also need to look at the service and product life cycles. Every service or product has a life cycle, which may be changed or become outdated after a time. When this happens, the need for information dealing with the product or service will change. As the business requirements and company processes change, aspects such as network security, location and relocation of resources, and the need for communication between individuals and groups may also change.

During the analysis of company processes, it is important to keep the following points in mind:

■ Make sure you are aware of the security tools available with Windows 2000, such as IPSec, Group Policy Objects, and NTFS permissions.

■ Plan for communication improvements constantly and allow AD to change with the times.

■ In looking at the planned business model, you must always analyze the frequency of change.

■ Always establish constants and guidelines for implementation with full documentation.

exam
⚙atch
There are a number of security tools and features in Windows 2000 that can aid in controlling the flow of information and communication. The Microsoft Distributed File System (Dfs) allows system administrators to enable users to access shared folders distributed throughout the network. Lightweight Directory Access Protocol (LDAP) is a protocol for accessing online directory services. It allows users to query and update Active Directory. IPSec secures communications within an intranet or virtual private network. Group Policy Objects (GPOs) allow you to control actions and settings for users and computers. Finally, NTFS is the New Technology File System, a secure file system for use within Windows 2000. Using such tools and features, you have increased control over the flow of communication and information within an organization.

QUESTIONS

2.03: Analyzing Company Processes

11. As shown in the following illustration, Murky Motors has offices in several countries. To share information, it uses a virtual private network (VPN). There is also a need for users at the headquarters in New York to access shared folders on the Toronto server, and for users at the European headquarters to access shared folders belonging to users on the European branch office servers. Which of the following would you use to secure communication over the VPN?

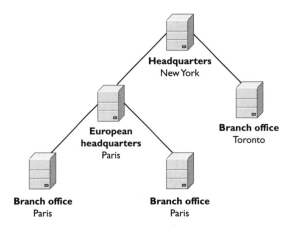

A. Because there are offices in Canada, IPSec cannot be used due to its encryption. Consequently, LDAP must be used. Dfs should be used to allow users easy access to shared folders.

B. Because there are offices in Europe, LDAP cannot be used due to its encryption and Dfs should be used. LDAP should also be used to allow users easy access to shared folders.

C. IPSec should be used to secure communications, whereas Dfs should be used to allow access to shared folders.

D. Dfs should be used to secure communications, whereas IPSec should be used to allow access to shared folders.

12. You are documenting the flow of communication in a company. Which of the following will you include in this documentation? (Choose all that apply.)

    A. How information is distributed

    B. Communication protocols like IPSec, NTFS, and LDAP

    C. Communication methods such as intranets and email

    D. Methods of securing information, such as Dfs and IPSec

13. A project group needs access to shared folders that are distributed throughout the network. Each member of the group has created documentation that will ensure the success of the project and placed the documents in folders they have created and shared. Which of the following allows system administrators to make it easy for these users to access and manage these files, regardless of where those files physically reside in the network?

    A. Dfs

    B. LDAP

    C. NTFS

    D. FAT

14. **Current Situation:** Murky Motors has started a new project to design a sports car. The project team is made up of individuals who will create their own documents and blueprints, but will need to share these files with other team members. They are concerned that members may be confused or that some information may be overlooked if only shared folders are used, so they want an organized method of accessing these files. One user will also have the occasional need to query Active Directory and perform updates. Due to the high security attributed to their designs, there is also concern about accessing the data over the company's intranet, and remote users accessing the data over virtual private networking.

    Required Result: Users will need secure communication over the intranet and virtual private network.

    Optional Desired Results:

    1. Certain users should be able to perform queries and updates to Active Directory.

    2. Users should be able to access shared folders distributed throughout the network.

Proposed Solution: Have each member of the project team create a shared folder containing the information they want to share. Use Dfs to create logical views of these directories and files. Use LDAP to ensure secure communication over the intranet and virtual private network. LDAP will also ensure a secure method of accessing online directory services.

What results are produced from the proposed solution?

A. The proposed solution produces the required result only.

B. The proposed solution produces the required result and only one of the optional results.

C. The proposed solution produces the required result and both of the optional results.

D. The proposed solution does not produce the required result.

TEST YOURSELF OBJECTIVE 2.04

Identifying Growth Strategy

As a company grows, the network will change. If a new division or unit with great needs is to be added in the future, then even a small growth in the company can have a profound impact on your network. Additional workstations will need to be added, network traffic will increase, network security will be adjusted to include new groups and user accounts, and new features and technologies will be added. In the case of acquisitions, a new company will be purchased, and there may be a need to integrate two disparate network infrastructures. In light of these possibilities, it is important to identify the projected growth and review the growth strategy of a company when you analyze business requirements.

Most companies have a business plan that shows what direction it will take over the next few years. Acquisition plans will provide information about new companies to be purchased, whereas growth plans detail proposed expansions within the business. Every company has implementation plans for such growth, with specific goals and priorities for each department. When growth occurs, processes such as evaluations, project tracking, change management, quality assurance, and quality control will all rely on proper security and collaboration to be successful. To be sure to meet the needs of the users during company expansion, you will need to interview all persons involved in the movement to grow, in addition to analyzing documentation.

When analyzing growth strategies, it is important to remember the following points:

- Shareholders and owners will consistently search for growth within the organization to determine the success of the company.

- Internal management team and customer expectations need to be determined before deciding on your security model.

Growth strategies will have a profound impact on a network so your design of Active Directory should be flexible enough to accommodate such changes. Remember that Active Directory stores information by organizing it into sections. These sections permit storage for a large number of objects, allowing scalability for your design. As the business grows, the directory can expand. Theoretically, a domain's Active Directory can contain ten million objects. Microsoft admits that one million objects is a more practical number, but this still shows that Windows 2000 Active Directory has the incredible ability to keep up with any changes your network experiences.

QUESTIONS

2.04: Identifying Growth Strategy

15. **Current Situation:** Murky Motors plans to buy a smaller company that manufactures brake lines. Murky Motors has 50,000 users, whereas the new company will add 10,000 additional users. 1,000 of these new users will be remote users who will be travelling around the country. At present the company is unsure whether the deal will go through, but you have been informed of this possibility so that you can consider this growth in your Active Directory design. You will also need to set up additional security to keep these new users from accessing data on the Murky Motors server.

    Required Result: Have as few domains as necessary, but ensure your design supports growth.

Optional Desired Results:

1. Set up security to keep users in the new company from accessing data on the Murky Motors server.

2. Implement a method to allow remote users to access data from laptops while on the road.

Proposed Solution: Due to this growth, the number of users will exceed those supported by Active Directory so multiple domains need to be implemented. The separate domains will also keep user accounts and groups separate, providing the necessary security. Implement virtual private networking to allow users to connect over the Internet.

What results are produced from the proposed solution?

A. The proposed solution produces the required result only.

B. The proposed solution produces the required result and only one of the optional results.

C. The proposed solution produces the required result and both of the optional results.

D. The proposed solution does not produce the required result.

16. You are designing a Windows 2000 Active Directory network for a small company. When you inquire about growth strategies, the owner states that there are no expectations that the company will grow over the next few years. Which of the following should you do? (Choose the best answer.)

A. Follow the owner's directions and not account for growth in your design.

B. Further analyze growth strategies by interviewing people within the organization and researching documentation.

C. Do nothing.

D. Create multiple domains from the beginning to account for the future possibility of large growth.

17. The company you have designed an Active Directory for experiences some growth. Which of the following will be affected by this growth? (Choose all that apply.)

A. Groups

B. Decreased file storage

C. Increased network traffic

D. User accounts

18. As seen in the following illustration, your company consists of three offices. The Atlanta and New York offices have existed for years. Recently, the San Diego office was opened. The New York and San Diego offices provide duplicate services to different parts of the company. Regularly the three offices work together on major projects. What is the best directory services solution?

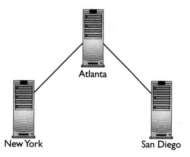

A. One domain with multiple sites

B. Two domains with multiple sites

C. One domain with one site

D. Multiple domains with no sites

LAB QUESTION

Objectives 2.01–2.04

Asimov Robotics, Inc., has offices in New York, San Diego, Hong Kong, and London. The headquarters is located in New York, whereas the other offices are responsible for manufacturing and marketing. While designing Active Directory for Asimov Robotics, the company purchases Positronic Robotics and Housewares. This smaller company consists of a single office in New Jersey that makes components geared toward home offices. Asimov Robotics manufactures components for corporate use. Information is sent between these companies over a virtual private network, but there is concern over the security of these communications.

1. During analysis of Asimov Robotics, Inc., what type of documentation would have indicated the purchase of Positronic Robotics and Housewares?

2. In establishing priorities for the project, what three elements will be traded off against one another?

3. Looking at the geographic scope of this corporation, what company model does Asimov Robotics fall into?

4. Looking at the geographic scope of this corporation, what company model does Positronic Robotics and Housewares fall into?

5. What will you use to secure communications between these two companies when they share data over the virtual private network?

QUICK ANSWER KEY

Objective 2.01

1. **B**
2. **A** and **D**
3. **A, B,** and **D**
4. **B**

Objective 2.02

5. **D**
6. **C**
7. **A**
8. **D**
9. **B**
10. **D**

Objective 2.03

11. **C**
12. **A** and **C**
13. **A**
14. **D**

Objective 2.04

15. **D**
16. **B**
17. **A, C,** and **D**
18. **A**

IN-DEPTH ANSWERS

2.01: Analyzing the Planned Business Models

1. ☑ **B.** The proposed solution produces the required result and only one of the optional results. At face value, it may seem that the required result isn't produced, as your team will identify decision-makers but not allow their place in the company to dictate design. However, political influences and egos of decision-makers shouldn't be a factor in your design. How the company itself is organized, hierarchical versus flat organization, departments and members, and other elements will factor into how you decide to design AD. As such, the required result has been produced. As your team doesn't have the equipment or experience to do a proper analysis and do upgrades to WAN technologies, outsourcing the work of network analysis is a viable option. Outsourcing is hiring other information technology professionals to perform information technology management functions. Such firms may be brought in to do specialized work, such as programming large applications, analyzing a network and doing upgrades, or other tasks.

    ☒ **A, C**, and **D** are incorrect because the proposed solution produces the required result and only one of the optional results. The result of implementing proper change management wasn't achieved. Changes should be implemented quickly, efficiently, and with minimal disruption to users.

2. ☑ **A** and **D** are correct. Both horizontal and flat organizational structures, as the names imply, have flat structures with different branches that enjoy a high degree of autonomy. You will see many different patterns of departmentalization, as companies will divide groups by function, divisions or units, or by a matrix or project-based strategy. This type of organizational structure is usually visible in the lower portions of a traditional organization chart.

    ☒ **B** and **C** are incorrect because a vertical or hierarchical structure has a pyramid command structure cascading from the point at the top down to the base. This is the most common design.

3. ☑ **A**, **B**, and **D** are correct. Setting priorities is a process of trading off one element of a project for another. The three elements that will be affected by these tradeoffs are resources, schedule, and features. Features are components of your project, including operating systems that will be installed, Active Directory design, and so forth. Resources include such things as budgets, facilities, and employees making up your project team. Schedule involves the time elements of the project, such as when part of a project will be completed. When one of these three elements is adjusted, it affects the other two.

   ☒ **C** is incorrect because a business model is a comprehensive description of business requirements and provides an overview of how the business works and what its requirements are. It provides insight into the needs of the business by looking at such factors as what the business does, how information flows, its organizational structure, and how decisions are made. Although designing the Active Directory may affect the business model, the business model itself will not be considered as a possible trade-off in setting priorities.

4. ☑ **B.** Outsource the work to a firm that will install fiber optics and improve network performance. Since another firm has the experience and knowledge to do the necessary work immediately, it will keep the project on schedule and allow the project to succeed.

   ☒ **A** is incorrect because the upgrades need to occur as soon as possible. Increasing funding to train the IT staff to install fiber optics and improve network performance would make scheduling a trade-off. The question states that scheduling is more important than other elements of the project, so this choice is incorrect. **C** is also incorrect because it uses scheduling as a trade-off. **D** is incorrect because features in Windows 2000 won't change the bandwidth of media and the ISDN lines will still be a bottleneck.

2.02: Analyzing the Company Geographic Scope

5. ☑ **D.** The proposed solution does not produce the required result. You need to determine which servers should be domain controllers so that the users will experience the best network performance. In this case, a domain controller should be placed in Atlanta, London, and Paris. Each of these offices is in a different country. If only one or two domain controllers were placed in these

locations, one or more of the locations would need to connect over a slow link to a domain controller, thereby degrading performance.

☒ **A**, **B**, and **C** are incorrect because the proposed solution does not produce the required result.

6. ☑ **C.** It follows the international model. domain controllers should be placed at both headquarters and at the Toronto branch office. The European headquarters and Toronto branch office should both have a domain controller because they are in different countries. The Toronto office also has a slow connection to its headquarters so it would need a domain controller. The branch offices in Paris do not need domain controllers because they can connect to the European headquarters easily with fiber optic connections.

☒ **A** is incorrect because this would degrade performance when users in other countries need to access GPOs or when they are logging on. **B** is incorrect because it is an international company. **B** and **D** are also incorrect because the branch offices in Paris do not need domain controllers since they can easily connect to the European headquarters.

7. ☑ **A.** Regional. Businesses with a regional geographic scope are the smallest, and generally the easiest, to plan and manage. They may be spread across large cities, counties, or regions.

☒ **B** is incorrect because national companies are spread across a country and provide greater challenges such as staffing and network management. **C** is incorrect because international companies offer many of the same challenges as regional ones, but on a greater scale. They also present issues such as differing languages, currencies, laws, and so on. **D** is incorrect because regional businesses are generally the easiest to plan and manage when designing a Windows 2000 Active Directory network.

8. ☑ **D.** WidgetSoft Sprockets and Gadgets is an international company with branch offices in Detroit and Toronto. Jennifer Carruthers Graphics is a new subsidiary. WidgetSoft is international because it has offices in both the United States and Canada. The graphics company is a subsidiary because it is a company that is owned by another company. A subsidiary is run as a separate business, generally purchased by a larger corporation. Finally, WidgetSoft Sprockets and Gadgets has branch offices. These are not separate companies, but smaller units of the business as a whole.

☒ **A** is incorrect because Jennifer Carruthers Graphics runs as a separate company and is therefore a subsidiary. It is also incorrect because WidgetSoft Sprockets and Gadgets is an international company with branch offices in Canada. **B** is also incorrect because WidgetSoft Sprockets and Gadgets is an international company. **C** is incorrect because the offices in Detroit and Toronto are still under the WidgetSoft Sprockets and Gadgets company, thus making them branch offices.

9. ☑ **B.** Atlanta and Toronto. Since the Atlanta and Detroit offices are connected by a high-speed connection, performance will not be adversely affected. Toronto should have its own domain controller since the connection is slowed by its being in another country, and it should not be completely reliant on the U.S. domain controller. This will also prevent redundancy. The new graphics company needs only occasional access, so it doesn't need a domain controller at its location.

☒ **A** is incorrect because this would place two domain controllers in one country, whereas only one is necessary. **C** and **D** are incorrect because the new graphics company does not need its own domain controller. It runs as a separate company and requires only occasional access to the domain.

10. ☑ **D.** E-commerce is a possible improvement that may be implemented in the future and should be considered in your design. Nationwide there is an increasing demand for e-commerce, quick delivery of products, and easy purchases. Consequently, such advances should be considered in your design.

☒ **A** is incorrect because Atlanta, Detroit, and Toronto are already connected by a fast WAN. It would not be an improvement to implement slower connections. **B** is incorrect because the graphics company is already a subsidiary. **C** is incorrect because users already have Internet access. This will be considered part of the current design, not as something that will be implemented in the future.

2.03: Analyzing Company Processes

11. ☑ **C.** IPSec should be used to secure communications, whereas Dfs should be used to allow access to shared folders. IPSec is the Internet Security Protocol and is an industry standard for encrypting TCP/IP. It provides secure

communications over intranets and virtual private networks. Dfs is Microsoft's Distributed File System used to organize shared folders that reside on different network computers. It provides users with a way of accessing shared folders that are distributed throughout the network. Using Dfs, system administrators can create logical views of directories and files, regardless of where those files physically reside in the network.

☒ **A** is incorrect because IPSec can be used in North America. LDAP is a protocol used to access Active Directory and is not used to provide secure communication. **B** is also incorrect because LDAP is not used as a security protocol or to allow easy access to distributed files and folders. It is also incorrect because Dfs is Microsoft's Distributed File System, not a security protocol. Dfs allows system administrators to enable users to access shared folders that are distributed throughout the network. **D** is incorrect because IPSec secures communications, whereas Dfs allow users to access shared folders.

12. ☑ **A** and **C** are correct. Communication flow shows how information is conveyed and the method and frequency with which it is distributed. Thus, you should document or diagram how information is distributed and the frequency of this distribution, and look into electronic communication methods like intranets and email.

☒ **B** is incorrect because NTFS is a file system used by Windows 2000. IPSec is used to secure communication within an intranet or virtual private network, whereas LDAP is a protocol for accessing online directory services. **D** is incorrect because Dfs is Microsoft's Distributed File System. It allows system administrators to enable users to access shared folders distributed throughout the network.

13. ☑ **A.** Dfs is an abbreviation for Microsoft's Distributed File System. Dfs organizes shared folders that reside on different network computers. It provides users with a way of accessing shared folders that are distributed throughout the network. Using Dfs, system administrators can create logical views of directories and files, regardless of where those files physically reside in the network.

☒ **B** is incorrect, because LDAP is the Lightweight Directory Access Protocol, a protocol for accessing online directory services. **C** and **D** are incorrect because NTFS and FAT are file systems that can be used on Windows 2000 Servers and Professional machines.

14. ☑ **D.** The proposed solution does not produce the required result. LDAP is the Lightweight Directory Access Protocol, a protocol for accessing online directory services. It allows users to query and update Active Directory, but does not secure communications within an intranet or virtual private network. To ensure security over intranets and virtual private networks, IPSec should be used.

    ☒ **A, B**, and **C** are incorrect because, although the optional results are met, the proposed solution does not produce the required result. Dfs organizes shared folders that reside on different network computers and provides a way of accessing shared folders distributed throughout the network. LDAP can be used to query and update Active Directory, but does not provide the security required in this case when sending data over the intranet and virtual private network.

2.04: Identifying Growth Strategy

15. ☑ **D.** The proposed solution does not produce the required result. Active Directory is scalable, so in theory, a domain's Active Directory can contain ten million objects, with one million objects being a more practical number. The proposed solution is also incorrect because Microsoft recommends that, whenever possible, only a single domain should be used.

    ☒ **A, B**, and **C** are incorrect because the proposed solution does not produce the required result. Implementing a VPN would allow users to connect to the network remotely. Windows 2000 security features, such as Group Policy Objects, would enable you to set what users can access. There is no need to create separate domains.

16. ☑ **B.** Further analyze growth strategies by interviewing people within the organization and researching documentation. Remember that even a small growth in the company can have a profound impact on your network. Although the owner may feel the company as a whole may not grow, individual departments or units within the business may expand.

    ☒ **A** and **C** are incorrect because you should always account for growth in your design. Each of these solutions fails to do this. **D** is incorrect because this solution would be overkill. Remember that, in theory, a domain's Active

Directory can contain ten million objects. To create multiple domains to account for growth in a small company, you would need to expect millions of objects in the company's domain structure.

17. ☑ **A, C**, and **D** are correct. Groups, user accounts, and network traffic are all aspects of a network that can be affected by growth. Other areas that can be affected are the need for additional workstations, adjustments to network security, increased file storage, reorganization of backups, and the addition of new features and technologies.

☒ **B** is incorrect because growth would result in increased need for file storage, not a decrease. If new users were added, they would be saving files to the network. If no new users were added, the growth would still result in additional documents and files being generated and saved.

18. ☑ **A.** One domain with multiple sites. Microsoft recommends a single domain whenever possible. By creating different sites within a single domain, you simplify administration.

☒ **B** and **D** are incorrect because Microsoft recommends a single domain whenever possible. Since it is possible to use a single domain with multiple sites, you should use that option. **C** is incorrect because if you created one domain with one site, one of these locations would be left out of the network.

LAB ANSWER

Objectives 2.01–2.04

1. Acquisition plans would have indicated the purchase of Positronic Robotics and Housewares. You will find that documentation plays a major role in the integration of the two companies, if their infrastructures are in fact to be integrated. Although this information is often confidential, you should inquire about such acquisitions to ensure your design will accommodate the changes.

2. Establishing priorities is a matter of tradeoffs. The three elements that will be affected by tradeoffs are resources, schedule, and features.

3. Asimov Robotics is an international company. It has branch offices in San Diego, Hong Kong, and London.

4. Positronic Robotics and Housewares is a subsidiary.

5. IPSec, Internet Protocol Security, is used to secure communications within an intranet or virtual private network.

3

Analyzing the Existing Windows NT Environment

I n many cases, you will not be performing clean installs of Windows 2000 nor designing your network where no network existed before. Because of this, analyzing an existing Windows NT environment is a common practice in designing Active Directory. The existing Windows NT network can, and probably will, have a significant impact on your design.

As we summarize in this chapter, you will need to document the details of the Windows NT environment. When documenting a Windows NT environment, you can start by investigating the domain architecture and working your way down to the server component details, or start with the individual components and work your way up to the overall design. This includes not only domain models and the physical network, but also operating system versions, hardware, and network services like DNS, DHCP, and WINS. These details will help you determine the upgrade or migration paths for your domains and servers.

TEST YOURSELF OBJECTIVE 3.01

Analyzing the Existing NT Environment

When documenting a Windows NT environment, you can start by investigating the domain architecture and working your way down to the server component details, or start with the individual components and work your way up to the overall design. In doing so, it is important that you document the domain structure of the Windows NT environment and any existing trusts. All domain models are built on one or more domains using specific trust relationships between them. There are four possible domain models: single domain, master domain, multiple master domain, or complete trust. In most cases you will find that there is a hybrid of models.

Trust relationships are an important aspect of Windows NT environments, and should be documented. While investigating trust relationships in legacy Windows NT environments, trusts in Windows NT 4.0 and earlier versions, you should remember that these trust relationships are nontransitive and unidirectional. In legacy Windows NT environments, a trust relationship cannot pass through one domain to another, and if one domain trusts another domain, the reverse is not automatically true. This is not the case in Windows 2000 networks. In Windows 2000, trust relationships are bidirectional and transitive. This means that both domains trust each other, and that this trust can pass from one domain to another.

In addition to domain models and trust relationships, you will also need to document software and hardware of computers on which Windows 2000 will be installed, and the geographic layout of the physical network. Documentation should include the number of users on the network, information on operating systems (such as type and versions), configurations (for example, IP addresses and protocols), as well as location and specifics of hardware and resources (such as printers). This information is an integral part of the research when planning your Windows 2000 network and Active Directory design.

When analyzing existing Windows NT environments, it is important to remember the following points:

- Document the logical architecture for your existing Windows NT domains and relate the result to one of the four domain models: single domain, master domain, multiple master domain, or complete trust.

- Document the physical architecture for your Windows NT environment by working from the global level down to the local area networks within buildings.

- Document the Windows NT operating systems, their versions, applied service packs, and the hardware on which they are installed.

exam
ⓦatch

Examining existing Windows NT environments requires an understanding of Windows NT domain models. There are four models: single domain, master domain, multiple master domain, and complete trust. The single domain is one domain that encompasses all user accounts and network resources in the Windows NT environment. All Windows NT servers have the role of a domain controller (either the PDC or one of the BDCs) or of a member server, and all workstations are members of the domain. The master domain model has a single master domain that contains user accounts and can contain network resources, with additional domains that contain network resources such as shared files and shared printers. Each resource domain trusts the master domain, allowing users in the master domain to be granted permissions to resources within any of the resource domains. However, should the resource domain administrator create a user account in the resource domain, that account cannot be granted permissions to resources within the master or any other resource domain. The multiple master domain model is similar to the master domain model except that it consists of multiple master domains. All of the master domains contain user accounts and have one or more resource domains that contain the network resources but no user accounts. Each resource domain is configured to trust each of the master domains, and all of the master domains trust each other. Finally, the complete trust domain model consists of two or more domains, with each domain containing user accounts and network resources. All domains in this model are configured to trust each of the other domains in the Windows NT environment.

QUESTIONS

3.01: Analyzing the Existing NT Environment

1. The following illustration depicts an existing Windows NT environment. This network consists of one domain containing user accounts and network resources, and two additional domains containing additional network resources. Arrows in this illustration show the direction of trust relationships. What domain model is being used in this Windows NT environment?

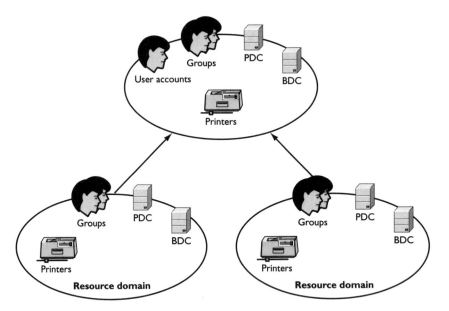

A. Single domain

B. Master domain

C. Multiple master domain

D. Complete trust

2. **Current Situation:** You are analyzing an existing Windows NT environment in a company running Windows NT Servers. The network consists of two Windows NT 4.0 domains, and the IT staff informs you that both domains trust each other. Each domain contains user accounts and network resources.

   Required Result: Identify the domain model being used by the Windows NT environment.

   Optional Desired Results:

   1. Verify that both domains trust each other and that the information you have been provided on trust relationships is correct.

   2. After performing your analysis, devise an upgrade path for the Windows NT environment. Your plan should inevitably lead to a Windows 2000 domain running in Native mode so that only Windows 2000 domain controllers are supported.

   Proposed Solution: You identify the domain model as being a "complete trust." You decide to use User Manager to determine the trust relationships. To upgrade the Windows NT environment, you migrate primary domain controllers (PDCs) but leave BDCs as they are.

   What results are produced from the proposed solution?

   A. The proposed solution produces the required result only.

   B. The proposed solution produces the required result and only one of the optional results.

   C. The proposed solution produces the required result and both of the optional results.

   D. The proposed solution does not produce the required result.

   Questions 3–5   The next three questions are based upon the scenario that follows. Read the following case study and then answer the questions. You may refer to this case study as often as needed.

   You are designing a Windows 2000 Active Directory network for a company that currently has a Windows NT 4.0 network. The network consists of three domains, with each domain containing all user accounts and network resources. The following illustration shows the domain model and trust relationships of the legacy Windows NT environment. Arrows in this illustration point out the direction of trust relationships, while circles depict the domains themselves.

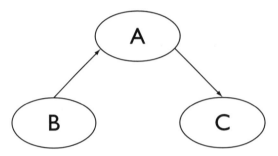

3. What domain model does the legacy network use?

   A. Single domain with trusts established between the domains

   B. Master domain with trusts established between the domains

   C. Multiple master domain

   D. Complete trust

4. In documenting the trust relationships between the domains, which of the following is true?

   A. Domain A trusts Domain B

   B. Domain B trusts Domain A

   C. Because Domain B trusts Domain A, and Domain A trusts Domain C, then Domain B and Domain C also have a trust relationship

   D. Domain C trusts Domain A

5. If you were to keep this domain model and trust relationship structure when you upgraded the network to Windows 2000, which of the following would be true? (Choose all that apply.)

   A. Domain A trusts Domain B

   B. Domain B trusts Domain A

   C. Because Domain B trusts Domain A, and Domain A trusts Domain C, then Domain B and Domain C also have a trust relationship

   D. Domain C trusts Domain A

Analyzing Existing Network Services

When documenting a Windows NT environment, you will also need to analyze existing network services that run natively on Windows NT. One such service is the Domain Name System (DNS). DNS is a hierarchically distributed database that maps host names to IP addresses. Windows 2000 requires DNS because Active Directory uses it as the locator service enabling clients and servers to locate Windows 2000 servers. However, if it is already running in an existing Windows NT environment, the DNS Service you are using may not run the same way on Windows 2000. Windows NT's DNS Service does not support dynamic updates or service resource records, whereas Windows 2000 DNS does support dynamic updates and requires service resource records.

Dynamic Domain Name System (DDNS) is a new enhancement to DNS, allowing clients to register their own host name and IP address in the DNS database and other DNS resource records. This creates maps called *A* or address resource records. Self-registration by users reduces administration by eliminating the need to manually register resource records. In addition to DDNS, DHCP can reduce administration of a network. DHCP is the Dynamic Host Configuration Protocol, used to assign IP addresses to client computers. Because the DHCP Service in Windows 2000 supports DDNS, DHCP has the ability to register records on behalf of DHCP clients.

Whereas DNS is used to map host names to IP addresses, the Windows Internet Name Service (WINS) is used to map NetBIOS names to IP addresses. You may come across this service when upgrading because Windows NT Servers use NetBIOS names, and Windows NT environments use WINS extensively. In a pure Windows 2000 environment, the presence of WINS is not necessary for the system to work. It is important to identify WINS Services when upgrading so you can then use the Windows 2000 version of WINS until such time as you are ready to remove WINS.

When analyzing existing network services, it is important to keep the following points in mind:

- When documenting DNS, make certain to find out whether the existing DNS Service supports service resource records, dynamic updates, and incremental zone transfers.

- DHCP Services also need to be documented. If a DHCP Service is provided on a different operating system, check to see if it supports DDNS.

■ WINS is not required in a pure Windows 2000 environment because Windows 2000 uses DNS for service location, but most environments will continue to have Windows NT 4.0 and Windows 9*x* workstations for many years.

exam
♨atch

If you have used the Internet, you are probably already familiar with DNS, even if you are not aware of having used it. DNS has a treelike structure, with its "root" depicted at the top, commonly shown as a single dot (.). The servers below the root are domains, which are represented by a name followed by a two- or three-letter abbreviation. Common domains include .com (for commercial organizations), .edu (for educational institutions), .gov (for nonmilitary U.S. government agencies), .mil (for U.S. military), .net (for network backbones), and .org (for nonprofit organizations). Each of these top-level domains is divided into smaller domains that are registered by organizations for their own use. This is called a namespace and must be unique. The namespace can be further divided into zones. Zones are partitions of the DNS database that is housed on a server, called the primary server. Zone information is replicated to secondary servers. When an entire zone is replicated, it is called a zone transfer, whereas updates since the last zone transfer are called incremental zone transfers. Windows 2000 has the added capability of storing zone information in Active Directory. This is called an Active Directory integrated zone and uses AD's own replication features to exchange zone information.

QUESTIONS

3.02: Analyzing Existing Network Services

6. **Current Situation:** You are designing a Windows 2000 network and Active Directory for a company that has a large user base, but a small IT staff to support users. Because of the small IT staff, it is important that administration of the Active Directory network be reduced. The staff remembers that a significant amount of time was spent manually entering IP addresses, subnet masks, and gateway information on client computers during the initial setup of the current Windows NT network. They would like to avoid having to do this in the future. The staff is also concerned about having to manually enter DNS resource records, as well as about issues regarding DNS replication. The current network does

not use DNS, and the IT staff is worried about having to manage replication of zone information between servers.

Required Result: Devise a method so that static IP addresses and other information needed to use the TCP/IP network does not need to be manually assigned to clients.

Optional Desired Results:

1. Reduce administration of DNS.

2. Design the network so that replication of zone information is automated.

Proposed Solution: Implement DDNS to reduce DNS administration. Design Active Directory to use Active Directory integrated DNS. Implement DHCP to have IP addresses automatically assigned to users.

What results are produced from the proposed solution?

A. The proposed solution produces the required result only.

B. The proposed solution produces the required result and only one of the optional results.

C. The proposed solution produces the required result and both of the optional results.

D. The proposed solution does not produce the required result.

7. The following illustration depicts the DNS Server used by Howsaboutit University. Based on the information provided in this diagram, what is the domain name of Howsaboutit U.?

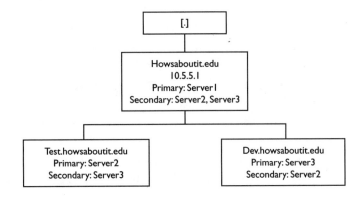

A. 10.5.5.1

B. [.]

    C. howsaboutit.edu

    D. Server1

8. Murky Motors has been using DNS on the Windows NT network. At present, each host name and IP address must be entered manually into DNS. Upon upgrading to Windows 2000, the network administrator would like clients to register their own host name and IP address in the DNS database and other DNS resource records. Which of the following would be implemented to allow this to happen?

    A. DDNS

    B. WINS

    C. DHCP

    D. DNS

TEST YOURSELF OBJECTIVE 3.03

Analyzing Existing Network Security and Reliability

Network security and reliability is always an important issue when analyzing existing Windows NT environments. If security is a problem, an unauthorized person could access a user's account and damage data or the network's integrity. Security within an existing Windows NT environment is composed of resource access permissions granted or denied to people who administer and use the Windows NT environment and the policies created for the domain. If network reliability is a problem, an existing problem in the current Windows NT network may not be fixed with the upgrade. Your upgrade to Windows 2000 could be considered a failure, even though the problem was one that existed in the legacy environment.

    Passwords are an important part of network security. On Windows NT 4.0 Servers, password security policies are found in the User Manager for Domains utility. This utility allows you to control such aspects as password length, age, number of attempts at logging in before locking the account out, and more. Password security policy is applied at the domain level only. If a group needs a different password policy, it will have its own domain.

Key tools to monitor the reliability of an Windows NT environment are event logs and Performance Monitor. Each time a failure occurs an event log is written, and these logs can then be viewed with a tool called Event Viewer. Event Viewer allows you to view the system log (for operating system errors), security log (for domain security policy violations), and application log (for application problems). Performance Monitor is another tool, which allows you to view the real-time performance of your server and network. This tool enables you to monitor suspected problem areas so you can determine if they are functioning as expected.

When analyzing existing network security and reliability, you should keep the following points in mind:

- The domain security policies for passwords and account lockout are found in the User Manager for Domains utility.

- Setting a policy to change passwords more often will reduce the security risk but increase the administrative overhead for end users who forget their passwords.

- Monitor the server's reliability through the Event Viewer and Performance Monitor utilities.

exam
⚙atch

An important part of analyzing a network's security and reliability is knowing what tools you will use to perform the analysis. User Manager for Domains allows you to view password security policies. You can look for possible security problems, which may enable an unauthorized person to hack their way into your system. In terms of reliability, Event Viewer allows you to view logs that will provide information on system, security, and application errors. The application log lists errors, warnings, audit results, and informational messages for applications. The security log lists security violations, audit results, and alerts that are related to the local or domain security policy. Finally, the system log lists errors, warnings, and informational messages for services that are part of the operating system. Performance Monitor is also vital to monitoring a server's reliability. It provides a graphical user interface that allows you to view a server's performance in real time. Before taking the exam, you should be familiar with each of these tools.

QUESTIONS

3.03: Analyzing Existing Network Security and Reliability

9. You are analyzing the existing network reliability. Windows NT Server seems to be experiencing a number of errors and you have decided to investigate the matter further. Which of the following logs would you view to obtain information on errors, warnings, and informational messages dealing with software solutions running on a Windows NT 4.0 Server?

    A. Software log

    B. System log

    C. Application log

    D. Security log

10. **Current Situation:** You are analyzing the reliability and security of a small network running Windows NT 4.0 Servers and Workstations. In the past, there have been security breaches by hackers, who accessed user accounts by continually trying a variety of possible passwords. There is also some concern about the reliability of the servers because fatal errors have occurred in the operating system on several occasions.

    Required Result: Analyze existing password security and determine the number of incorrect passwords a user is allowed to enter before the account is locked out.

    Optional Desired Results:

    1. Determine what errors, warnings, and informational messages for operating system services have occurred.

    2. Follow up on this analysis by viewing the server's performance while it is running.

    Proposed Solution: Use User Manager for Domains and document the duration an account is locked out after a predetermined number of incorrect logons. Use Event Viewer to view the server's performance in real time and view the security log to view errors, warnings, and informational messages for services that are part of the operating system.

What results are produced from the proposed solution?

A. The proposed solution produces the required result only.

B. The proposed solution produces the required result and only one of the optional results.

C. The proposed solution produces the required result and both of the optional results.

D. The proposed solution does not produce the required result.

11. The following illustration shows a tool commonly used when analyzing the reliability of a server running Windows NT 4.0. What is the name of this tool?

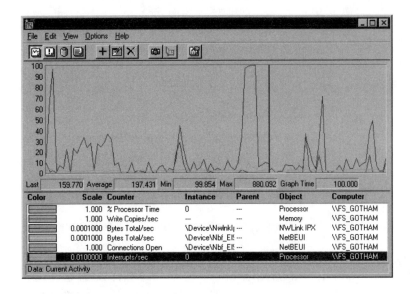

A. Server Monitor

B. Event Viewer

C. User Manager for Domains

D. Performance Monitor

TEST YOURSELF OBJECTIVE 3.04

Analyzing Existing Applications

Applications are an important part of any network, and some applications currently running on an existing Windows NT environment may not run or run properly after upgrading to Windows 2000. Some applications require the Windows NT security to work and may not be compatible with Active Directory. Others may need specific registry keys that do not exist or are in a different registry location in Windows 2000. It is important to analyze what software exists so you can determine whether to upgrade, migrate, replace, or retire applications.

During your analysis, you should determine whether an application is mission-critical. If users are unable to perform their jobs without certain software and current applications will not run on Windows 2000, then you will need to replace the software with a similar application. Once you have replaced the software, you will need to ensure that any data used by the old software is transferred to the new application. In cases where an application is not mission-critical, duplicates the functionality of other applications, has no upgrades available for it, or has few or no users accessing it, you should simply retire the application.

When analyzing existing applications, it is important to remember the following points:

- You should always list the applications that are mission-critical to end users.

- Generally, if an application is mission-critical but cannot be upgraded to Windows 2000, its function should be replaced by a similar application from a different manufacturer.

- When an application is no longer used, it can be retired.

exam
ⓦatch

Analysis of existing applications running in a Windows NT environment determines whether the software needs to be in place on the new system, and whether it will function after upgrading to Windows 2000. You can determine which applications may not function after the upgrade by running the Windows 2000 Readiness Analyzer program. To start this program, run the setup application on your Windows 2000 Server setup CD with the switch /CHECKUPGRADEONLY. This is the same procedure used to determine if the server itself can be upgraded to Windows 2000. Analyzing existing applications is an objective of the Microsoft exam, so it is important that you remember the WINWindows NT32 /CHECKUPGRADEONLY command and what it is used for.

QUESTIONS

3.04: Analyzing Existing Applications

12. The following illustration shows the user interface of a tool that determines which applications can run on your system after upgrading to Windows 2000. Which of the following command lines would you use to start this tool?

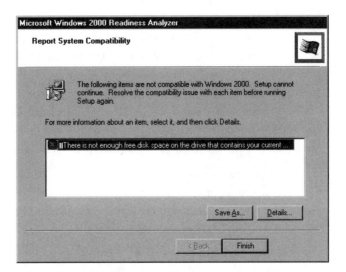

A. SETUP /CHECKUPGRADEONLY

B. WINWindows NT /CHECKUPGRADEONLY

C. WINWindows NT32 /CHECKUPGRADEONLY

D. WINWindows NT32 /CHECKUPGRADE

13. You are analyzing existing applications running in a Windows NT environment. In doing so, you come across mission-critical software, without which people cannot do their jobs. A client portion of the program runs on workstations throughout the organization, whereas the server runs a server-side

portion of the program and stores data. This application will not run on Windows 2000. What will you do?

A. Retire the application.

B. Upgrade the application and server operating system with a service pack.

C. Replace the application and transfer the data to the new application.

D. Migrate the application.

14. **Current Situation:** You are analyzing existing applications running in a Windows NT environment to determine which should be upgraded, migrated, replaced, or retired. In your analysis you find the following information. Application1 runs on the server and is used for internal email. It is used by everyone in the company and is listed as compatible with Windows NT as well as Windows 2000. Application2 is antivirus software that runs on the Windows NT 4.0 Server and Workstations. Application3 is CAD software that runs on several Windows NT Workstations. It does not install on Windows NT, but new software from the manufacturer is available that is specifically designed for Windows 2000. Application4 is a SQL Server client application that was last used September 8, 1997. Client software accesses a database on the server.

Required Result: Devise a plan so that server applications are migrated, replaced, upgraded, or retired. Server applications being used regularly that need to be available on the server are available when Windows NT Server is upgraded to Windows 2000.

Optional Desired Results:

1. Determine a plan to migrate, replace, upgrade, or retire existing software running on client computers so all applications being used regularly are available after the upgrade to Windows 2000 Active Directory.

2. Ensure that any software that is replaced or removed will not impact a user's ability to do his or her job.

Proposed Solution: Migrate Application1, retire Application3, upgrade Application4, and replace Application2 with new software that supports Windows 2000.

What results are produced from the proposed solution?

A. The proposed solution produces the required result only.

B. The proposed solution produces the required result and only one of the optional results.

C. The proposed solution produces the required result and both of the optional results.

D. The proposed solution does not produce the required result.

TEST YOURSELF OBJECTIVE 3.05

Analyzing Existing and Planned Upgrades and Rollouts

Analyzing existing and planned upgrades and rollouts is the next step after your analysis of existing applications in the Windows NT environment is complete. If you are retiring an application, you should do this analysis before upgrading to Windows 2000. Replacing or migrating applications should be done after Windows 2000 is installed. If the application is compatible with both Windows NT and Windows 2000, upgrade it prior to migration. However, if it is incompatible but still scheduled for an upgrade, upgrade the application after the migration to Windows 2000 is complete.

Another issue is the operating system software. There is no upgrade path for Windows NT 3.1 and Windows NT 3.5. You must therefore upgrade servers running these older versions of Windows NT to Windows NT 3.51 or Windows NT 4.0. Once this is done, you can then upgrade to Windows 2000. Then, before performing an upgrade on Windows NT 3.51 or 4.0, ensure that the latest service pack has been installed. This will reduce or resolve known problems in Windows NT and diminish the risk of problems you will encounter during the upgrade. Service packs for applications running on the Windows NT Server should also be applied.

■ Plan to apply service packs to both Windows NT Servers and applications prior to executing your Windows 2000 project.

- You must upgrade Windows NT 3.1 and Windows NT 3.5 Servers to newer versions, either Windows NT 3.51 or Windows NT 4.0, before executing the Windows 2000 upgrade.

- When an application must be upgraded and the application's upgraded version is supported by both Windows NT and Windows 2000, you should upgrade the application prior to upgrading the server's operating system.

exam **!**
ⓦatch

Minimal requirements are a favorite topic in Microsoft exams. Remember that before upgrading to Windows 2000, servers must be running either Windows NT 3.51 or 4.0. Even if a server is running Windows NT 3.51, you may want to consider upgrading to Windows NT 4.0 before your Windows 2000 upgrade. Windows NT 3.51 handles authentication and authorization differently than later versions. Windows NT 3.51 authenticates users and builds an access token using only security identifiers (SIDs) that are relative to the user's account domain and local groups. This access token cannot contain either a universal group outside the user's account domain or domain local groups from a resource domain. SIDs from other domains are excluded from the access token. This results in a denial of access to resources. To avoid this issue, you need to upgrade Windows NT 3.51 to Windows NT 4.0 before your Windows 2000 project starts.

QUESTIONS

3.05: Analyzing Existing and Planned Upgrades and Rollouts

15. The following illustration shows the servers currently running on the Murky Motors network. Based on the information provided in this illustration, which of the following servers must be upgraded to a later version before upgrading all servers to Windows 2000? (Choose all that apply.)

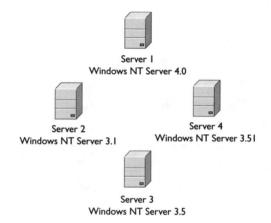

Server 1
Windows NT Server 4.0

Server 2
Windows NT Server 3.1

Server 4
Windows NT Server 3.51

Server 3
Windows NT Server 3.5

- A. Server1
- B. Server2
- C. Server3
- D. Server4

16. You are analyzing existing and planned upgrades and rollouts. There is a mission-critical application that is to be upgraded. The upgrade is compatible with both Windows NT and Windows 2000. When should the application be upgraded?

- A. Before upgrading the server to Windows 2000 Active Directory.
- B. After upgrading the server to Windows 2000 Active Directory.
- C. During the upgrade of the server to Windows 2000 Active Directory. An option will appear during this upgrade allowing you to run application upgrades and service packs.
- D. Run the Windows 2000 Readiness Analyzer before upgrading the server to Windows 2000 Active Directory. This program will allow you to upgrade the application safely.

17. **Current Situation:** You have finished analyzing existing applications running in a Windows NT environment. Windows NT 4.0 Servers and Windows NT 4.0 Workstations currently have Service Pack 4 installed, and there is another server running Windows NT 3.1 Server. You have decided that Application1

should be retired, Application2 should be replaced, and Application3 should be migrated.

Required Result: Determine when the applications should be migrated, upgraded, or replaced.

Optional Desired Results:

1. Determine what additional software should be installed before upgrading servers to Windows 2000 Server, and workstations to Windows 2000 Professional.

2. Determine whether all servers can be upgraded to Windows 2000 Server.

Proposed Solution: Application1 should be retired before upgrading to Windows 2000, whereas Application2 and Application3 should be replaced and migrated after Windows 2000 is installed. The servers and workstations running Windows NT 4.0 will not need to be upgraded or have additional software installed before upgrading them to Windows 2000. The Windows NT 3.1 Server will need to be upgraded to Windows NT 3.5 Server before it can be upgraded to Windows 2000 Server.

What results are produced from the proposed solution?

A. The proposed solution produces the required result only.

B. The proposed solution produces the required result and only one of the optional results.

C. The proposed solution produces the required result and both of the optional results.

D. The proposed solution does not produce the required result.

LAB QUESTION

Objectives 3.01–3.05

The existing Windows NT environment consists of three domains containing user accounts and network resources. Each of these domains trusts one another. There are additional domains that trust these three domains. These additional domains contain network resources such as shared files and shared printers, but no user accounts. Two of the domains have servers running Windows NT 4.0, and the third runs Windows NT 3.51. The Windows NT 4.0 Servers are running a service that maps NetBIOS names to IP addresses and runs antivirus software that uses specific Windows NT registry settings. The manufacturer does not support this service on Windows 2000.

1. What domain model does the existing Windows NT environment use?

2. What service is running on the Windows NT Servers to map NetBIOS names to IP addresses?

3. What will you use to determine password security policies used in these domains?

4. What actions should be taken regarding the antivirus software running on the Windows NT 4.0 Servers before upgrading to Windows 2000?

5. Which servers need to be upgraded before upgrading all servers to Windows 2000?

QUICK ANSWER KEY

Objective 3.01

1. B
2. B
3. A
4. B
5. A, B, C, and D

Objective 3.02

6. C
7. C
8. A

Objective 3.03

9. C
10. D
11. D

Objective 3.04

12. C
13. C
14. A

Objective 3.05

15. B and C
16. A
17. A

IN-DEPTH ANSWERS

3.01: Analyzing the Existing NT Environment

1. ☑ **B.** Master domain. The master domain model has a single master domain with additional domains containing network resources. The master domain contains user accounts and can contain network resources, while the resource domains contain network resources such as shared files and shared printers. Each resource domain trusts the master domain, so user accounts within the master domain can be granted permissions to resources within any of the resource domains. User accounts can be created within the resource domain, but these accounts cannot be granted permissions to resources within the master or any other resource domain.

    ☒ **A** is incorrect because the single domain model does not use resource domains. **C** is incorrect because the multiple master domain uses more than one master domain. **D** is incorrect because the complete trust domain model consists of two or more domains, with all domains configured to trust one another. The illustration shows two unidirectional trusts. Not all domains in this case trust one another.

2. ☑ **B.** The complete trust domain model consists of two or more domains. Each domain contains user accounts and network resources, and all domains are configured to trust each of the other domains in the Windows NT environment. To find out the trusts within the domain, you should look at the User Manager for Domains utility on either the PDC or a BDC. In User Manager's Options menu, choose the Trusts option and then view the trust relationships. Analyze which domains trust this domain and what domains this domain trusts.

    ☒ **A, C,** and **D** are incorrect because the proposed solution produces the required result and only one of the optional results. To upgrade the Windows NT environment, you will need to migrate the primary domain controller (PDC) before any backup domain controllers (BDCs). After upgrading the PDC to Windows 2000, you will then need to migrate all of the BDCs. This will change the Windows 2000 domain from Mixed mode to Native mode. Remember that Mixed mode supports legacy Windows NT BDCs and Windows 2000 domain controllers. In Native mode, only Windows 2000 domain controllers are supported.

3. ☑ **A.** The structure of this network consists of three single domains, with trust relationships set up between them. The single domain model is one domain that encompasses all user accounts and network resources in the Windows NT environment. All Windows NT Servers have the role of a domain controller (either the PDC or one of the BDCs) or of a member server, and all workstations are members of the domain.

☒ **B** is incorrect because a master domain model is a single master domain that contains user accounts and can contain network resources, with additional domains that act as resource domains. None of these domains is acting as a resource domain for the other domains. **C** is incorrect because the multiple master domain has the same qualities of a master domain model, but uses multiple master domains. An additional indicator that this is not a multiple master domain is that all of the master domains trust each other. In this case study, two domains do not trust each other. **D** is incorrect because a complete trust domain model consists of two or more domains, with all domains configured to trust one another. Since two domains do not trust each other, a complete trust does not exist.

4. ☑ **B.** Domain B trusts Domain A. Of the trust relationships of the legacy network, the following trust relationships exist: Domain B trusts Domain A and Domain A trusts Domain C.

☒ **A** and **D** are incorrect because legacy Windows NT trust relationships are unidirectional. This means that if one domain trusts another domain, the reverse is not automatically true. **C** is incorrect because legacy Windows NT trust relationships are nontransitive. This means that a trust relationship cannot pass through one domain to another. Just because Domain B trusts Domain A, and Domain A trusts Domain C, this trust does not pass through to establish a trust relationship between Domain B and Domain C.

5. ☑ **A**, **B**, **C**, and **D** are correct. All of the choices are true because trust relationships in Windows 2000 are bidirectional and transitive. Being bidirectional means that both domains trust each other. Therefore, Domain A

and Domain B trust one another, and Domain A and Domain C trust one another. Being transitive means the trust relationship passes from one domain to another. Consequently, because Domain B trusts Domain A, and Domain A trusts Domain C, then Domain B and Domain C also have a trust relationship.

3.02: Analyzing Existing Network Services

6. ☑ **C.** The proposed solution produces the required result and both of the optional results. Implementing DHCP will allow IP addresses to be automatically assigned to clients in addition to other information they will require to use the TCP/IP network. DDNS is the Dynamic Domain Name System, a new enhancement to DNS. With DDNS, clients can register their own host name mapped to their own IP address in the DNS database and other DNS resource records. These maps are called *A* or address resource records. Client self-registration reduces the administrative overhead of DNS. If DDNS were not used, you would need to manually enter each resource record in the DNS database. Windows 2000 has the added capability to store zone information in Active Directory. This is called an Active Directory integrated zone, and it uses AD's own replication features to exchange zone information. Because the DHCP service in Windows 2000 supports DDNS, DHCP has the capability to register records on behalf of DHCP clients.

    ☒ **A, B,** and **D** are incorrect because the proposed solution produces the required result and both of the optional results.

7. ☑ **C.** howsaboutit.edu is the domain name. The domain name identifies the domain and appears in the DNS tree below the root. It is represented by a name followed by a two- or three-letter abbreviation.

    ☒ **A** is incorrect because this is the IP address. **B** is incorrect because the "root" of the DNS tree is depicted at the top, commonly shown as a single dot (.). **D** is incorrect because this is the name of the server on which this domain resides.

8. ☑ **A.** DDNS is the Dynamic Domain Name System. It is a new enhancement to DNS, allowing clients to register their own host name and IP address in the DNS database and other DNS resource records.

    ☒ **B** is incorrect because WINS is the Windows Internet Name Service. It is used to map NetBIOS names to IP addresses. **C** is incorrect because DHCP is the Dynamic Host Configuration Protocol, used to automatically assign IP addresses and configuration information to client computers. **D** is incorrect because DNS is not necessarily dynamic and will not automatically allow clients to register unless it has the capabilities (such as with Windows 2000) and has been configured to do so.

3.03: Analyzing Existing Network Security and Reliability

9. ☑ **C.** The application log lists errors, warnings, and informational messages for applications. This log is viewed with the Event Viewer. Event Viewer is used to view logs that will provide information on system, security, and application errors.

    ☒ **A** is incorrect because there is no software log. **B** is incorrect because the system log lists errors, warnings, and informational messages for services that are part of the operating system. **D** is incorrect because the security log lists security violations, audit results, and alerts that are related to the local or domain security policy.

10. ☑ **D.** The proposed solution does not produce the required result. Using User Manager for Domains, you should have documented the account lockout threshold. This is the threshold number of incorrect password attempts at which point an account is locked out. User Manager for Domains also allows you to set the duration an account is locked out after a predetermined number of incorrect logons, but this is the time a user is locked out after the account lockout threshold is met.

    ☒ **A**, **B**, and **C** are incorrect because the proposed solution does not produce the required result. In addition, neither of the optional requirements is met. Event Viewer does not allow you to view a server's performance in real time. To do this, Performance Monitor is used. Also, the security log does not list errors, warnings, and informational messages for services that are part of the operating system. The system log lists this information.

11. ☑ **D.** Performance Monitor is a tool used to monitor the reliability of a Windows NT 4.0 Server. It allows you to view areas of your server in real time so you can determine performance and reliability issues.

☒   **A**, **B**, and **C** are incorrect because the figure shows the user interface of Performance Monitor.

3.04: Analyzing Existing Applications

12.   ☑   **C.** You can determine which applications may not function after the upgrade by running the Windows 2000 Readiness Analyzer. This is run by using the Windows 2000 setup application (WINWindows NT32) with the switch /CHECKUPGRADEONLY. This tool is also used to check your system to ensure it meets the requirements for upgrading a computer to Windows 2000.

☒   **A**, **B**, and **D** are incorrect because they are invalid command lines. They will not determine which applications can run on your system after upgrading to Windows 2000.

13.   ☑   **C.** Replace the application and transfer the data to the new application. Since the application is mission-critical, users are unable to perform their jobs without it. Since the application will not run on Windows 2000, it must be replaced with a similar application. Once you have replaced the application, you will need to ensure that any data used by the old software is transferred to the new application.

☒   **A** is incorrect because retiring the application and not replacing it means users will be unable to do their jobs. **B** is incorrect because the application will not run on Windows 2000 and installing service packs will not change this situation. **D** is incorrect because the application cannot be migrated since it will not run on Windows 2000.

14.   ☑   **A.** The proposed solution produces the required result only. The required result is satisfied because Application1 is to be migrated, and Application2 is to be replaced with new software. Consequently, server applications being regularly used will still be available after upgrading to Windows 2000.

☒   **B**, **C**, and **D** are incorrect because only the required result was met. Neither of the optional results was met because Application3 should have been upgraded and Application4 should have been retired. In the proposed solution these were reversed. Because this will affect the ability of users to perform their jobs and will not satisfy the requirement of ensuring regularly used applications are available after the upgrade, neither of the optional requirements was met.

3.05: Analyzing Existing and Planned Upgrades and Rollouts

15. ☑ **B** and **C** are correct. Server2 is running Windows NT 3.1 and Server3 is running Windows NT 3.5. There is no upgrade path available for either of these previous versions of Windows NT to Windows 2000. Therefore, each of these servers would need to be upgraded to Windows NT 3.51 or migrated to Windows NT 4.0 before upgrading to Windows 2000.

    ☒ **A** and **D** are incorrect because both of these servers can be upgraded to Windows 2000.

16. ☑ **A.** Upgrading an application prior to migrating to Windows 2000 should be done when the application upgrade is compatible with both Windows NT and Windows 2000. This will most likely happen only for servers installed with Windows NT 4.0, since there are more significant changes between Windows NT 3.5*x* and Windows 2000 than between Windows NT 4.0 and Windows 2000.

    ☒ **B** is incorrect because you should upgrade an application that is compatible with Windows NT and 2000 before migrating to Windows 2000. **C** is incorrect because there is no option during the Windows 2000 upgrade to install application upgrades and service packs. **D** is incorrect because the Windows 2000 Readiness Analyzer is not used to upgrade applications.

17. ☑ **A.** The proposed solution produces the required result only. Retiring an application should be done before upgrading to Windows 2000, whereas replacing or migrating applications should be done after Windows 2000 is installed.

    ☒ **B**, **C**, and **D** are incorrect because the proposed solution produces the required result only. The Windows NT 3.1 Server needs to be upgraded to Windows NT 3.51 or Windows NT 4.0 before it can be upgraded to Windows 2000 Server. Servers and workstations should have the latest service packs installed before upgrading to Windows 2000. By applying the latest Windows NT service pack to Windows NT before upgrading to Windows 2000, there will be less risk of problems during the upgrade.

LAB ANSWER

Objectives 3.01–3.05

1. Multiple master domain. The multiple master domain model has one or more
   master domains. All of the master domains contain user accounts and have one
   or more resource domains that contain the network resources but no user
   accounts. Each resource domain is configured to trust each of the master
   domains, and all of the master domains trust each other.

2. The Windows Internet Name Service (WINS) is used to map NetBIOS names
   to IP addresses. Windows NT environments use WINS extensively, so it is
   important to identify WINS Services when upgrading.

3. User Manager for Domains is a tool in Windows NT 4.0 that allows you to
   view and set password security policies.

4. Before upgrading the Windows NT operating system to Windows 2000, you
   should remove the antivirus software. Applications that use specific registry
   keys in Windows NT may not function properly once the server has been
   upgraded to Windows 2000.

5. None. Each of the servers is running Windows NT 3.51 or Windows NT 4.0
   and has upgrade paths available to it. If any of the servers were running
   Windows NT 3.1 or Windows NT 3.5, you would need to upgrade them
   to Windows NT 3.51 or Windows NT 4.0.

4

Analyzing Technical Requirements of a Directory

Regardless of any initial ideas you have about how you will design Active Directory, you may find your design limited by technical aspects of the network infrastructure. In such cases, applications, hardware, and network connectivity may need to be upgraded, replaced, or removed, and new technologies may need to be added. In doing so, you may need to work with other project teams and coordinate your results with theirs. You will also need to determine how the resources added, replaced, or removed by such projects will be distributed.

One of the greatest influences on a network and Active Directory design is the size of the company. Size is not limited to geographic scope. It also includes elements of a business, like the number of users, how they are distributed throughout the network, and the applications used by these people. This information is then applied to analyzing the distribution of the company's resources, thereby determining where servers and network services should be placed and how to allocate bandwidth to support applications and data sharing.

TEST YOURSELF OBJECTIVE 4.01

Analyzing Company Size

As we have discussed in previous chapters, a domain's Active Directory can theoretically contain ten million objects. Microsoft has acknowledged one million objects as being a more practical number, and you should consider two or more domains when Active Directory reaches 100,000 objects. The reason for this is that although AD can store millions of objects in its database, you will need the physical infrastructure to support it. Active Directory needs extra hard drive space available to support a database of this size and additional network capacity to support replication.

Although objects may include a number of different elements, a large number of objects comprising your Active Directory will be users. When analyzing a company's size, you should look at not only the current number of users, but also how this number will grow over time. You will also need to examine how these users are distributed across the network. By doing so, you will be able to determine which areas will need increased network capacity, storage space, and so forth.

In addition to determining the number of users on your network, you should also make an inventory of applications running on the network. As we discussed in the previous chapter, this will provide you with an understanding of what programs need to be upgraded, migrated, replaced, or retired. To determine the compatibility of applications, you can use the Windows 2000 Readiness Analyzer. This is started from the Windows 2000 setup CD with the command line WINNT32 /CHECKUPGRADEONLY. Programs such as Systems Management Server (SMS) can also be used to assist in creating an inventory. SMS can be used to gather information about applications by scanning host drives for .EXE files.

When analyzing a company's size, you should remember the following points:

- AD can hold millions of objects.
- Microsoft SMS can be used to gather software and hardware inventories.

exam
ⓦatch

Users, applications, and hardware are three major components to evaluate when analyzing a company's size. For users, it is important to consider growth over time. Just because a company has a set number of users now and experienced little or no growth over the last number of years, does not mean the number of users will not increase in the future. For applications, it is important to create an inventory, and Systems Management Server is useful in this regard. To determine software and hardware compatibility with Windows 2000, you can run the WINNT32 setup program with the /CHECKUPGRADEONLY switch. To determine hardware compatibility, you should also use the Hardware Compatibility List (HCL), located on Microsoft's Web site.

QUESTIONS

4.01: Analyzing Company Size

1. **Current Situation:** Murky Motors has hired you to design their Windows 2000 Active Directory network. It has 45,000 network users. The CEO of the company says he expects this number of users to grow by 50 percent, whereas the head of Human Resources does not expect any growth at all over the next few years.

   Required Result: You must design your Windows 2000 Active Directory so that it uses the fewest number of domains possible.

Optional Desired Results:

1. Determine the number of users who will use this network over the next three years.

2. Inventory the applications used on this network.

Proposed Solution: Because Active Directory has an administrative limit of 40,000 users, a minimum of three domains must be used. As the head of Human Resources does not expect any growth at all, use the current number of 45,000 users in your design. Use Windows 2000 Readiness Analyzer to assist in creating an inventory of applications being used.

What results are produced from the proposed solution?

A. The proposed solution produces the required result only.

B. The proposed solution produces the required result and only one of the optional results.

C. The proposed solution produces the required result and both of the optional results.

D. The proposed solution does not produce the required result.

2. As shown in the following illustration, the company you are designing a Windows 2000 Active Directory for has four servers, each of which is a domain controller for four separate domains. T1 lines connect these domains, and there are sufficient hardware requirements to accommodate the 50 percent increase in the number of users that is expected over the next three years. Based on this information, which of the following is true? (Choose all that apply.)

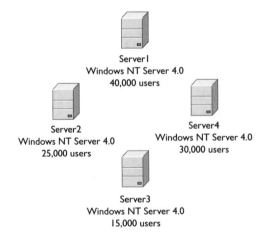

Server1
Windows NT Server 4.0
40,000 users

Server2
Windows NT Server 4.0
25,000 users

Server4
Windows NT Server 4.0
30,000 users

Server3
Windows NT Server 4.0
15,000 users

A. Server2 and Server3 can be consolidated so that one Windows 2000 Server will support the maximum 40,000 users. Server1 and Server4 can be upgraded since they are already at or near the 40,000 user limit.

B. You will need to accommodate the projected 50 percent increase in users over the next three years in your design.

C. You should use the current number of users in the design of your Active Directory. If this number actually increases, you can redesign the AD at a later date.

D. The servers can all be consolidated because Active Directory can accommodate millions of objects.

TEST YOURSELF OBJECTIVE 4.02

Analyzing Company Resource Distribution

After assessing the size of a company, you can apply information about the number of users accessing the network and their geographic location to your analysis of company resource distribution. The goal is to ensure that each location has adequate resources to support its userbase and workload. This includes not only printers, scanners, and other tools, but also servers. Because Windows 2000 is tightly integrated with DNS, users need DNS to locate domain controllers and other services, such as global catalogs. By analyzing the distribution of your company's resources, you can determine where to place servers and network services and how to allocate bandwidth to support applications and data sharing.

Since Active Directory is a database that will be stored on your server's hard drive, you need to inventory your current server hardware. This includes CPU type, memory, mass storage, BIOS, video card, sound card, and network interface card (NIC). Analyzing this information will ensure that servers meet or exceed the recommended resource requirements of Windows 2000. You should also consider the role that the servers will play in the Windows 2000 Active Directory network, such as domain controller or Web server. In Windows 2000, you can promote servers to be or demote servers from being domain controllers using a wizard called DCPROMO.EXE. This option was not available in Windows NT. Once a Windows NT Server was made a domain controller it could not be changed from that role without reinstalling the operating system. We will discuss DCPROMO in greater detail in Chapter 13.

When analyzing company resource distribution, you should always keep the following points in mind:

■ If there is inadequate network connectivity, position resources close to the users that use them.

■ Windows 2000 clients require access to a DNS Service because Windows 2000 AD is tightly integrated with DNS.

exam
ⓦatch

It is important to inventory server components to ensure that the hardware requirements to run Windows 2000 are met. Windows 2000 requires at least a 133MHz Pentium-compatible processor, 128MB of RAM, and a 2GB hard disk with 1GB free space. These requirements are considerably more than for Windows NT 4.0 Server. Consequently, just because Windows NT can run on the server, it does not necessarily follow that Windows 2000 can. If the minimum requirements are not met, the hardware will need to be replaced or upgraded. In real-world situations, it is also important to realize that the minimum requirements may not suit your needs, and additional memory, storage space, or other resources may be required for your server to perform adequately.

BIOS compatibility is another important factor with Windows 2000. Advanced power management and configuration (Plug-and-Play) in the form of Advanced Configuration and Power Interface (ACPI) is dependent upon a compatible BIOS. If the BIOS is incompatible, it could cause system stability problems.

QUESTIONS

4.02: Analyzing Company Resource Distribution

3. The company you work for has servers in a centralized location at the company's main building. Because of lack of facilities, it has offices located in a

separate building across the street and in another office one block away. These offices are connected with routers and an ISDN connection because there is not enough money in the budget to use faster methods of connectivity. When users at offices across the road attempt to send and receive email, they find it incredibly slow. They also find it slow accessing applications on the server. When users in the offices one block away try to access large files and applications on the server, they have to wait a significant amount of time. Which of the following can you do to improve this situation?

A. Move all users to facilities in the main building.

B. Because Windows 2000 can support millions of objects in Active Directory, keep the servers in a centralized location.

C. Add a server to each office location. A server at the offices across the road can be an application and email server, and the server at the office down the block can store files for common use.

D. Do nothing. The only thing that can be done is improve network connectivity.

4. You have a Windows NT Server that is acting as a domain controller. When the Windows 2000 network is in place, you will no longer need this server as a domain controller, but you still want this server to be available for network file storage. Which of the following will you do?

A. Before upgrading to Windows 2000 Server, demote the domain controller.

B. Before upgrading to Windows 2000 Server, run DCPROMO to demote the domain controller.

C. Upgrade the Windows NT Server to Windows 2000 Server, and then run WINMSD to demote the domain controller.

D. Upgrade the Windows NT Server to Windows 2000 Server, and then run DCPROMO to demote the domain controller.

Assessing Existing and Planned Upgrades and Rollouts

In Chapter 3 we discussed how important it is to determine what applications and service packs are being added, upgraded, or removed and when this will occur in your Windows 2000 project. In addition to this, you may find that projects are currently in the works involving upgrades to network media and connectivity, hardware upgrades, and so forth. When this occurs, you will need to determine if your Active Directory rollout coincides with other IT projects and coordinate your efforts with those of other project teams.

The key is to stay in contact with other project teams and coordinate your efforts with them. This may involve regular IT meetings, allowing members or leaders of each team to discuss their plans and current status. Another option is to designate a liaison to work with other teams. The goal is to ensure a consistent and accurate flow of information among project teams.

When assessing existing and planned upgrades and rollouts, it is important to remember the following points:

- Watch for current upgrades and rollouts and how they may impact the directory.
- Work with other project teams to coordinate your efforts.

exam
ⓦ**atch**

In coordinating your efforts, you will need to give some projects priority over others, postpone other projects, or put them ahead of Windows 2000 upgrades. If the application is compatible with both Windows NT and Windows 2000 or if it is being retired, then the installation, upgrade, or removal of that application should occur prior to migration. If an application is compatible but still planned for upgrading, you should plan this upgrading to take place after Windows 2000 is installed. The same applies to replacing or migrating applications, which should also be done after Windows 2000 is installed. In addition to application rollouts and upgrades, you should be aware of other projects, such as upgrades to network connectivity, which will have an impact on your project.

QUESTIONS

4.03: Assessing Existing and Planned Upgrades and Rollouts

5. The IT staff of Murky Motors has several projects currently under way. The Graphics Department is to install several stand-alone Macintosh computers. The IT training staff will also install a small training network, allowing users to learn on computers before becoming part of the actual network. A Research and Development project has decided to upgrade software in the finance department that is not compatible with Windows 2000, and it has developed in-house software that will run on servers and is designed to work with Windows 2000. A new hardware upgrade project plans to upgrade the current hard drives on servers and workstations. Which of the projects will have an impact on your Windows 2000 Active Directory project? (Choose all that apply.)

    A. The Macintosh computers being installed

    B. The network being installed in the training room

    C. The finance software to be installed by R&D

    D. The in-house software developed by R&D

    E. The hardware upgrade project

6. **Current Situation:** Asimov Robotics, Inc., currently has a Windows NT environment and has several IT projects currently under way. You are in charge of upgrading the environment to Windows 2000 Active Directory. A hardware project is replacing 15-inch monitors with 17-inch monitors. An application project is installing several applications that are compatible with both Windows NT and Windows 2000. There is another project to remove an unused program from servers and workstations.

    Required Result: Determine what IT projects will affect your Active Directory upgrade project and what teams you will need to coordinate with.

Optional Desired Results:

1. Determine what effect hardware upgrades will have on your Active Directory design.

2. Determine when installation of applications by other project teams should occur.

Proposed Solution: The only IT project that will affect your upgrade is the application project. You will need to coordinate your efforts with this team. Each of the applications should be removed or installed after the Windows 2000 upgrade. The hardware project will have no effect on your upgrade. What results are produced from the proposed solution?

A. The proposed solution produces the required result only.

B. The proposed solution produces the required result and only one of the optional results.

C. The proposed solution produces the required result and both of the optional results.

D. The proposed solution does not produce the required result.

TEST YOURSELF OBJECTIVE 4.04

Assessing Available Connectivity

Assessing available connectivity requires knowledge of network technologies and topologies. The ability of workstations and servers to connect to one another is an important factor of a network. When evaluating network connectivity and performance, we need to look at three different criteria: reliability, capacity, and delay.

Reliability refers to the dependability of the network link both in the past and in the present. An unreliable link can result in packets of data needing to be resent or the link being unavailable. It can also cause poor performance or users being unable to connect at all to the rest of the network.

Capacity refers to the capability of a network connection to transmit packets of data. It can be broken down into two components: bandwidth and throughput. The capacity of a network medium is usually measured in bandwidth, which is the theoretical capacity of a network connection. For example, the following table shows examples of media bandwidth. Throughput is the actual capacity of the link. Actual capacity is theoretical capacity minus overhead (the administrative data needed to flow over the link). To illustrate this, if you used a T1 line with a bandwidth of 1.544 Mbps, the actual capacity (throughput) may be only 1 Mbps or less. It is throughput, or the actual capacity of the media, that is used to determine if a link can handle replication traffic generated by AD.

Media	Bandwidth
Unshielded twisted pair (UTP)	1–155 Mbps (typically 10 Mbps)
Shielded twisted pair (STP)	1–155 Mbps (typically 16 Mbps)
Coaxial cable	10 Mbps
Fiber optic	2 Gbps (typically 100 Mbps)
T-carriers	T1 (1.544 Mbps) T2 (6.312 Mbps) T3 (44.736 Mbps) T4 (274.176 Mbps)

Finally, delay or latency refers to how long it actually takes for packets of data to travel from point to point on the network. There are several tools available to measure this, including PING and PINGPATH. PING is used to check connectivity and latency (delay). It sends a message and then waits for a reply. The result displayed is the time it took for each packet to travel from the source to the destination. PINGPATH is a Windows 2000 tool that combines the features of PING with those of TRACERT, which allows you to view route information.

Network diagrams can be useful tools to analyze network connectivity. When creating a diagram, you need to note whether a link is dial-on-demand or always available. When diagramming the physical network, you should denote physical locations, the communication links between locations, network devices such as routers and switches, protocols, addressing schemes such as the subnet addresses and address ranges for each segment, network address translation (NAT), RAS connections, and Internet connections. For logical network diagrams, you should include Windows NT domains, trust relationships, WINS (Windows Internet Name Service) Service locations, replication topology, DNS namespace, DHCP Services, and any implementations of Kerberos that may exist on the network.

When assessing available connectivity of a network, you should keep the following points in mind:

- Delay is the amount of time it takes data to travel from point A to point B.
- Network address translation (NAT) is used to translate a private IP address to a public address.
- Windows 2000 clients attempt to locate resources close to them on the network using AD site definitions.

exam

⑩atch

Read questions carefully because issues dealing with available connectivity may be hidden within the question. For example, unreliable links may be the actual issue addressed in the question, but the surrounding material may mislead you. You should also keep in mind the differences between bandwidth capacity and throughput capacity. Bandwidth capacity is the theoretical capacity of a connection. It is the amount of data the media should transfer in a perfect world. Throughput is the actual capacity, less overhead. When looking at bandwidth and throughput, you will generally find throughput to be less than the theoretical bandwidth. When designing your Active Directory, you should look at throughput capacity, as it will show if a link can handle AD replication.

QUESTIONS

4.04: Assessing Available Connectivity

Questions 7–9   The next three questions are based upon the scenario that follows.

Read the following case study and then answer the questions. You may refer to this case study as often as needed.

As shown in the following illustration, Positronic Robotics and Housewares has offices in New York and Los Angeles. Recently, it has opened a second office in Los Angeles, which is depicted here as LA2. When assessing available connectivity, you find that the capacity of the T1 line between NY and LA ranges between 850 and 900 Kbps, and the connection between the main LA office and LA2 has been going down regularly. When this happens, users are unable to resolve hostnames to IP addresses and are also unable to access Active Directory.

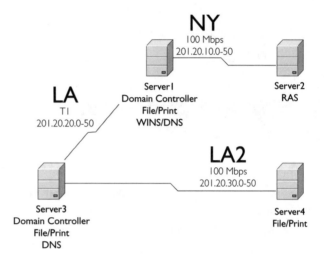

7. Which of the following will solve the problem LA2 is having resolving hostnames to IP addresses and using Active Directory?

   A. Add an additional domain controller that will also act as a DNS Service at the LA office to service the LA2 office.

   B. Add an additional domain controller that will also act as a DNS Service at the NY office to service both LA and LA2.

   C. Promote Server4 to a domain controller, and make it a DNS Service.

   D. Promote Server4 to a domain controller, and install the WINS Service.

8. In looking at the capacity of the T1 line between NY and LA, what is being measured?

   A. The theoretical capacity of the network media

   B. Throughput

   C. Bandwidth

   D. The actual capacity of the network media, including overhead

9. Which of the following can be used to measure latency between LA and LA2? (Choose all that apply.)

    A. TRACERT

    B. PINGPONG

    C. PINGPATH

    D. PING

TEST YOURSELF OBJECTIVE 4.05

Assessing the Net Available Bandwidth

If your network does not have available the bandwidth that it needs, then the performance of your network will decrease. This is generally because of having media with inadequate bandwidth to support your network, or having so many users and resources using the network that the throughput falls to such a degree that performance suffers. If the media does not have the capacity to support Active Directory, users will experience delays in trying to log on and access resources. Your network can become so bogged down that users, services, and resources cannot function properly.

Network Monitor is a useful tool for analyzing network traffic and assessing the net available bandwidth. It is shipped with Windows NT 4.0 and Windows 2000, allowing you to monitor your network before and after upgrading to Windows 2000. This tool allows you to gather information on the number of bytes sent and received per second, as well as packets sent and received per second. Other features include the ability to capture data related to transmit and receive errors. The version of Network Monitor that comes with Windows 2000 is limited to analyzing traffic originating from, or destined to, the host on which it is running. The full version of Network Monitor is shipped with Systems Management Server. This full version can operate in "promiscuous mode," allowing it to listen for all traffic on the network segment to which the host is attached.

Regardless of the version you are using, you should capture traffic during peak periods and slow periods, so that you can have a baseline for your network. A baseline measures performance under what is considered a normal load. It provides a record of how the network is currently responding, so that you can make a comparison when changes or problems occur.

When assessing the net available bandwidth of your network, it is important to remember the following points:

- Available bandwidth is required to replicate portions of the directory database.
- Network Monitor can be used to analyze LAN traffic.

e x a m
ⓦa t c h

Available bandwidth is an important issue for Active Directory because of replication. Remember that Active Directory is a distributed database, meaning that parts of it exist on different servers across the network. The distributed database design reduces the load on any single server. It also facilitates the delegation of administration through domain boundaries and provides fault tolerance in the event of a single server failure. The distributed database design of AD provides numerous benefits, but it also requires that the servers holding pieces of the database must communicate with one another. Because AD is a multimaster database, writes to the database are allowed on any server holding the relevant partition of the directory. In order for the other servers hosting that partition to receive an update, replication needs to occur, and this takes up bandwidth.

QUESTIONS

4.05: Assessing the Net Available Bandwidth

10. Which of the following best describes Active Directory and the effect that net available bandwidth will have on it?

   A. Active Directory can be hosted only on a single server. Because of this, AD is immune to the effects of poor bandwidth.

   B. Active Directory is a multimaster database. Because it is stored on multiple servers, it needs enough bandwidth to properly replicate changes or even the entire database between servers.

C. Active Directory can be stored only on a single server. Because each server stores an entire copy of the database, AD relies on the net available bandwidth to replicate changes.

D. Active Directory is a multimaster database. This means that multiple copies of the AD database are stored on a single server, and only the portions required by other servers are replicated across the network. Because this is such a small data transfer, net available bandwidth has no impact on AD.

11. The following illustration shows the user interface of a program used to assess net available bandwidth. This tool is shipped with Windows 2000 Server. What application is this, and what is it used for?

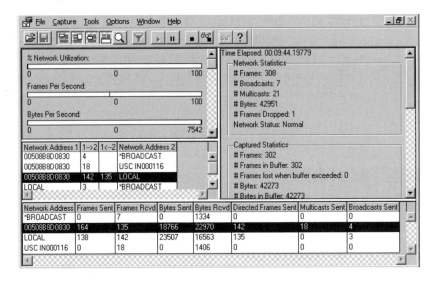

A. Network Manager, used for gathering information on the number of bytes sent and received per second

B. Network Monitor, used for monitoring network traffic

C. Network Monitor, used for assessing the impact that net available bandwidth currently has on Active Directory

D. Network Manager, used for monitoring network traffic

TEST YOURSELF OBJECTIVE 4.06

Analyzing Performance Requirements

Performance is always an issue in a network. When analyzing performance requirements, you must determine what resources and technologies need to be present to meet the level of performance expected. For example, you may need to improve the processor speed of servers, use multiprocessing, or implement faster methods of connectivity. A number of companies have Service Level Agreements (SLAs) in place that give some guarantee of performance and reliability. To better reflect the demands and functionality requirements of Windows 2000, these SLAs should be reviewed and, if necessary, revised.

As mentioned in the previous section, a baseline is important in detecting network performance declines. A baseline can provide a record of how the network performs when it is running properly and not bogged down. When the network performs poorly, you can then compare your findings to this baseline.

There are two tools that are useful for monitoring network performance: Network Monitor and Performance Monitor. We discussed Network Monitor in the previous section, including how it can be used to view information on current network utilization, frames per second, and so forth. Performance Monitor is used to view how your server is performing. A version of Performance Monitor is shipped with both Windows NT 4.0 and Windows 2000 Server, so you can view a server's performance both before and after upgrading to Windows 2000. The tool can monitor most aspects of your Windows server and can present information about the server in the form of charts, reports, and logs.

When analyzing performance requirements, keep the following points in mind:

- Service Level Agreements (SLAs) are used to guarantee a level of performance.

- Performance Monitor and Network Monitor are two tools useful in monitoring network performance.

When analyzing network performance, you need to ensure that the technologies and resources in place meet the company's needs. If a company is using video streaming, NetMeeting, or ERP applications like SAP, does the present media in use allow these applications to access data and function quickly? If not, is faster media necessary, or will placing servers closer to the users who use these applications meet their needs? You should also consider redundancy when analyzing performance. If a T1 or T3 line goes down and users absolutely must access data across these lines, you should consider implementing a second link. An Integrated Services Digital Network (ISDN) line or a fully redundant link (such as a second T1 connection) would allow users to continue their work in these cases.

QUESTIONS

4.06: Analyzing Performance Requirements

12. **Current Situation:** Asimov Robotics, Inc., has offices in New York City, Atlanta, and Toronto. Each of these sites is connected with an ISDN line. The company has recently implemented an intranet. The intranet has a Web page that users can access to view video streaming of training sessions. Because of the anticipated success of this, company board members have decided to meet with the management of these offices using NetMeeting.

    Required Result: Users in Atlanta and Toronto should be able to view video streamed training sessions and use NetMeeting without performance problems.

    Optional Desired Results:

    1. Users in Atlanta and Toronto should still be able to access data on the New York servers even if the T1 line goes down.

    2. Devise a method of monitoring network performance issues.

Proposed Solution: Upgrade the existing ISDN lines to T1 lines. Have an additional ISDN line between Atlanta and New York, and between Toronto and New York. Use Performance Monitor and Network Monitor to monitor network performance.

What results are produced from the proposed solution?

A. The proposed solution produces the required result only.

B. The proposed solution produces the required result and only one of the optional results.

C. The proposed solution produces the required result and both of the optional results.

D. The proposed solution does not produce the required result.

13. As shown in the following illustration, Murky Motors has its headquarters in Detroit. It has just started a project with its partner, Muddy Mufflers, whose offices are in Oklahoma. Muddy Mufflers supplies all the mufflers used in Murky Motors automobiles, but now the two companies will work together designing exhaust systems for the cars. The two companies are already connected through the network. They are connected through a T1 line, but there is some concern over network reliability and availability. Which of the following will you do to deal with this issue?

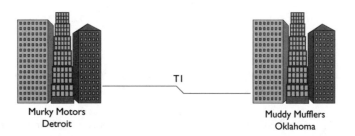

Murky Motors
Detroit

T1

Muddy Mufflers
Oklahoma

A. Upgrade the T1 line to a T3 line.

B. Put domain controllers with DNS at each location.

C. Install a redundant network connection between the locations.

D. Remove the T1 line and have separate LANs.

TEST YOURSELF OBJECTIVE 4.07

Analyzing Data and System Access Patterns

An important part of researching a network is determining when and where users access data and systems. When we discussed creating baselines, we saw that it is important to identify customary peak and slow periods so you can properly assess network performance and net available bandwidth. Identifying these periods is also useful to scale and locate servers and to determine replication and site links for Active Directory, so that replication of the directory does not overwhelm network connections.

Windows 2000 uses site definitions as boundaries of good network connectivity. A site is one or more TCP/IP subnets. When users log on, Active Directory clients locate AD servers in the same site as the user. If the connectivity between two sites is less than optimal, each location should be defined as a separate site in Active Directory.

A benefit of site-to-site communication is that the replication traffic generated by Active Directory can be scheduled. You can set when replications will occur and how often. This means that Active Directory replication can be scheduled to occur during off-hours, when there is little or no network activity. Another benefit is that replication data is compressed, meaning there will be less data from replication to take up your network bandwidth. Users will not have to compete with Active Directory for network bandwidth.

When analyzing data and system access patterns, it is important to remember the following points:

- Examining how and when users access resources helps place and scale servers and network links.

- AD site-to-site replication is compressed and can be scheduled to avoid peak user access periods.

exam
Watch

Because Active Directory is a distributed database, data must be replicated between servers. You can schedule when replication occurs so that you do not transmit this data across the network when a majority of users are online. Compression decreases the size of replicated data sent across the network. You can also decrease the frequency with which replication occurs to prevent unnecessary data transmission, thereby freeing up network bandwidth.

Another way to decrease network traffic, and thereby allow users to access data and services, is to use incremental zone transfers. A zone is a domain, or a domain with child domains. The zone is a subtree of the DNS database, administered as a separate entity. If the zone is Active Directory integrated, changes in zones are replicated to other DNS Services when AD is replicated. If it is not AD integrated, then zone transfers are used. To decrease traffic, you can set incremental zone transfers, so that only differences between the source and replicated versions are transferred. In other words, only changes are sent to other DNS Services.

QUESTIONS

4.07: Analyzing Data and System Access Patterns

14. Your Windows 2000 network consists of several sites and zones that are connected with slow links. The zones are Active Directory integrated. Which of the following will improve performance so that users are better able to access data and services across the network? (Choose all that apply.)

   A. Lower the frequency with which replication occurs.

   B. Raise the frequency with which replication occurs.

   C. Use incremental zone transfers.

   D. Schedule replication during off-hours.

15. You have two subnets as part of your existing Windows NT network. These two subnets are connected with a slow, unreliable link. In upgrading to Windows 2000, how will your design deal with these subnets so that performance is not decreased and users will be better able to access data and systems?

   A. Combine both subnets into a single site in Active Directory.

   B. Define each subnet as a separate site in Active Directory.

   C. Make replication occur more frequently between the subnets.

   D. Schedule replication to occur during peak hours.

TEST YOURSELF OBJECTIVE 4.08

Analyzing Network Roles and Responsibilities

As your network changes, roles and responsibilities on the network will also change. Management should work with individuals to determine what their current skill set is and prepare for what their roles and responsibilities will be once Windows 2000 is deployed. In most cases, administration of the network will need to be reorganized, and users and IT staff will need to be retrained. This applies not only to those who administer the network, but also to support staff. You should determine what support will be available to users when the new system rolls out, analyze what experience and knowledge support staff such as help desk personnel have, and determine what additional training they will require.

Active Directory also changes roles and responsibilities by allowing you to assign administrative authority in a more precise way. In Windows NT, the tasks a user performed often required him or her to be a member of the Domain Administrators group. This often meant the user was given more security than they required. In Windows 2000, you can use organizational units (OUs). OUs are containers in Active Directory used to organize objects in a domain into logical administrative groups. OUs can contain such objects as user accounts, groups, computers, printers, applications, file shares, and so forth. You can arrange these organizational units so they mirror the functional or business structure of an organization. Once you have organized the objects into OUs, you can then use them to enforce separate security policies or administrative boundaries.

When analyzing network roles and responsibilities, you should always keep the following points in mind:

- Make sure your technical support team is properly trained on Windows 2000.
- AD administrators will need to work closely with DNS and network administrators.

When implementing Windows 2000 Active Directory on your network, roles and responsibilities will ultimately change. This is particularly evident when considering DNS and WINS. Prior to Windows 2000, WINS (Windows Internet Name Service) was commonly used on Microsoft networks to resolve NetBIOS names to IP addresses. If a member of your IT staff administrated WINS on the Windows NT network, his or her usefulness may end once Windows 2000 is in place. Although Windows 2000 supports WINS, it is no longer needed on a pure Windows 2000 network. DNS (Domain Name System) is used as the locator service, resolving host names to IP addresses. It allows clients to locate domain controllers, or to find global catalog servers to initiate enterprise directory searches. If a company with an NT environment is using DNS, it may be running some version of Berkeley Internet Name Domain (BIND) on Unix-based servers. BIND is a proven and reliable DNS Service, and a Windows version of BIND was available with Windows NT 4.0. When it comes to choosing a DNS Service, IT departments have the following choices: BIND running on Unix, Windows 2000 DNS, or a hybrid solution of Windows 2000 DNS and BIND. Regardless of the implementation, WINS administrators may need retraining on DNS, and DNS administrators may need to upgrade their knowledge to understand Windows 2000 DNS. Because Active Directory and DNS are so closely related, you may also experience overlapping responsibilities between existing DNS administrators and Windows administrators.

QUESTIONS

4.08: Analyzing Network Roles and Responsibilities

16. The company you work for uses only Windows NT 4.0 Servers and Workstations. The network uses WINS to resolve NetBIOS names to IP addresses, and this is administered by a member of the IT staff. DNS is not used on the network because there has never been a need for this service. Your plan is for all servers to run Windows 2000 Server, and all workstations to run Windows 2000 Professional. The Windows administrator, WINS administrator, and help desk personnel have no experience or knowledge of these operating systems. Which of the following will you need to do? (Choose all that apply.)

    A. Keep WINS for name resolution after upgrading the network to Windows 2000.

    B. Remove WINS from the network, and use DNS for all name resolution.

    C. Train the WINS administrator on DNS. Make this IT staff member the DNS administrator.

    D. Train the Windows administrator on WINS. Make this IT staff member an additional WINS administrator.

17. You are concerned about the level of security certain users have on the network. To perform certain tasks, a number of these users have been made members of the Domain Administrators groups. In upgrading all servers on your network to Windows 2000, how will you resolve this situation?

    A. Use organizational units to delegate administrative control.

    B. Use DNS to delegate administrative control.

    C. Use WINS to delegate administrative control.

    D. Use zone replication to delegate administrative control.

TEST YOURSELF OBJECTIVE 4.09

Analyzing Security Considerations

When analyzing security considerations, you should document as many aspects of security that apply to your environment as possible. This includes authentication mechanisms such as Internet, intranet, and dial-up, Service Level Agreements (SLAs), existing Windows NT Security Groups and permissions, backup schemes, disaster recovery procedures, and security account synchronization with other operating systems such as Unix. These elements will be applied to your design of Active Directory and your Windows 2000 network.

As mentioned in the previous section, OUs can be used to delegate administrative authority at various levels. When you design OUs into your domain structure, you should create a common group of organizational units that can be contained in all domains. Separate security policies can then be applied to each level. However, in doing so, you should try to keep your design simple because administrative duties will grow with the number of OUs you create.

Security protocols are another important part of analyzing security considerations. Kerberos is the default and preferred authentication mechanism for Windows 2000. Windows 2000 uses Kerberos, version 5, which is an industry standard security protocol. It encrypts passwords that are sent across the network, so that passwords are secure. It handles authentication of user or system identity and supports mutual authentication, so that the server and client must each provide authentication. It also supports delegated authentication, so that a user's credentials are tracked. Another important protocol is Internet Protocol Security (IPSec), an industry standard protocol for encrypting TCP/IP. It provides secure communication within a network or virtual private network (VPN).

Finally, smart cards used in computers should be documented, since they provide an alternate method of authentication. A smart card is a credit card–size device with an embedded chip that interfaces with a smart card reader attached to a PC. Group policy settings can be used to specify whether a user must log on using a smart card. When this specification has been set, three types of logons can be used: interactive logon, client authentication, and remote access. To enhance security, the smart card hosts a certificate issued by a certificate authority, and the owner of the smart card must enter a personal identification number (PIN) to identify the user as the owner of the smart card.

When analyzing security considerations you should keep the following points in mind:

■ A Windows 2000 domain defines the security boundary that determines account policy.

■ Kerberos is the default and preferred authentication mechanism for Windows 2000.

exam
⚠atch

Windows NT relied on a less secure protocol called NTLM. With Windows 2000, Kerberos, version 5, is the default authentication mechanism. Kerberos uses tickets and ticket requests to facilitate logon authentication and access to resources. Each Windows 2000 domain controller runs a Kerberos Distribution Center (KDC) service that handles ticket creation and authorization. The KDC validates users against their object in AD and then issues the client a Kerberos ticket that is good for a predefined amount of time.

QUESTIONS

4.09: Analyzing Security Considerations

18. You have just upgraded your NT environment to a pure Windows 2000 network. Which of the following is the default authentication protocol that will be used, and what must be running on Windows 2000 Server?

A. NTLM 1.0. DNS must be running on the server for this authentication protocol to function.

B. NTLM 2.0. DNS must be running on the domain controller for this authentication protocol to function.

C. Kerberos, version 1. Each server must be running the Kerberos Distribution Center (KDC) service.

D. Kerberos, version 5. Each domain controller must be running the Kerberos Distribution Center (KDC) service.

19. Which of the following is an alternate method of authentication in which group policy settings specify whether a user must logon with this alternate method?

    A. Kerberos

    B. IPSec

    C. Smart card

    D. Dumb card

LAB QUESTION

Objectives 4.01–4.09

Asimov Robotics, Inc., has a population of 40,000 users. The CEO of the company says that he expects a 25 percent increase in users over the next three years because of a new contract they have acquired. The Human Resources Manager believes there will be only a 10 percent increase in users, whereas other managers have estimated a growth increase of 15 percent. Part of the network is in a small building, and because of the slow and unreliable connection, most of the network in this building is on a separate LAN. Because WINS is used on this separate network, it does not use the DNS Service, which is available to the major portion of the network. Currently, the small building's LAN has its own server, and the main building has several other servers.

1. What is the number of current users and projected users that you should consider when designing Active Directory?

2. What effect will the location of the DNS Service have on your Windows 2000 Active Directory design?

3. Where should a new DNS Service be placed?

4. What tool is available with Windows 2000 and Windows NT 4.0 that you can use to check network traffic? On which servers would you use this tool?

5. What can be done to improve the reliability and availability of the connection between the buildings?

A QUICK ANSWER KEY

Objective 4.01
  1. **D**
  2. **B** and **D**

Objective 4.02
  3. **C**
  4. **D**

Objective 4.03
  5. **C, D,** and **E**
  6. **B**

Objective 4.04
  7. **C**
  8. **B**
  9. **C** and **D**

Objective 4.05
  10. **B**
  11. **B**

Objective 4.06
  12. **C**
  13. **C**

Objective 4.07
  14. **A** and **D**
  15. **B**

Objective 4.08
  16. **B** and **C**
  17. **A**

Objective 4.09
  18. **D**
  19. **C**

IN-DEPTH ANSWERS

4.01: Analyzing Company Size

1. ☑ **D.** The proposed solution does not produce the required result. Theoretically, a domain's Active Directory can contain ten million objects, with one million objects being a more practical number. In Windows NT 4.0, there is an administrative limitation on how big the Security Account Manager (SAM) account database can get. This limitation is 40MB, which equates to about 40,000 users. With the introduction of Active Directory (AD), this administrative limitation no longer exists.

   ☒ **A, B,** and **C** are incorrect because the proposed solution does not produce the required result. In determining growth of network users over time, you should use the highest projection. Whether this number is reached or not, your design will be able to handle it. The choice of programs to help create an inventory is also incorrect. The Windows 2000 Readiness Analyzer is used to determine the compatibility of applications before upgrading to Windows 2000.

2. ☑ **B** and **D** are correct. You should take not only the current number of users into account in your design, but also the projected growth of users as well. If you want to consolidate servers, you can in this case. Active Directory can support millions of objects. If, as in this case, the physical infrastructure can support consolidation, then you can decrease the number of servers to one, two, or three servers running Windows 2000.

   ☒ **A** is incorrect because AD can store millions of objects in its database, and the physical infrastructure has the ability to support the current and projected number of users. **C** is incorrect because you should take not only the current number of users into account in your design, but also the projected growth of users as well.

4.02: Analyzing Company Resource Distribution

3. ☑ **C.** Add a server to each office location. A server at the offices across the road can be an application and email server, and the server at the office down the block can store files commonly used. Because there is inadequate network connectivity, it is important to position resources close to the users that use them.

   ☒ **A** is incorrect because the reason these users are in different offices is that there is a lack of facilities at the main building. **B** is incorrect because this solution would not place resources close to the users that need them. **D** is incorrect because this solution does nothing to improve the users' access to resources.

4. ☑ **D.** Upgrade the Windows NT Server to Windows 2000 Server, and then run DCPROMO to demote the domain controller. When inventorying servers, you should consider the role servers will play in the Windows 2000 Active Directory network. DCPROMO is a wizard in Windows 2000 that allows you to promote servers to be domain controllers or demote domain controllers back to servers.

   ☒ **A** is incorrect because once you make a Windows NT server a domain controller you cannot change it from that role without reinstalling the operating system. **B** is incorrect because DCPROMO is a tool available only with Windows 2000 Server. You need to upgrade the server to Windows 2000 before using it. **C** is incorrect, because WINMSD is a tool that allows you to view current hardware configuration, but it has nothing to do with the promotion or demotion of servers and domain controllers.

4.03: Assessing Existing and Planned Upgrades and Rollouts

5. ☑ **C**, **D**, and **E** are correct. The finance software that is not compatible with Windows 2000, the in-house software developed to work with Windows 2000, and the hardware upgrade project will all have an effect on the design of your Windows 2000 Active Directory project. The finance software will not work with Windows 2000, so you will need to work with the Research and

Development team to choose software that will work with Windows 2000. The in-house software will be installed on the Windows 2000 servers, and you will need to determine how it will affect security, network traffic, storage, and other issues. Because the Active Directory is a database requiring storage space, and because Windows 2000 requires minimum hard disk space, you will also need to coordinate your efforts with the hardware upgrade project.

☒ **A** is incorrect because the stand-alone Macintosh computers will not be part of your Windows 2000 Active Directory network. **B** is incorrect because the training network is being installed as a separate network.

6. ☑ **B.** The proposed solution produces the required result and only one of the optional results. Since the hardware project upgrades only monitors, it will have no impact on your project. The application project will affect your AD project, and you should coordinate your efforts with them.

☒ **A, C**, and **D** are incorrect because the proposed solution produces the required result and only one of the optional results. If the application is compatible with both Windows NT and Windows 2000 or if it is being retired, the installation, upgrade, or removal of that application should occur prior to migration.

4.04: Assessing Available Connectivity

7. ☑ **C.** Promote Server4 to a domain controller, and make it a DNS Service. If there is an unreliable link between headquarters and a remote location, then resources such as domain controllers and DNS need to be placed at the remote site. This will allow users to access the domain controller and resolve hostnames to IP addresses.

☒ **A** is incorrect because locating the domain controller and DNS Service at the LA office will not prevent LA2 from being cut off from the network when the link between LA and LA2 is down. This means LA2 will not have access to the domain controller or DNS. **B** is incorrect because if the link between LA2 and LA is unreliable, then when this link is down, LA2 will be cut off from both NY and LA. **D** is incorrect because WINS resolves NetBIOS names to IP addresses. DNS is needed to resolve hostnames to IP addresses.

8. ☑ **B.** Throughput is the actual capacity of the network, less overhead. Overhead is the administrative data needed to flow over the link. Because T1

lines can theoretically transmit 1.544 Mbps of data, it cannot be bandwidth that is being measured here. Therefore, the capacity given here is the throughput.

☒ **A** and **C** are incorrect because bandwidth is the theoretical capacity of a network medium. Since T1 lines can, in theory, transmit 1.544 Mbps of data, and the network medium has the capacity of carrying only 850–900 Kbps of data, the measurement given in this scenario cannot be bandwidth. **D** is incorrect because capacity can be bandwidth or throughput. Throughput is the actual capacity of the network media, less overhead.

9.   ☑   **C** and **D** are correct. PING and PINGPATH can be used to measure latency between LA and LA2. Latency or delay is how long it actually takes for packets of data to travel from point-to-point on the network. PING is an older program. To use it you type PING at the command prompt followed by the IP address of the destination computer. PINGPATH is a Windows 2000 tool that combines the features of PING with those of TRACERT. You can check not only connectivity, but also route information with PINGPATH. Both PING and PINGPATH send a message and then wait for a reply. The result displayed to you is the time it took for each packet to travel from the source to the destination.

☒ **A** is incorrect because TRACERT is used to view the route a packet takes to a destination computer. **B** is incorrect because there is no such program called PINGPONG in Windows that allows you to check connectivity and how long it takes for a packet to be sent to a destination computer.

4.05: Assessing the Net Available Bandwidth

10.   ☑   **B.** Active Directory is a multimaster database. Consequently, writes to the database are allowed on any server holding the relevant partition of the directory. In order for the other servers hosting that partition to receive an update, replication needs to occur, and this takes up bandwidth.

☒ **A** is incorrect because AD is a distributed database, and portions of it can be stored on multiple servers. Because it needs the bandwidth to replicate changes or perhaps even the entire database between servers, net available bandwidth is an important issue. **C** is also incorrect because, although it is true that AD does need the net available bandwidth to replicate changes, the AD database is distributed across multiple servers. **D** is incorrect because AD relies on net available bandwidth to replicate changes.

11. ☑ **B.** Network Monitor is a tool that is useful for monitoring network traffic and assessing net available bandwidth. It allows you to gather information on the number of bytes sent and received per second and the number of packets sent and received per second, as well as to capture data related to transmit and receive errors.

☒ **A** and **D** are incorrect because there is no tool that is shipped with Windows 2000 called Network Manager. **C** is incorrect because Network Monitor does not provide information on how net available bandwidth currently affects Active Directory.

4.06: Analyzing Performance Requirements

12. ☑ **C.** The proposed solution produces the required result and both of the optional results. Upgrading the existing ISDN lines to T1 lines will improve the speed of data transfer between these sites. Having additional ISDN lines in place between Atlanta and New York, and between Toronto and New York, will provide redundancy. If the T1 lines go down, users will still be able to access data on the New York servers. Finally, Performance Monitor and Network Monitor are both tools that can be used to monitor network performance.

☒ **A, B**, and **D** are incorrect because the proposed solution produces the required result and both of the optional results.

13. ☑ **C.** Install a redundant network connection between the locations. If the T1 connection between the sites failed, the companies would still be able to use the redundant link to exchange data.

☒ **A** is incorrect because although upgrading the T1 line would increase the speed between the sites, it would do nothing to improve reliability and availability. **B** is incorrect for the same reason. Since the sites are connected but on separate networks, this option would do nothing to improve reliability and availability of the connection between the sites. **D** is incorrect because removing the T1 line removes the link, thereby completely removing reliability and availability.

4.07: Analyzing Data and System Access Patterns

14. ☑ **A** and **D** are correct. Lower the frequency with which replication occurs and schedule replication during off-hours. Lowering the frequency of replication means Active Directory replication will occur less often. This will decrease the amount of traffic caused by AD while users are attempting to access data and services over the network. Scheduling replication during off-hours will also assist in this, because replication will occur when little or no users are logged on.

   ☒ **B** is incorrect because raising the frequency of replication could decrease performance. **C** is incorrect because the zone type is Active Directory integrated. Although incremental zone transfers will lower traffic because only changes to zones will be transferred across the network, AD-integrated zones have zone information contained within the Active Directory. This means that zone data is replicated with AD replication.

15. ☑ **B.** If the connectivity between two sites is less than optimal, each location should be defined as a separate site in Active Directory. A site is one or more TCP/IP subnets that use a good connection to the Windows 2000 network.

   ☒ **A, C**, and **D** are incorrect because of the slow, unreliable connection. Each of these choices will decrease performance and make it more difficult to access data and systems.

4.08: Analyzing Network Roles and Responsibilities

16. ☑ **B** and **C** are correct. Because a network consisting of Windows 2000 Servers and Windows 2000 Professional Workstations does not need WINS for name resolution, you should remove it from the network. Active Directory does rely on DNS, and Windows 2000 networks use DNS to locate domain controllers, other hosts, and resources. By training the WINS administrator on DNS, this person will be useful when the network is upgraded.

☒ **A** is incorrect because a pure Windows 2000 network does not need WINS for name resolution. Because WINS is not needed, there is no reason to train other members of the IT staff on WINS. Therefore, **D** is also incorrect.

17. ☑ **A.** In Windows 2000, you can use organizational units (OUs) to delegate administrative control. OUs can contain such objects as user accounts, groups, computers, printers, applications, file shares, and so forth. Once you have organized these objects into OUs, you can then delegate administrative authority over them.

☒ **B**, **C**, and **D** are incorrect because WINS and DNS are not used to delegate administrative control.

4.09: Analyzing Security Considerations

18. ☑ **D.** Kerberos, version 5, is the default and preferred authentication mechanism for Windows 2000. Each Windows 2000 domain controller must run the Kerberos Distribution Center (KDC) service that handles ticket creation and authorization. The KDC validates users against their object in AD and then issues the client a Kerberos ticket that is good for a predefined amount of time.

☒ **A** and **B** are incorrect because NTLM was an authentication protocol used in previous versions of Windows NT. It is also incorrect because this protocol does not require DNS to be running. **C** is incorrect because Windows 2000 supports Kerberos, version 5.

19. ☑ **C.** Smart cards provide an alternate method of authentication. Group policy settings are used to specify whether a user must log on using a smart card. When this specification has been set, three types of logons can be used: interactive logon, client authentication, and remote access. The smart card hosts a certificate issued by a certificate authority, and the owner of the smart card must enter a personal identification number (PIN) to identify the user as the owner of the smart card.

☒ **A** and **B** are incorrect because neither IPSec nor Kerberos requires group policy settings to specify whether the user must log on with these protocols. **D** is incorrect because there is no such thing as a dumb card.

LAB ANSWER

Objectives 4.01–4.09

1. 40,000 current users and 50,000 projected users over the next three years should be considered when designing Active Directory. When estimating projected growth of a userbase, you should use the highest estimated growth percentage.

2. Windows 2000 clients require access to a DNS Service because Windows 2000 AD is tightly integrated with DNS. Pure Windows 2000 networks do not require WINS. Therefore, you will need to connect the main network with the network section currently operating separately.

3. Because of the unreliable link between the small building and the main building, you will need to place a Windows 2000 DNS Service in that small building. An alternate solution would be to replace the unreliable link with a reliable one, or install a second line.

4. Network Monitor is a tool that allows you to check network traffic. It is shipped with Windows 2000 and Windows NT 4.0. However, the version of Network Monitor that comes with Windows 2000 and Windows NT 4.0 is limited to analyzing traffic originating from, or destined to, the host on which it is running.

5. To improve reliability and availability between the two buildings, you can install a second link. If the line between the buildings went down, a separate line would then be available to keep the sites connected.

MICROSOFT CERTIFIED SYSTEMS ENGINEER

5

What Is Active Directory?

I n this chapter, we summarize the purpose, function, and architecture of Active Directory (AD). AD is Windows 2000's mechanism for providing directory services. A directory is a collection of information about objects related to one another in some way. In Active Directory, these objects include such things as servers, printers, applications, databases, and users. The directory is used to identify users and resources on a network, so that users can find, and administrators can manage, the objects contained in the directory.

Since Windows NT 3.51, domains have been considered a directory service because they act as repositories for objects and allow directory information to be distributed throughout an enterprise. In Windows 2000, many of the limitations and concepts are changed from what you may be familiar with in NT environments. AD holds information about network objects in a distributed database. Like many directory services, AD is based on the design of X.500, which was developed as a definition of distributed database services by the International Standards Organization (ISO). As we see in this chapter, the design of Active Directory provides open standards support, support for standard name formats, scalability, and simplified administration.

TEST YOURSELF OBJECTIVE 5.01

Understanding the Purpose of Active Directory

Active Directory is a distributed database and serves as a repository for information about the Windows 2000 network. Information is stored in Active Directory in what is called an object, and these objects contain attributes. To put this in terms of a database, an object would be analogous to a single record, and an attribute would be comparable to a field in that record.

Theoretically, Active Directory can store millions of objects in its hierarchy. Many companies will not have this much information to store about users or resources; consequently, AD's capacity can accommodate significant company growth. As your company grows, the amount of objects contained in AD will grow. Organizing resources is another important part of AD design that allows you to organize objects by organizational or geographic boundaries. This provides your business with the opportunity to create an organizational hierarchy if one does not already exist, or organize resources by location.

Active Directory provides a single point of management and administration. Generally, a Windows 2000 network will have group policies, user profiles, and network services stored in the Active Directory. This means that rather than having to log on to multiple computers, the administrator needs to log on only once to change settings and access and manage resources such as printers and file servers. In addition to managing resources, AD also allows centralized administration for managing user access to these resources. The administrator creates organizational units containing users and resources and then delegates administrative control of these organizational units to site or line-of-business administrators, or power users for particular workgroups of users.

In comparing Windows NT domains to AD, you will notice a number of similarities and differences. Windows NT uses the Security Account Manager (SAM) database to store user accounts. Windows 2000 also uses the SAM to store user accounts on a member server, except when it is promoted to a domain controller, when it uses the Active Directory for storing user accounts. Accounts stored in AD are replicated among all domain controllers. Another similarity deals with access control. Like NT domains, Active Directory uses groups and group membership to control access to resources. Permissions to resources should be assigned using local groups. Local groups should then contain global groups, to which users are assigned. You should never assign users directly to resources. Unlike Windows NT domains, an Active Directory domain in Native mode gives you the ability to use universal groups. Universal groups span domains in an Active Directory forest (which we describe later in this chapter) and can also be used to assign access to local groups.

To help understand the purpose of Active Directory, try to keep the following points in mind:

- Active Directory allows you to organize your directory service by organization or by geography, or both.

- Active Directory has the ability to store millions of objects.

- Management and control of resources is simplified with the ability to delegate administration.

- You need to log on only once to access all resources managed by Active Directory.

- Group policies enable an administrator to control and manage users and workstations in Active Directory.

exam
Watch

With Active Directory, many limitations you may have experienced with Windows NT domains are gone. With Windows NT, each resource had to authenticate a user in order for that user to access the resource. With Windows 2000, a single logon is all that is needed to access and manage resources. As we mentioned in previous chapters, NT domains had an administrative limit of 40MB (or about 40,000 users), but AD can hold millions of objects. Rather than needing to create multiple domains, Active Directory allows large enterprises to use a single domain. In NT environments, you needed to manage trust relationships between domains manually. Trusts in Active Directory are implicit and transitive, meaning that when you set up Active Directory domains, they all trust one another by default. Also, delegation of administration has improved with AD. In Windows NT, administrators often received greater levels of access than needed. For example, users often had to be made members of the Domain Administrators group in order to be able to perform tasks. Active Directory uses organizational units, which groups users and resources together into units and provides the ability to delegate administration at a granular level. This allows you to control what the administrator can and cannot do with more precision.

QUESTIONS

5.01: Understanding the Purpose of Active Directory

1. **Current Situation:** The company for whom you are designing a Windows 2000 Active Directory network has 80,000 employees and uses two Windows NT domains. Each employee has a user account stored in Windows NT's SAM database. Due to the projected growth of users, the company was considering adding a third domain. Upon deciding to upgrade to Windows 2000, they reconsidered the addition of the third domain. Administration of the existing domains has been problematic for them, and they would like to use as few domains as possible. In these domains, Domain A trusts Domain B, but Domain B does not trust Domain A. If a new domain, Domain C, is created in the upgrade to Windows 2000, it needs to trust and be trusted by the other two domains.

Required Result: Design a Windows 2000 network that uses as few domains as possible.

Optional Desired Results:

1. Determine what trust relationships need to be in place.

2. Determine whether the design of the new Windows 2000 Active Directory network should use only Windows 2000, or a mix of Windows NT Servers and Workstations and computers running Windows 2000 Server and Professional.

Proposed Solution: Because of the number of users, create three domains. Since trust relationships are implicit and transitive, Domain C will trust the other domains by default. Given that the SAM databases contain user accounts, the company should continue using Windows NT Servers. New Windows 2000 Servers will be added to the network, and NT Workstations will be upgraded to Windows Professional.

What results are produced from the proposed solution?

A. The proposed solution produces the required result only.

B. The proposed solution produces the required result and only one of the optional results.

C. The proposed solution produces the required result and both of the optional results.

D. The proposed solution does not produce the required result.

2. A new company has just installed Windows 2000 Servers and Windows 2000 Professional workstations for its network. You are responsible for assigning control access to resources in Active Directory. How will you assign these permissions?

A. Assign permissions to global groups. These global groups will then contain local groups, to which users will be assigned.

B. Assign permissions to local groups. These local groups will contain global groups, to which users will be assigned.

C. Assign users directly to resources.

D. None of the above. Active Directory does not use groups or group membership to control access to resources.

3. As shown in the following illustration, Murky Motors has three domains running Windows NT 4.0. Domain A trusts Domain B, and Domain A and Domain C trust each other. Another company would like to copy the Murky Motors network structure. All servers and workstations in this other company will run Windows 2000. They would like three domains, but want all domains to trust one another. What will you do?

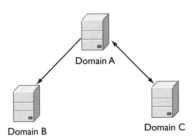

A. Active Directory trusts require that trusts be managed manually between domains. You will need to set up two-way trusts between each domain.

B. By default, Active Directory domains do not trust one another. There is no way to set up trusts. Since Active Directory supports millions of objects, you should create a single domain.

C. Trusts in Active Directory are implicit and transitive. All domains in Active Directory will trust one another by default.

D. Trust relationships are an element of Windows NT environments. They do not exist in Windows 2000 Active Directory networks.

4. The company you work for currently uses Windows NT 4.0 Servers on its network. It has one primary domain controller, two backup domain controllers, and three member servers. After upgrading to Windows 2000 Server, which of these servers will continue to use the SAM database to store user accounts?

A. The domain controllers will use SAM.

B. The member servers will use SAM.

C. Both the domain controllers and member servers will use SAM.

D. Neither the domain controllers nor member servers will use SAM.

TEST YOURSELF OBJECTIVE 5.02

Understanding Directory Parts

As we have mentioned, Active Directory is made up of a number of objects and containers. Objects can include such elements of a network as users, groups, computers, domains, sites, and organizational units. These objects contain attributes, which are details related to the object. For example, if you were to look at a user object, you would find such attributes as first name, last name, age, sex, email address, and so on. Some of the objects in AD are known as containers, because they can contain other objects. An example of a container would be a domain, as it can hold users, computers, and other objects.

All objects of the Active Directory are defined by rules, which are called schema. The schema is a list of definitions that define the kind of objects that can be stored in AD and what attributes an object must contain and may contain. There are two types of definitions in the schema: attributes, discussed above, and classes. A class is a logical grouping of objects, used to describe the possible AD objects that can be created. Object classes can be used to represent user accounts, groups, computers, domains, or organizational units. Each class is a collection of attributes that describes the object.

In learning to understand the parts making up the directory, it is important to remember the following points:

- Information is stored in Active Directory as objects.
- The container object is used to organize other objects.
- The schema is the blueprint of Active Directory. It defines the objects and attributes contained in Active Directory.

exam
ⓦatch

Objects, containers, and schema are the main parts making up Active Directory. The schema defines Active Directory, because it is a listing defining both the types of objects and the information about these objects that can be stored in AD. These definitions themselves are stored as objects in AD, so that AD can manage the schema as it would any other object. The schema contains classes, logical groupings of objects that can created, and attributes, information relating to the objects. When you create an object, the schema maintains rules relating to the object. An example of a rule could be that a user must have the attributes of a first and last name, but does not require a middle initial. As we saw when we discussed organizational units, container objects are used to organize and manage objects in AD. Without containers, the task of managing AD could quickly become overwhelming.

QUESTIONS

5.02: Understanding Directory Parts

5. The following illustration shows the properties of a network user. Which of the following is true? (Choose all that apply.)

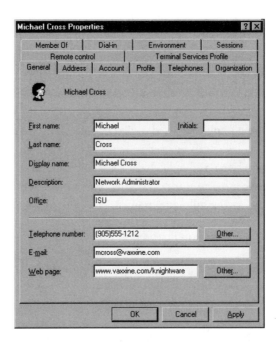

A. The container is the user account, whereas the objects are the information about the user. Objects about this user include first name, last name, and so on.

B. Attributes are the information about the user (first name, last name, and so on), and these are contained within the user object.

C. Schema is information about the user (first name, last name, and so on) and is contained within the attributes.

D. Objects and attributes, such as those shown here, are defined by the schema.

6. **Current Situation:** Muddy Mufflers has a Windows 2000 Active Directory network. Although it has a single domain, Muddy Mufflers has two subsidiary companies that run as separate businesses. The two subsidiaries are sites within Active Directory. Each site has its own administrator, and administration of users must occur at the site level. A single Personnel Department handles hiring for Muddy Mufflers and its subsidiaries. The Personnel Department has contacted you to have a new field added to each user's properties. They would like a field that shows whether the user is a full-time employee or a co-op student.

   Required Result: Design container objects in Active Directory such that delegation of administration occurs at the site level.

   Optional Desired Results:

   1. Create a field for each user's property sheet to show employment status.

   2. Make it a requirement that the employment status field be filled out when user accounts are created for new employees, and that it be updated by the personnel department for existing employees.

   Proposed Solution: Create site containers that allow delegation of administration to that level. Create line-of-business containers within the site containers so that users and computers can be organized for that particular line-of-business. Add an attribute to the user object in the schema so that the user properties indicate the user's employment status as full-time or co-op. Making this a required attribute enables personnel to update each user object accordingly.

   What results are produced from the proposed solution?

   A. The proposed solution produces the required result only.

   B. The proposed solution produces the required result and only one of the optional results.

   C. The proposed solution produces the required result and both of the optional results.

   D. The proposed solution does not produce the required result.

7. You are designing the Active Directory for a small company. You realize that containers can be used to organize different objects in AD. Which of the following would be considered containers? (Choose all that apply.)

   A. Organizational units

   B. Groups

    C. Domains

    D. Computers

8. Which of the following are contained within the schema? (Choose all that apply.)

    A. Attributes

    B. Containers

    C. Classes

    D. User information

TEST YOURSELF OBJECTIVE 5.03

Understanding Active Directory versus X.500

Active Directory is based on the X.500 set of design specifications. X.500 was developed by the International Standards Organization (ISO) as a set of specifications used in creating directory services. It ensures that directory services following these specifications interoperate with other directory services.

Being X.500-like, Active Directory makes use of Directory User Agents and Directory System Agents. When clients request information from Active Directory, they make their request with a specific protocol. A Directory User Agent (DUA) uses this protocol to communicate with a Directory System Agent (DSA). The DSA then uses the protocol to interface with and obtain information from Active Directory. In the case of Active Directory, the DSA is the domain controller.

Although Active Directory is X.500-like, it is not compliant. It uses different protocols to communicate than those specified by X.500. X.500 defines four protocols to communicate with an X.500-compliant directory service. These are DSP (Directory System Protocol), DISP (Directory Information Shadowing Protocol), DAP (Directory Access Protocol), and DOP (Directory Operational Binding Management Protocol). DSP and DISP are protocols used by X.500 to communicate information between DSAs. In Active Directory, neither of these is used to communicate information between domain controllers. Instead, AD uses either Remote Procedure Calls (RPCs) or Simple Mail Transfer Protocol (SMTP) or both. DOP is used to communicate operational connections, such as hierarchy layout and replication, between DSAs in X.500-compliant directory services. DAP is used to communicate between a DUA and a DSA in an X.500-compliant directory service. Microsoft does not use this protocol, but instead uses the Lightweight Directory Access Protocol (LDAP).

When understanding and comparing X.500 to Active Directory, it is important to remember the following points:

- Active Directory, like most directory services, gets its roots from X.500 design specifications.

- An X.500-compliant directory service uses four protocols to communicate: Directory System Protocol (DSP), Directory Information Shadowing Protocol (DISP), Directory Access Protocol (DAP), and Directory Operational Binding Management Protocol (DOP).

- Active Directory is not considered X.500-compliant because it does not use the X.500 transport protocols.

- Active Directory domain controller is like a Directory System Agent (DSA).

- Active Directory uses Lightweight Directory Access Protocol (LDAP) because of its speed of accessing a directory service and its support for TCP/IP.

exam
Watch

LDAP is a simplified version of DAP and is the primary access protocol for Active Directory. LDAP is used in most directory services currently available and provides interoperability between Active Directory and other directory services. Active Directory supports LDAP, versions 2 and 3, which are versions fully supported by the Transmission Control Protocol/Internet Protocol (TCP/IP). TCP/IP support is an important reason that the X.500 protocols are not used by Active Directory, and protocols like LDAP are. The X.500 protocols are dependent on Open Systems Interconnection (OSI) networking, which is an alternative to Transmission Control Protocol/Internet Protocol (TCP/IP). TCP/IP is the most widely used protocol on networks today. Transporting OSI across a TCP/IP network is less efficient than using TCP/IP directly because there is overhead in enveloping OSI in TCP/IP. Consequently, LDAP is used because it provides the most important functions offered by DAP and DSP.

QUESTIONS

5.03: Understanding Active Directory versus X.500

9. **Current Situation:** A company is considering upgrading to Windows 2000. They have called you in as a consultant for this possible upgrade. Members of the IT staff that meet with you are familiar with X.500 and realize that Active Directory is based on X.500 specifications. Thus, they would like information regarding the compliance of AD with X.500 and what protocols will be used. At present, NWLink, NetBEUI, and TCP/IP are used on their network. Depending on your answers to their questions, they will either upgrade to Windows 2000, or use existing Windows NT Servers but switch to Novell NetWare as the network operating system.

   Required Result: Determine what protocols will be used by Active Directory to communicate with other domain controllers.

   Optional Desired Results:

   1. Determine what protocols will be used to communicate between clients and domain controllers.

   2. Determine what transport protocol should be used.

   Proposed Solution: DSP and DISP are protocols that will be used by domain controllers to communicate with one another. LDAP will be used to communicate between clients and domain controllers. TCP/IP should be used as the transport protocol on the network.

   What results are produced from the proposed solution?

   A. The proposed solution produces the required result only.

   B. The proposed solution produces the required result and only one of the optional results.

C. The proposed solution produces the required result and both of the optional results.

D. The proposed solution does not produce the required result.

Questions 10–12   The next three questions are based upon the scenario and illustration that follow. Read the following case study, and then answer the questions. You may refer to this case study and illustration as often as needed.

Muddy Mufflers is a medium-sized company that has a significant number of users. It has two domain controllers running Windows 2000, and, as shown in the following illustration, users connect to these domain controllers to access Active Directory. The domain controllers also connect to each other to share information.

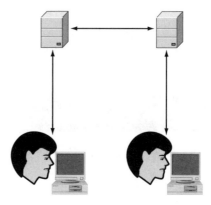

10. Which of the following is true about the illustration shown above?

A. Clients map to Directory User Agents in Active Directory and use DAP to communicate with domain controllers.

B. Clients map to Directory System Agents in Active Directory and use LDAP to communicate with domain controllers.

C. Clients map to Directory User Agents in Active Directory and use LDAP to communicate with domain controllers.

D. Components in Active Directory do not map to X.500. Clients use DAP to communicate with domain controllers.

11. When mapping components to X.500, what role does the domain controller play in Active Directory?

   A. Directory System Agent.

   B. Directory User Agent.

   C. Directory Service Agent.

   D. None of the above. Components of an Active Directory network do not map to X.500.

12. Which of the following protocols are used to communicate information between domain controllers? (Choose all that apply.)

   A. Directory System Protocol

   B. Directory Information Shadowing Protocol

   C. Remote Procedure Calls

   D. Simple Mail Transfer Protocol

TEST YOURSELF OBJECTIVE 5.04

Understanding Active Directory Architecture

Active Directory is made up of a logical hierarchy. This hierarchy consists of organizational units, domains, trees, and forests. AD also relies on a number of physical elements, including domain controllers, global catalog servers, and sites.

Organizational units (OUs) are the smallest units of organization in Active Directory. They contain users, groups, and other objects, including other OUs. OUs allow you to group such objects together in a single container, which you can then use to delegate administration and apply group policies. By using OUs, you can organize Active Directory organizationally, geographically, or functionally. However, you should try to keep the organizational structure of OUs as flat as possible and avoid nesting them too deeply. Nesting multiple levels of OUs can be confusing to administer, and the deeper they are nested, the slower performance will be when users in the OUs are authenticated. This is because AD will check and apply group policies at every level.

Domains are used to logically group objects within a security or administrative boundary. In other words, they are used to group objects to make administration of those objects easier, or to enforce security policies. Because you can have only one security policy per domain, if additional security policies are needed, you will need to create additional domains. In AD, domains are laid out in a hierarchical design called a domain tree, which is a group of domains within a contiguous DNS namespace. So when more than one domain exist, they become a domain tree. The domains in the tree are connected by transitive, bidirectional trust relationships, meaning they have complete trust among one another. There are two types of trusts available in AD. A transitive trust is an automatic, two-way trust that is created by Active Directory. Explicit trusts are manual, one-way trusts created to enhance performance in large tree structures. In addition to the trust relationships, domains in a domain tree also share a global catalog and have the same schema.

Forests are the largest units of organization in AD. Forests are groups of one or more domain trees that trust one another. Forests allow you to logically group together AD trees so that the trees can easily communicate with one another. All trees in a forest share a common schema and global catalog. Because the forest allows trees to trust one another, administrative overhead is reduced in the creation of trust relationships.

A global catalog (GC) is used to find objects across the many partitions that may be used in Active Directory. It holds all objects in a forest, but holds only a subset of the attributes of those objects. This enables quick response to queries, and when replication between global catalog servers occurs, not as much information needs to be replicated. Unlike domain controllers that replicate within a domain, GC servers are the only servers that replicate between domains in a forest. Because of this fact, there must be at least one GC per domain, and it is always a domain controller. It is always part of the replication process, and thereby has an updated copy of every object in the forest.

domain controllers are different in Active Directory than in Windows NT domains. In Windows NT, there is a primary domain controller (PDC) and backup domain controllers (BDC). These functioned in a top-down replication approach, with all changes happening on the PDC, and the PDC replicating those changes down to the BDC. In Active Directory, domain controllers (DCs) are peers to one another, and use multimaster replication. When an administrator makes changes on any DC, these changes will be replicated to all of the other DCs in a domain. Each DC has replication partners to ensure that changes are replicated around the entire domain.

A site is one or more well-connected subnets using TCP/IP and a physical partitioning of Active Directory. Sites are not replication boundaries, but boundaries for managing the replication process. They allow you to schedule when replication occurs and what protocol is used for replication. Replication within a domain requires the use of Remote Procedure Calls (RPCs), but replication between sites can use Simple Mail Transfer Protocol (SMTP) or RPCs. Sites help reduce network traffic by controlling authentication processes and allowing users to log on to domain controllers in their physical location. Group policies can also be applied at the site level, allowing you to control user and computer settings based on physical locations. Domains can be spread over multiple sites, and multiple domains can be located in one site.

In understanding Active Directory, it is important to keep the following points in mind:

- A forest is a group of one or more Active Directory trees that trust one another.

- A domain is a security and administrative boundary.

- Domains are logical collections of objects.

- A domain tree is a collection of domains in a contiguous namespace.

- Active Directory domains are linked together by trusts.

- Active Directory trusts by default are transitive and bidirectional.

- Organizational units (OUs) are used as administrative partitions within an Active Directory domain.

- Administration can be delegated to OUs at a granular level.

- Group policies can be applied to OUs.

- All domain controllers are peers to one another in Active Directory.

- Active Directory uses multimaster replication.

- Each Active Directory domain must have at least one global catalog server.

- The global catalog holds every object in the forest, but only a subset of the object attributes.

- A site is a physical partitioning of Active Directory.

Although domain controllers are peers to one another, different DCs may have different roles. There are five roles a DC might have, and a domain controller may have one or all of the roles. When a DC has one or more of these roles, it is called an operations master. The first type of operations master is a schema master, which is the only server that can make changes to the schema. Because the schema is shared by a forest, there can be only one schema master in a forest. A domain-naming master is responsible for controlling changes to the DNS namespace. It ensures that when a domain is added or removed, the namespace is updated. Like the schema master, there is only one domain-naming master in a forest. A RID (relative identifier) master ensures that security identifiers (SIDs) in a domain are unique. An infrastructure master is used in managing group membership between domains by keeping references to objects located in other domains. There is only one RID master and infrastructure master per domain. Finally, a PDC emulator is used when Windows 2000 is in Mixed mode, that is, when Windows 2000 and Windows NT domain controllers are used. To understand a PDC emulator, you need to remember that Active Directory is a distributed database that uses multimaster replication in order that every domain controller has a read/write copy of the Active Directory. Changes to AD are replicated to other domain controllers. However, in Windows NT changes can be made only on the primary domain controller (PDC) and then replicated to backup domain controllers (BDCs). When Windows 2000 runs in Mixed mode, the PDC emulator will replicate changes down to the Windows NT BDCs. When Windows 2000 is in Mixed or Native mode, the PDC emulator accepts changes to the AD from down-level clients such as Windows NT and Windows 9x.

QUESTIONS

5.04: Understanding Active Directory Architecture

13. **Current Situation:** A company with 95,000 users has a Windows NT environment with four domains, and it has hired you to assist with designing and upgrading to Windows 2000 Active Directory. The company would like

the Active Directory to be organizationally driven, not geographically. The programmers in the company have asked you to determine how many servers will be required to control changes to the schema, since they would like to create new object classes for applications. The network administrator, who is currently learning Windows 2000, has concerns about how many servers will be necessary to control changes over the DNS namespace.

Required Result: Determine the best design to meet the requirements of the business, including the number of forests, trees, and domains.

Optional Desired Results:

1. Determine how many schema masters will be required by the network.

2. Determine how many domain-naming masters will be required by the network.

Proposed Solution: Create one forest, with one tree and one domain. Create OUs to further partition the domain for the organizational structure. Only one schema master and one domain-naming master will be required.

What results are produced by the proposed solution?

A. The proposed solution produces the required result only.

B. The proposed solution produces the required result and only one of the optional results.

C. The proposed solution produces the required result and both of the optional results.

D. The proposed solution does not produce the required result.

14. Which of the following is used to manage group membership between domains by keeping references to objects located in other domains?

A. Schema master

B. Infrastructure master

C. RID master

D. Domain-naming master

15. As shown in the following illustration, Asimov Robotics is composed of two domains in two separate sites. The network administrator wants to create a third domain. Which of the following options will the network administrator have in creating this third domain? (Choose all that apply.)

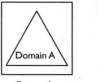

Site A   Site B

   A. The network administrator can create multiple domains in a single site.

   B. The network administrator can create multiple sites in a single domain.

   C. The network administrator can spread the new domain over multiple sites.

   D. The network administrator can create multiple sites in a single domain, or spread the new domain across multiple sites.

16. The Human Resources Department of your company has just added a reference number to each employee's user object, so that the employee file and user object can be cross-referenced. When they try searching by this reference number, they get no results. Why?

   A. You cannot add attributes to user objects.

   B. The attribute for the reference number has not been designated as an attribute to be replicated throughout the forest.

   C. The object associated with this number has not been replicated throughout the forest.

   D. The global directory has not been installed with Active Directory.

LAB QUESTION

Objectives 5.01–5.04

Murky Motors has a Windows 2000 network consisting of three domain controllers and one member server. Recently, it has acquired another business. It would like to keep these companies separated and use noncontiguous namespaces. However, on occasion, they will need to use each other's network resources. Because of the new resources the acquisition brings to Murky Motors, IT staff would like to track computer serial number information for inventory purposes and add a field to the properties of the computer object.

1. What would be used to add new attributes to the computer object?

2. What protocol will DUAs use to communicate with DSAs in Active Directory?

3. Where are user accounts stored on the Windows 2000 member server?

4. When the Windows 2000 member server is promoted to a domain controller, where will user accounts be stored?

5. What will you do to keep the two companies separate in Active Directory so that they use noncontiguous namespaces?

QUICK ANSWER KEY

Objective 5.01
1. **D**
2. **B**
3. **C**
4. **B**

Objective 5.02
5. **B** and **D**
6. **C**
7. **A** and **C**
8. **A** and **C**

Objective 5.03
9. **D**
10. **C**
11. **A**
12. **C** and **D**

Objective 5.04
13. **C**
14. **B**
15. **A** and **C**
16. **B**

IN-DEPTH ANSWERS

5.01: Understanding the Purpose of Active Directory

1. ☑ **D.** The proposed solution does not product the required result. As few domains as possible need to be created to fulfill the required result. Windows NT domains had an administrative limit of 40,000 users, but AD can hold millions of objects. Rather than necessitating the creation of multiple domains, Active Directory allows large enterprises to use a single domain. The situation states that projected growth of users is the only reason a new domain was going to be added, therefore no additional domains need to be created.

   ☒ **A, B**, and **C** are incorrect because the proposed solution does not produce the required result. Trusts in Active Directory are implicit and transitive. This is different from Windows NT environments, where trust relationships between domains needed to be managed manually. The solution offered for the second optional requirement is incorrect, because upon upgrading Windows NT domain controllers to Windows 2000, user accounts in the SAM database will be transferred to Active Directory.

2. ☑ **B.** Permissions to resources should be assigned to local groups. Local groups should then contain global groups, to which users are assigned.

   ☒ **A** is incorrect because permissions should be assigned to local groups. These groups can contain global groups to which users are assigned. **C** is incorrect because you should never assign users directly to resources. **D** is incorrect because Active Directory uses groups and group membership to control access to resources.

3. ☑ **C.** Trusts in Active Directory are implicit and transitive, meaning that when you set up Active Directory domains, they all trust one another by default.

☒   **A** is incorrect because this solution describes how to set up domains in Windows NT environments. In Windows NT networks, you need to manage trust relationships between domains manually. In Active Directory, trusts are implicit and transitive. **B** is incorrect because when you set up Active Directory domains, they all trust one another by default. **D** is incorrect because Windows 2000 Active Directory networks use trust relationships.

4.   ☑   **B.** The member servers will use SAM. Windows NT Servers use the Security Account Manager (SAM) database to store user accounts. Windows 2000 also uses the SAM to store user accounts on a member server. However, domain controllers use Active Directory for storing user accounts, which are replicated between all domain controllers.

5.02: Understanding Directory Parts

5.   ☑   **B** and **D** are correct. Attributes are details relating to an object. Objects can include such elements of a network as users, groups, computers, domains, sites, and organizational units. For example, if you look at a user object, you would find such attributes as first name, last name, age, sex, email address, and so on. The schema is a listing defining both the types of objects and the information about these objects that can be stored in AD.

☒   **A** is incorrect because details about the object are attributes. Containers are used to organize objects. **C** is incorrect because the schema defines both the types of objects and the information about these objects that can be stored in AD.

6.   ☑   **C.** The proposed solution produces the required result and both of the optional results. Creating site containers allows delegation of administration to the site level. Line-of-business containers within the site containers permit the organization of users and computers for that particular line-of-business. To add the new field, you would extend the schema to include the new user object attribute. Since this is a required attribute, new users cannot be added to Active Directory without this field being filled out. Existing users would be updated by the personnel department.

☒   **A**, **B**, and **D** are incorrect because the proposed solution produces the required result and both of the optional results.

7. ☑ **A** and **C** are correct. Containers are objects that contain and organize other objects in Active Directory. Organizational units and domains function in this capacity, hence, organizational units and domains are containers.

   ☒ **B** is incorrect because although groups contain users and other groups, groups are not used for organization in Active Directory. Groups are used for access control. **D** is incorrect because a computer is an object, not a container.

8. ☑ **A** and **C** are correct. When you create an object, the schema maintains rules relating to the object. These rules are contained in classes (describing objects that can be created) and attributes (information relating to the objects). An example might be that a user must have the attributes of a first and last name, but does not require a middle initial.

   ☒ **B** is incorrect because the schema does not contain containers. **D** is incorrect because the schema does not include information on users.

5.03: Understanding Active Directory versus X.500

9. ☑ **D.** The proposed solution does not produce the required result. DSP (Directory System Protocol) and DISP (Directory Information Shadowing Protocol) are protocols used by X.500 to communicate information between DSAs. However, in Active Directory, these protocols are not used to communicate information between DSAs (domain controllers). Active Directory uses Remote Procedure Calls (RPCs), Simple Mail Transfer Protocol (SMTP), or both for this purpose.

   ☒ **A, B,** and **C** are incorrect because the proposed solution does not produce the required result. TCP/IP is the most used protocol on the network and is used by Active Directory instead of OSI. Lightweight Directory Access Protocol (LDAP) is used to communicate between clients and domain controllers to access Active Directory.

10. ☑ **C.** Clients map to Directory User Agents in Active Directory and use LDAP to communicate with domain controllers.

    ☒ **A** is incorrect because DAP is not used to communicate with domain controllers. **B** is incorrect because domain controllers map to Directory System

Agents. **D** is incorrect because components of Active Directory and X.500 do map to one another, and clients do not use DAP to communicate with domain controllers.

11. ☑ **A.** Domain controllers are Directory System Agents (DSAs) in Active Directory.

   ☒ **B** is incorrect because Directory User Agents (DUAs) are the client components of X.500. **C** is incorrect because there is no such component as a Directory Service Agent. **D** is incorrect because components of an Active Directory network do map to X.500.

12. ☑ **C** and **D** are correct. Remote Procedure Calls (RPCs), Simple Mail Transfer Protocol (SMTP), or both are used by DSAs (Directory Service Agents) to communicate information between each other in a Windows 2000 Active Directory network.

   ☒ **A** and **B** are incorrect because DSP (Directory System Protocol) and DISP (Directory Information Shadowing Protocol) are protocols used to communicate information between DSAs in an X.500-compliant system. These protocols are not used in Active Directory to communicate information between domain controllers.

5.04: Understanding Active Directory Architecture

13. ☑ **C.** The proposed solution produces the required result and both of the optional results. Creating one forest, with one tree and one domain, and OUs to further partition the domain for the organizational structure, will meet the needs of the business. Microsoft recommends that you attempt designing AD with only one domain. If you are upgrading a Windows NT environment to Windows 2000, do not be unduly influenced in your design by the presence of multiple domains. Windows NT networks often contain multiple domains because of the 40MB limitation of the SAM database and the division of administration. These limitations no longer exist in Windows 2000 Active Directory.

   Only one schema master and domain-naming service is required in a forest. The schema master is the only server that can make changes to the schema.

Since the forest shares the schema, only one schema master is required. A domain-naming master is responsible for controlling changes to the namespace and ensuring that when a domain is added or removed, the namespace is updated.

☒ **A**, **B**, and **D** are incorrect because the proposed solution produces the required result and both of the optional results.

14. ☑ **B.** An infrastructure master is used to manage group membership between domains by keeping references to objects located in other domains. There is one per domain.

☒ **A** is incorrect because the schema master is the only server that can make changes to the schema. **C** is incorrect because a RID (relative identifier) master ensures that security identifiers (SIDs) in a domain are unique. **D** is incorrect because a domain-naming master is responsible for controlling changes to the namespace. It ensures that when a domain is added or removed, the namespace is updated.

15. ☑ **A** and **C** are correct. The network administrator can create multiple domains in a single site, or spread the new domain over multiple sites. The important thing to remember is that sites are physical and domains are logical.

☒ **B** and **D** are incorrect because domains can be contained in sites, but sites cannot be contained in domains.

16. ☑ **B.** The attribute for the reference number has not been designated as an attribute to be replicated throughout the forest. The global catalog does not replicate every attribute of an object throughout the forest. Any additional attributes must be flagged to be replicated.

☒ **A** is incorrect because attributes can be added to user objects. **C** is incorrect because the global catalog holds all objects in a forest, but holds only a subset of the attributes of those objects. **D** is incorrect because the global directory is not a component or service that needs to be installed by the user.

LAB ANSWER

Objectives 5.01–5.04

1. The schema can be used to add new attributes and new objects to Active Directory. The schema can be extended by developers and network administrators who wish to define new classes and attributes.

2. DUAs use Lightweight Directory Access Protocol (LDAP) to communicate with DSAs in AD because of its speed of accessing a directory service and its support for TCP/IP.

3. Windows 2000 still uses the SAM to store user accounts on a member server.

4. When the Windows 2000 member server is promoted to a domain controller, it will use the Active Directory for storing user accounts. Accounts stored in AD are replicated between all domain controllers.

5. Create one forest so that objects and schema are shared between the namespaces, and create two trees to accommodate the need for noncontiguous namespaces.

MICROSOFT CERTIFIED SYSTEMS ENGINEER

6

Analyzing the Impact of Active Directory

A nalyzing the impact of Active Directory is an important part of implementing Windows 2000. Any changes to a network will impact how it functions in the future. Changes to the network will affect services and server applications, as well as end user needs. This analysis requires assessing the impact on both the existing and planned technical environment, and on the technical support structure. It is also important to analyze existing and planned network and systems management, as well as issues that will directly affect the end users. This requires analyzing business requirements for client computer desktop management, examining end user work needs, identifying their technical support needs, and establishing the required client computer environment.

TEST YOURSELF OBJECTIVE 6.01

Analyzing the Impact on the Existing Technical Environment

You should take into consideration what impact current network applications will have on a new installation or upgrade to Windows 2000 Active Directory. As we discussed in Chapter 3, applications and Windows NT operating systems should have the latest service packs installed, and be upgraded whenever possible to a version that is compatible with Windows 2000. This should be done prior to your upgrade to Windows 2000. If the facilities and equipment are available, you should also consider creating a test lab. This is a small network with the same operating systems, applications, services, and hardware that your actual network uses. By upgrading the test lab's network, you can practice upgrading to Windows 2000 Active Directory and determine any issues or problems that may result when the actual network is upgraded.

It is vital that any existing issues with the network be documented. This includes any slow or unreliable links, media speeds, recurring power failures, and so forth. You will also need to analyze protocols and addressing used on the existing network. Windows 2000 Active Directory and many of its services (such as DNS, which is used for name resolution) require the Transmission Control Protocol/Internet Protocol (TCP/IP). Such services and protocols may conflict if more than one operating system is being used on your network. In heterogeneous environments, you need to consider and document other operating systems, such as Novell NetWare, Unix, or Linux.

Other factors in your analysis are security and policies, since administration of these has changed with Windows 2000. With Active Directory, security and policies are managed through Microsoft Management Console (MMC) using "snap-ins." Snap-ins are tools that are loaded into the console so that the functionality you need is accessible through a program. The Security Templates snap-in allows you to generate and configure security templates, which are used to control security settings on local systems. The Security Configuration and Analysis snap-in uses these templates to configure and analyze security settings for each system. It replaces the Windows NT 4.0 Security Configuration Editor. A command-line version called SECEDITY.EXE is available to run batch files or scripts. Finally, the Security Settings extension snap-in is used to enhance Group Policy editor, allowing the implementation of security processes to impact groups.

When analyzing the impact on the existing technical environment, you should remember the following points:

- It is important to take into consideration what impact your current network applications will have on a new installation of Windows 2000 and Active Directory.

- It is imperative to ensure the current network applications are in tiptop shape prior to considering the installation of Windows 2000 and Active Directory.

- Because of the way network applications are accessed across a network, it is important to take into consideration how this information will flow through your directory services model.

- With Windows 2000 and Active Directory, any problems relating to the integration of heterogeneous environments (that is, the use of multiple operating systems such as Novell, Unix, and Linux) require careful consideration.

- The Microsoft Management Console (MMC) is one of six software components introduced in Windows 2000 that had their beginnings in the Zero Administration Initiative. Others are Active Directory, Systems Management Server (SMS), the Zero Administration Kit (ZAK), the Web Administration Utility for Windows NT Server, and the Windows Scripting Host.

exam
ⓦatch

Security Configuration and Analysis is a Microsoft Management Console snap-in that is used to configure and analyze security, view results, and resolve discrepancies that are exposed by the analysis. This snap-in uses a database containing computer-specific information, allowing you to import security templates created with the Security Templates snap-in. The system is configured with the levels of security specified in the template. When an analysis is done, this tool reveals current system settings with recommendations. It will display and highlight settings that do not match proposed levels of security.

QUESTIONS

6.01: Analyzing the Impact on the Existing Technical Environment

1. **Current Situation:** You are concerned about problems that may result upon upgrading your existing Windows NT 4.0 environment to Windows 2000. You have installed Windows 2000 Server only on computers in a test lab, and these were clean installs. You have never upgraded actual servers on your network. The network is using NWLink and NetBEUI, and Windows NT Servers are currently using Service Pack 3. Several mission-critical applications running on the servers do not use service packs, but Web sites related to this software say that service packs are available to make the software Windows 2000 compatible. Several other applications that run on the server have not been used since 1998, whereas two others are not Windows 2000 compatible and have no service packs available.

   Required Result: Determine any problems that may occur when upgrading the network from Windows NT 4.0 to Windows 2000.

   Optional Desired Results:

   1. Determine what applications should be upgraded, migrated, or retired before upgrading to Windows 2000, and which applications will need service packs.

   2. Determine which protocols should be used on the network.

Proposed Solution: On the test lab network, install Windows NT 4.0 Server and other operating systems used on your network. Try to make the test lab resemble your network as closely as possible. Install all applications on the test lab network, since these will be used on the upgraded actual network, and apply service packs. Apply the latest service packs to Windows NT Servers. These service packs should also be applied to the software and Windows NT operating systems running on the actual network before upgrading to Windows 2000. Use the existing protocols after upgrading to Windows 2000.

What results are produced from the proposed solution?

A.   The proposed solution produces the required result only.

B.   The proposed solution produces the required result and only one of the optional results.

C.   The proposed solution produces the required result and both of the optional results.

D.   The proposed solution does not produce the required result.

2.   A friend of yours is a network administrator on a Windows 2000 network. Recently, security settings on a Windows 2000 Server running SQL Server needed to be changed because a developer on the IT staff needed to have greater permissions to run a series of queries and test a server application he created. To resolve this issue, the network administrator changed security levels temporarily, but she cannot remember if she changed these security settings back after the user was done. She knows that Microsoft Management Console can be used to check this, but she can not remember what snap-in to use. Which snap-in will you suggest she use?

A.   Security Templates

B.   Security Configuration and Analysis

C.   Security Configuration Editor

D.   Security Settings

TEST YOURSELF OBJECTIVE 6.02

Analyzing the Impact on the Planned Technical Environment

When analyzing the impact on a planned technical environment, it is important to pay attention to the method in which all parts of the network are prepared for implementation. You should ensure there is proper connectivity, power (uninterrupted power supplies for servers, grounded outlets, and so forth), and network addressing. You will also need to ensure that software is compatible. You can check the compatibility of software by checking Microsoft's Web site or by running the Windows 2000 Readiness Analyzer program.

Software management in Windows 2000 begins with ensuring the Active Directory network is organized properly. This involves creating the sites and organizational units that your business requires. It will also be necessary to create the proper groups and group policies to which you will add the software settings. In creating group policies, it is important to remember that new policies are unconfigured by default. The reason they are unconfigured is so that existing settings are not overridden.

When analyzing the impact on the planned technical environment, you should remember the following points:

- The creation of the necessary sites and organizational units is a prerequisite to beginning a software management solution.

- When creating new group policies for each of these units, keep in mind that with new policies each setting is unconfigured by default.

- It is important to verify the capability of applications to run on Windows 2000 prior to planning application purchases.

exam
Ⓦatᴄh

Group policies are collections of settings used to configure users and computers. These settings allow you to specify the behavior of a user's desktop. To configure Group Policy in Windows 2000, Microsoft Management Console (MMC) is used with the Group Policy snap-in. This is used to create Group Policy Objects (GPOs), which are collections of Group Policy settings. Each computer running Windows 2000 has a local GPO and may be affected by nonlocal GPOs in the Active Directory. Nonlocal GPOs are linked computers, sites, domains, and organizational units (OUs) in Active Directory. Any new policies that are created are unconfigured by default, so existing settings are not overridden.

QUESTIONS

6.02: Analyzing the Impact on the Planned Technical Environment

3. You are preparing to upgrade your network to Windows 2000. You are concerned that some programs currently running in your Windows NT environment may not be compatible with Windows 2000. Which of the following could you use to analyze whether these applications are compatible? (Choose all that apply.)

    A. Microsoft Management Console

    B. Microsoft Web site

    C. Windows 2000 Readiness Analyzer

    D. Windows NT Readiness Analyzer

4. Your network has had all Windows NT machines upgraded to Windows 2000. You want to configure the behavior of a group of users' desktops by creating group policies. After modifying the local GPO on Windows 2000 machines, you find that certain settings are working as they should but others are not working properly. Which of the following might be causing this? (Choose all that apply.)

    A. Any new policies that are created are unconfigured by default.

    B. Local GPOs are being affected by unconfigured group policies.

    C. The local GPO is being affected by nonlocal policies.

    D. Group policies are not used in Windows 2000. They are used only in mixed Windows NT/Windows 2000 environments.

TEST YOURSELF OBJECTIVE 6.03

Analyzing the Technical Support Structure

When designing Windows 2000 Active Directory, it is important to remember that user support is an essential role of your project team. Implementing Active Directory will cause many changes to your network, so it is important that you work with support staff early in the project. This will give support staff time to provide feedback, create methods for end user feedback, set up help desk initiatives, create documentation, implement training, and perform other tasks dealing with technical support. You should analyze the current support structure, including procedures and software used to provide technical support, and assess the skills and abilities of the support staff. In most cases, the support staff will need some additional training on Windows 2000 so that they can deal with problems that users will encounter.

Auditing is useful in identifying the activities of users. It tracks the activity of users and records these activities in the security log of a server or workstation. An audit policy is used to determine what security events should be recorded. Because it can be a helpful tool in troubleshooting and providing technical support, auditing should be kept enabled.

Windows 2000 provides a number of other practical features, including Microsoft Management Console (MMC), Group Policy, and Terminal Services. MMC is a framework used to create, save, and open administrative tools, which are called *consoles*. Consoles do not provide management functions, but are used to host individualized consoles called snap-ins. For example, Active Directory Users and Computers is a console run through MMC. It hosts an application for managing users and computers in AD.

Another console is for Group Policy and is used to create Group Policy Objects (GPOs). GPOs provide the capability to group users and computers, and to control factors related to them, such as system security, user access, updating applications, and locking down systems.

Lastly, Terminal Services allows client computers to act as terminals. The Terminal Server software running on Windows 2000 Server provides a multisession environment so that Windows-based software being used by client machines is run on the server instead of on the client machine. The Terminal Server presents a display to the client, including the user interface and results of processing. Using Terminal Services, Windows 2000 can be used on 16- and 32-bit clients. Client machines running Windows 3.x, Windows 9x, and Windows NT can thereby use a Windows 2000 operating system and applications because their session of Windows 2000 is running on the server and not on the client. Clients are presented with merely a display of this session.

When analyzing the technical support structure, you should always keep the following points in mind:

- It is important to work together with support staff far in advance of implementing Windows 2000 and Active Directory.

- When implementing a Windows 2000 network, it is a good idea to keep auditing enabled.

- The Microsoft Management Console is a customizable framework for a number of administrative tools available in Windows 2000.

- Group Policy enables the automation and centralization of administrative tasks by grouping both users and computers, and by granting or denying capabilities.

- Terminal Services allows client software to run as a session on the server, so the clients function as terminals rather than independent systems.

exam

ⓦatch

Terminal Services can be a difficult and odd topic for both novice and experienced computer professionals. Older computer users and history buffs may remember dumb terminals that were commonly used decades ago. Dumb terminals were end user devices that had little or no software. They accessed the operating system and applications from a mainframe. This arrangement was replaced by client/server technology, but terminal emulation remained popular. An example of a system that used terminal emulation software was the bulletin board system (BBS). With BBS, a predecessor of the Internet, a user dialed in to another computer and used terminal emulation software to connect with BBS software. The BBS server displayed a user interface and offered access to applications and files on the BBS. Although Terminal Services was founded in this history, improvements have made it a more useful and exciting technology.

Terminal Services enables Windows-based applications to run on a server and be displayed on a client computer acting as a terminal. Terminal emulation software allows applications to be accessed from a Windows-based terminal, a remote PC, or even a non-Windows device such as one running Unix or an Apple Macintosh operating system. The Windows 2000 desktop and applications can therefore be presented to any number of devices. Older computers that would not normally be able to use Windows 2000 software because of inadequate hardware requirements can now access these applications. Another benefit is that administrators can manage Windows 2000 Servers from any device using Terminal Services Client software.

QUESTIONS

6.03: Analyzing the Technical Support Structure

5. You want to modify Group Policy and have been told to use Microsoft Management Console. You open MMC and see what is shown in the following illustration. What is incorrect?

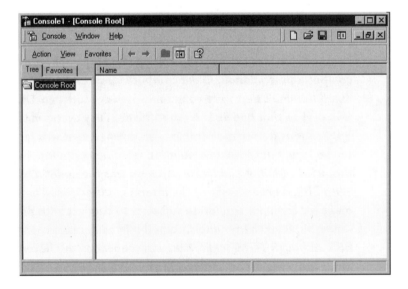

A. Microsoft Management Console is not used to modify group policies. Use Policy Editor.

B. The Group Policy snap-in needs to be loaded.

C. The Active Directory Users and Computers snap-in needs to be loaded.

D. The Active Directory User and Group Policy snap-in needs to be loaded.

6. You are about to leave on vacation for the first time since your network has been upgraded to Windows 2000. You want the ability to access the Windows 2000 Server from your Windows CE device in case a problem evolves in your absence. Which of the following will you install on your Windows CE device, and what will you need running on your Windows 2000 Server?

A. Terminal Services must be running on your Windows CE device. Nothing needs to be running on the Windows 2000 Server.

B. Terminal Services needs to be running on the Windows 2000 Server. GPO needs to be running on the Windows CE device.

C. Terminal Services needs to be running on the Windows 2000 Server. Terminal Services Client software needs to be running on the Windows CE device.

D. Nothing. Windows 2000 software cannot be run on a Windows CE device.

TEST YOURSELF OBJECTIVE 6.04

Analyzing Existing Network and Systems Management

There are a number of useful tools available when analyzing existing network and systems management. Among these are Systems Management Server (SMS) and Network Monitor. Each of these can provide vital insight when preparing to deploy Windows 2000 and after Windows 2000 has been implemented on a network.

Network Monitor is a tool that is shipped with Windows NT and Windows 2000 and is used to detect problems on local area networks (LANs). This tool enables you to detect network traffic problems, and it is a valuable troubleshooting tool. It captures frames (packets) from the network, which can then be displayed, filtered, saved, or printed. The version of Network Monitor that comes with Windows NT and Windows 2000 is not a full version of the program. It can capture only packets that are destined for the machine on which Network Monitor is installed. A full version of Network Monitor, available with Systems Management Server, allows you to place your network adapter in "promiscuous mode" so that your computer can capture packets destined for other computers on a network segment.

When using Network Monitor, it is important to capture and save information when your network is performing properly, and not merely when you are experiencing problems. Such historical information of how your network is supposed to behave is used to create a base line. When a problem is suspected, you can then collect data through Network Monitor to compare to the base line data collected when the network was functioning properly. This will enable you to determine if your network is working properly and help you forecast the impact of changes on your network or additions you may be planning.

Systems Management Server (SMS) has a number of valuable features, including the capability to take control of a computer, monitor hardware and software usage, and perform license monitoring so that your organization adheres to licensing agreements. A particularly important feature is its capability to manage and distribute software packages throughout your network. Not only can you schedule and perform unattended installations of applications, but you can also use SMS to deploy Windows 2000 to clients and servers. It enables you to push installation on a system without physically visiting it. This is advantageous when you need to distribute software on a network with a large geographic scope.

When analyzing the existing network and systems management, you should keep the following points in mind:

- Network Monitor is an administrative tool that ships with Windows NT and Windows 2000. This program captures packets on a network that are destined for the machine on which it is installed.

- If you purchase Microsoft's Systems Management Server, you will be able to use the full version of Network Monitor that allows you to place your network adapter in "promiscuous mode," enabling your computer to view every packet on your segment of the network.

- Systems Management Server (SMS) from Microsoft allows a network administrator to distribute software packages throughout the network.

exam
Watch

Although Systems Management Server (SMS) is not shipped with Windows 2000, it is important enough that you will see it mentioned in a number of Microsoft MCSE exams. SMS is available for use with both Windows NT and Windows 2000, and it provides a number of important features for analysis, troubleshooting, and network management. It can be used to inventory hardware by gathering information on local and remote computers over a LAN. It also has the capability to inventory software by generating a list of all applications installed on PCs throughout the network. This inventory is used in installations so that only compatible systems install software. With SMS, you can perform unattended installs and even schedule when they will occur.

QUESTIONS

6.04: Analyzing Existing Network and Systems Management

7. You suspect a bad network card on a server called Server1. You sit at another server called Server2, and you decide to use Network Monitor to capture packets destined for Server1 so that you can analyze them. Both servers are running Windows 2000 Server, and no server on your network is running Systems Management Server. When you attempt to troubleshoot this way, you find it does not work. Why?

   A. Systems Management Server is the only Windows 2000 tool that can capture packets for analysis.

   B. Network Monitor comes only with Systems Management Server and is not shipped with Windows 2000.

   C. The version of Network Monitor that comes with Windows 2000 can capture only packets that are destined for the machine on which Network Monitor is installed.

   D. The version of Systems Management Server that comes with Windows 2000 can capture only packets that are destined for the machine on which Systems Management Server is installed.

8. **Current Situation:** Your network has just been upgraded to Windows 2000. Server1 has Systems Management Server installed, whereas Server2 does not. The finance department of your company would like you to provide an inventory of software and hardware on the computers for which your IT staff is responsible. They have also asked you to install a number of programs on the computers in the finance department when you have time. While creating this inventory, you think it would also be beneficial to create a log of server behavior on the network so that you have information to compare to when a problem occurs.

   Required Result: Create a base line of Server1's network behavior.

Optional Desired Results:

1. Create an inventory of hardware and software.

2. Install the applications the finance department has asked for.

Proposed Solution: Run the Network Monitor installed on Server2 and place your network adapter in "promiscuous mode" so that packets destined for other computers on a network segment can be captured. Use SMS on Server1 to create hardware and software inventories, and install the applications remotely.

What results are produced from the proposed solution?

A. The proposed solution produces the required result only.

B. The proposed solution produces the required result and only one of the optional results.

C. The proposed solution produces the required result and both of the optional results.

D. The proposed solution does not produce the required result.

TEST YOURSELF OBJECTIVE 6.05

Analyzing Planned Network and Systems Management

Windows 2000 provides a number of valuable features for network and systems management. As part of Microsoft's Zero Administration Initiative, Windows Management Instrumentation (WMI) provides the capability to control and monitor the hardware on local workstations. WMI is an extension of the Windows Driver Model (WDM). It provides an interface through which hardware components can communicate so that these devices can supply information and notification. Devices communicate bi-directionally with WMI, so administrators can view alerts when the device is experiencing problems or is down.

Microsoft's Web Administration utility allows you to manage servers remotely over the Internet. Using this utility, you can perform administrative tasks on shares, accounts, sessions, servers, and printers. Because it works through a compatible Web browser, it does not matter what platform you are working from, so you can perform management tasks from Windows, Unix, or Macintosh computers.

In the previous section, we mentioned that Systems Management Server allows you to deploy software, but that it must be purchased separately from Windows 2000. With Active Directory, software can be deployed to your network through the use of group policies. You can use Group Policy to publish or assign packages to users and computers. When an application is assigned to a user, it is advertised to the user when he or she logs on. This advertisement follows the user, regardless of what computer this person is using. The first time the user starts the application or opens a file associated with the software, the application is installed. If the application is assigned to a computer, the application is advertised and installed when the computer starts up. When an application is published to a user, it does not appear as installed software. There are no shortcuts on the desktop or Start menu. No changes appear in the registry, but the advertised attributes are instead stored in Active Directory. For the application to be installed, the user must install it using the Add/Remove Programs applet in Control Panel, or by opening a file that is associated with the software.

When analyzing the planned network and systems management, it is important to keep the following points in mind:

- Windows Management Instrumentation allows network administrators to become more effective with disaster prevention, responding to end users, automating managerial tasks, managing operations, increasing effectiveness with the installation of upgrades, and performing preventative maintenance.

- The Web Administration utility will allow you to remotely perform administration on shares, accounts, sessions, servers, and printers.

- With Active Directory, software can be deployed to your network through the use of group policies.

- Software can only be assigned to a computer.

- Software can be both assigned and published to a user.

exam
ⓦatch

Windows Management Instrumentation uses drivers to allow compliant devices to communicate with Windows 2000 Server. When a device needs to communicate with the server, information is sent to a WDM Mini Driver that is supplied by the manufacturer. The mini driver passes this information to a standard WDM driver supplied by Microsoft. The WDM driver then sends the information to the WMI interface on the server. WMI gathers together all of the information from hardware, drivers, and applications, and delivers it to a centralized management store. Network administrators can then access this store and view information about the device.

QUESTIONS

6.05: Analyzing Planned Network and Systems Management

Questions 9–11   The next three questions are based upon the scenario that follows. Read the following case study, and then answer the questions. You may refer to this case study as often as needed.

You are the network administrator for a new company. You have two Windows 2000 Servers, and all workstations use Windows 2000 Professional. You have been asked to install new software on a number of computers. All users on your network will use the new word processing software, but only members of the finance department will use the spreadsheet application. In addition to taking on these tasks, you are scheduled to attend a meeting out of town. The facility where the meeting is held uses Macintosh computers, and no PCs are available. There is some concern about what will happen if there is a problem, as you are the only person currently employed at the company who knows how to manage the network.

9. You want to distribute the spreadsheet application only to computers in the finance department. The application should automatically install when the computer starts up. What will you do?

  A. Assign the application to a user.

  B. Assign the application to a computer.

  C. Publish the application to a user.

  D. Publish the application to a computer.

10. You want to distribute word processing software to users, such that the application is advertised to users when they log on, regardless of what computer they are using. The application should be installed when the user opens a

document associated with the application, or the first time the user starts the application. How will you do this?

A. Assign the application to the user.

B. Assign the application to the computer.

C. Publish the application to the user.

D. Publish the application to the computer.

11. While out of town at your meeting, you are given a message. You are told that some users of your network need access to a directory on the server, and that no one at the company knows how to do this. Which of the following can you use to solve this problem?

A. Network Monitor

B. Macintosh Management Console

C. Microsoft Management Console

D. Microsoft Web Administration utility

TEST YOURSELF OBJECTIVE 6.06

Analyzing Business Requirements for Client Computer Desktop Management

Analyzing business requirements for client computer desktop management involves determining what the company needs to control a user's desktop. At face value, this may seem somewhat trivial in the grand scheme of designing an Active Directory network. However, users are the largest element of a network, and they require the greatest amount of time to support. By controlling what users can do to their desktops, you decrease the need for support, and lower the company's total cost of ownership.

Group policies are an excellent way of managing client desktops. By installing software through Active Directory, visits to client computers to perform installations, upgrade software to the latest versions, or remove unwanted applications are decreased. It also eliminates the possibility of a client installing an application incorrectly, or of users breaking licensing agreements by installing software on additional machines. When applications are deployed through Group Policy, Windows Installer application installation packages are used. The software vendor provides a package file, which is a database with the .MSI extension. It contains information on application components, shortcut information, registry settings, file type associations, and services to be installed. If an .MSI file isn't available, then you must create a .ZAP file to distribute the application files.

Another effective method of desktop management is to use Group Policy Objects (GPOs) to "lock down" a client computer. Locking down a computer prevents users from making changes to their machines. By assigning a policy to prohibit users from making such changes, time is not wasted on trying to discover what settings the user has changed when you are troubleshooting a problem on their machine.

Disk quotas allow you to control the amount of information a user stores on a hard drive. Windows 2000 has the feature of allowing you to assign the drive space on volumes formatted as NTFS to users or groups, so they are limited in how much hard disk space they are allowed to use. Because disk quotas are a Windows 2000 feature for use with NTFS drives, they are unavailable on systems running on Windows NT, Windows 9x, and Windows 3.x.

When analyzing business requirements for client computer desktop management, you should remember the following:

- The implementation of software management with Windows 2000 begins with making sure that your networks, by way of the Active Directory, are organized in a proper manner. The creation of the necessary sites and organizational units is a prerequisite to beginning your software management solution. It will also be necessary to create the proper groups and group policies to which you will add the software settings.

- Microsoft has created the Windows Installer application installation package. This package allows you to create package files that have an .MSI extension.

- The software vendor provides the .MSI database. If one is not available, it will be necessary to create a .ZAP file to allow the distribution of these files using group policies.

- Active Directory allows network administrators to "lock down" a client computer. This is accomplished through the use of Group Policy Objects.

- Disk quotas allow centralized management of the amount of space a user can utilize on a hard drive.

- Windows 2000 allows assignment of drive space to users, or groups of users, on volumes that are formatted with NTFS. Please note that disk quotas are unavailable on systems running Windows NT, Windows 9x, and Windows 3.x.

Disk quotas allow you to limit the amount of space a user can use on the file server. To implement disk quotas on your Windows 2000 Server, you would use Microsoft Management Console and the Group Policy snap-in. This is a Windows 2000 feature and is available only for drives formatted with NTFS. Therefore, disk quotas are not available on systems running Windows 3.x, Windows 9x, and Windows NT. When disk quotas are activated on existing drives, Windows calculates the space used by each user that has files on it. It then uses this information to create quota limits and warning levels. However, when creating limits and warnings, you should be aware of roaming profiles used on your network. Since roaming profiles allow users to retain their settings from machine to machine, the disk quota will also follow them. This means a user could move to a particular machine and, when attempting to save work, discover that their profile and documents may not fit on the server.

QUESTIONS

6.06: Analyzing Business Requirements for Client Computer Desktop Management

12. **Current Situation:** Your company has several Windows 2000 Servers and over three hundred workstations running Windows 2000 Professional, Windows 98, and Windows NT Workstation. Members of your IT staff are having difficulty finding the actual problem with a computer, because users

are making changes to their computers. Management has also expressed concerns about the fact that users are putting backgrounds on their desktops of inappropriate cartoons and images containing nudity. This makes the office look unprofessional. Some users are also providing installation CDs to other users and installing the software incorrectly. Management is worried that the company may be sued over licensing agreements. You have considered installing software through Group Policy, but a number of applications do not have .MSI files. An additional problem exists, in that some users are using a large amount of disk space for personal files. These users have been scanning family photos and storing them on their hard drives and the hard disks of the server.

Required Result: Install all software through Active Directory so that users will not need access to installation CDs nor can they improperly install applications.

Optional Desired Results:

1. Control the ability of users to change backgrounds and other settings on their desktops.

2. Control the amount of disk space used by users on the network.

Proposed Solution: Use Group Policy to install applications. For applications without .MSI files, create .ZAP files. Use GPOs to lock down the client computers. Use disk quotas to control the amount of disk space being utilized by users on all servers and workstations.

What results are produced from the proposed solution?

A. The proposed solution produces the required result only.

B. The proposed solution produces the required result and only one of the optional results.

C. The proposed solution produces the required result and both of the optional results.

D. The proposed solution does not produce the required result.

13. You have set disk quota limit and warning levels, as shown in the following illustration. Which of the following is true? (Choose all that apply.)

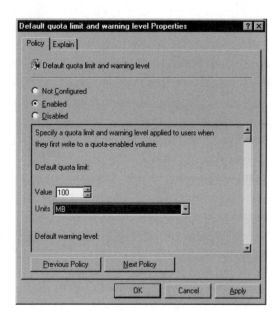

A. The limit will apply to all new users.

B. The limit will not apply to users with roaming profiles.

C. The limit will apply to all users on all volumes, regardless of actual volume size.

D. If disk quotas are not enforced, users can exceed this limit.

TEST YOURSELF OBJECTIVE 6.07

Analyzing End User Work Needs

Since users are the customers of IT, and since many users will have specific requirements of any Active Directory you design, it is important that you satisfy your customers by analyzing their work needs. This includes determining if users will need roaming profiles, and following proper procedures when deploying software.

Although applications can be deployed through SMS and Active Directory, there is a deployment process that must be followed. The Testing and Development stage is the part of this process wherein applications are tested prior to being deployed. This stage reveals a number of issues to your team that help determine what problems may result when users actually use the program. The Pilot Deployment stage involves deploying the application to a small number of users and computers so that you can see how it actually works on the network. Finally, in the Production Deployment stage the applications are rolled out to the various users requiring the software.

Often, users are not using a single desktop computer, but are moving from workstation to workstation. Roaming profiles allow users to retain their desktop settings, regardless of the machine they are working on. There are different types of user profiles available in Windows 2000. Local user profiles are stored on a user's local workstation and affect only their system. Roaming user profiles are stored on a server and accessed by users from any desktop. Mandatory roaming profiles are roaming profiles that cannot be permanently changed by users. Like roaming user profiles, mandatory roaming profiles are stored on the server and accessed from any desktop. If Terminal Services is being used, you can create roaming user profiles for use with Terminal Services clients. This type of profile is not replicated to a server until the user logs off and the interactive session is closed. Other types of roaming profiles are automatically replicated through Active Directory.

All versions of Windows 2000 have support for using different languages. Regardless of the language used for the user interface (UI), Windows 2000 will let users edit and process text in all languages, as well as run applications that have the UI in any or all languages. Single UI language versions of Windows 2000 are released in all supported UI languages. These single UI language versions differ mainly in the language. There is also a multilanguage user interface (MUI) version of Windows 2000, which has resources for each supported UI language. The MUI allows users to set the user interface language according to their preferences, provided the required language was added to the system. This allows users of different languages to share the same workstation.

When analyzing end user work needs, you should remember the following points:

- The three stages of software deployment are Testing and Development stage, Pilot Deployment stage, and Production Deployment stage.
- There are different types of user profiles, including local user profiles, roaming user profiles, and mandatory roaming profiles.
- Windows 2000 allows users to work in their own languages.

Roaming profiles are used to control user desktop settings and contain user work environments. Settings contained in a roaming profile include screen colors, mouse settings, window size and position, and network and printer connections. A roaming profile is downloaded from the server whenever and wherever the user logs on a computer. Since roaming profiles can take up a significant amount of disk space, especially when a user copies files directly to the desktop, you should consider using disk quotas when implementing them.

QUESTIONS

6.07: Analyzing End User Work Needs

14. Dianne is a member of your IT staff. You ask her to create a roaming profile for a user of Terminal Services. Dianne decides to open Active Directory Users and Computers and access the property sheet of the user. After making changes, she shows what has been done by showing you the following illustration. What will you tell her?

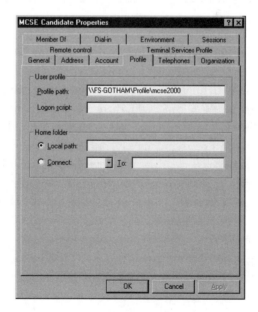

A. The roaming profile has been created correctly.

B. The profile created is a local user profile. Active Directory Users and Computers is not used for creating roaming profiles.

C. The profile created is not for Terminal Services.

D. No profile has been created.

15. You are planning to deploy an application through Active Directory. At present, you are at the stage where the application has been deployed to a small group of users on the network. Which of the following stages in the deployment process is this?

A. Preliminary Planning

B. Testing and Development

C. Pilot Deployment

D. Production Deployment

TEST YOURSELF OBJECTIVE 6.08

Identifying Technical Support Needs for End Users

Training end users is an important part of any information technology project and should be considered early in your project plan. This will give team members a chance to identify training issues and make proper training plans. By training end users properly on Windows 2000, there will be fewer help desk calls, and users will be able to adjust to the new system and use it effectively. This approach will allow you to deal with support needs proactively, rather than reacting to user problems as they occur.

As we discussed earlier, Windows Management Instrumentation (WMI) is a management infrastructure providing the capability to control and monitor system resources so that administrators are alerted to hardware issues before receiving complaints from end users. It provides interfaces between client hardware and a Windows 2000 Server. WMI also allows you to configure premade packages that contain dial-up configurations for remote users. It also provides control of power-management features so that you can configure power-management settings from a centralized location. As well, WMI provides greater controls of failed services, allowing you to restart a service, run a specific program, or reboot the system when a service fails.

There are several tools in Windows 2000 that are WMI enabled. One such tool is the WMI Control, used to perform Windows Management configuration tasks. This allows you to set permissions for users and groups, back up the object repository, and control logging of WMI. Services is a tool accessed through MMC with the Services snap-in added. It is used to manage services, allowing you to view and configure services, as well as view other services on which a particular service is dependent. The final three WMI enabled tools are accessed through the Computer Management (Local) snap-in for MMC. Logical Drives is a tool for managing mapped drives and local drives on remote and local computers. Using this WMI tool, you can change drive labels, view Drive Properties, and change security settings on drives. System Information is a tool used to collect and display information about your system. The last tool, Systems Properties, is used to view and configure system properties on local and remote computers. Using this tool, you can reboot a remote computer to apply system settings or detect new hardware. It is particularly useful for viewing the computer name and domain information for network computers, and for changing settings for the virtual memory paging file on computers.

When identifying technical support needs for end users, you should consider the following:

- End user training will help network administrators move from reactive management to proactive management.

- WMI is a set of instructions that allows Windows 2000 client hardware to communicate with a Windows 2000 server. It can become a very powerful tool for those who take the time to learn how it works.

exam

Watch

You configure and control the WMI service on your Windows 2000 Server using Microsoft Management Console with the WMI Control snap-in. By viewing the properties of the WMI Control, you will see a dialog box with several tabs. The General tab provides information about the server and WMI service, and it allows you to change what user account is used to connect to the service. The Logging tab allows you to specify the level of logging (disabled, errors only, or verbose), maximum size of the log files, and location of the logs. The Backup/Restore tab allows you to control when and where the WMI repository is backed up, and it allows you to perform manual backups and restores of WMI. The Security tab allows you to set namespace specific security, and the Advanced tab allows you to specify advanced settings in Windows Management on a Windows 2000 or Windows NT computer.

QUESTIONS

6.08: Identifying Technical Support Needs for End Users

16. You are configuring the WMI service on a new Windows 2000 Server. As shown in the following illustration, you open MMC with the WMI snap-in and bring up the properties of the WMI Control. On which tab would you view information about the WMI version and location?

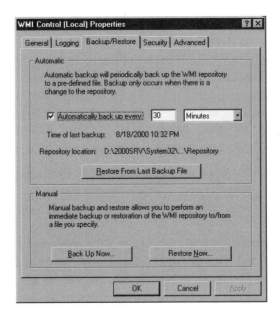

A. General

B. Logging

C. Security

D. Advanced

17. Cathy is a user located in another building from the central office, where you currently are. The computer she is working on is running Windows 2000, and she is using a number of applications that require a significant amount of memory. She complains that the computer is running slowly, and she is getting messages stating that memory is low. Which of the following would you use to change virtual memory paging file settings for her computer?

   A. WMI Control

   B. Services

   C. Systems Properties

   D. System Information

TEST YOURSELF OBJECTIVE 6.09

Establishing Required Client Computer Environment

Establishing the required client computer environment is an important part of designing a Windows 2000 Active Directory network. Just as the heart of programming is the manipulation of data, the soul of being a network administrator is ensuring the stability, reliability, and availability of data. This means not only ensuring that there is sufficient hard drive space, proper bandwidth, and so forth. It also requires making certain that the data a user needs is available through the right applications.

Applications have a life cycle that can be broken into four stages. Each of these is managed in Active Directory through the use of Group Policy. The Preparation stage includes the proper packaging of the application using Windows Installer. In this stage you prepare the .MSI or .ZAP files for distribution. In the Deployment stage, the package is deployed to the domain, site, or organizational unit as a GPO (Group Policy Object). As we discussed earlier, this deployment can be assigned or published based on specific operational requirements. The Maintenance stage involves maintenance of proper versions and updates. Group policies are used to apply updated versions or service packs at this stage. The Removal stage is the end of the life cycle of an application. When the application is no longer of use, group policies are used to perform automatic removals by running a Windows Installer uninstall routine.

Whether you are installing or uninstalling an application, it is important to keep users informed. End users need to know what applications are available to them, and you need to know what applications are currently being used or no longer needed. If a new application is being installed, users should be kept abreast of when it is expected to be available, and they should receive proper training to use it.

When establishing the required client computer environment for a network, it is important to remember these points:

■ The life of an application can be broken into four stages: Preparation stage, Deployment stage, Maintenance stage, and Removal stage.

■ By informing users about the installation process and assuring them that they will be able to access required applications, you will save yourself a lot of questions and concern.

exam ⚡
ⓌatcH

There are three tools provided with Windows 2000 Server for the installation and maintenance of software. Add/Remove Programs is an applet available in Control Panel that allows users to manage the software on their computer. Windows Installer is used to install software that is packaged in Windows Installer files. Finally, and perhaps most importantly to network administrators, the Software Installation extension of the Group Policy snap-in is used by administrators to install and manage software. This is the primary tool for managing software on a Windows 2000 network, and it is used to deploy and remove applications. It can also be used to apply mandatory and nonmandatory upgrades, patches, and fixes for software.

QUESTIONS

6.09: Establishing Required Client Computer Environment

18. You want to add an additional component to an application that is already installed on a user's computer. Since it is a single client machine this will be

installed on, you decide to use the installation CD for that application. Which of the following will you use?

A. Software Installation applet in Control Panel

B. Windows Installer extension of the Group Policy snap-in

C. Add/Remove Programs applet in Control Panel

D. Windows Installer applet in Control Panel

19. **Current Situation:** Your network has grown and been upgraded since initially running Windows NT 3.51. You have just upgraded the network from Windows NT 4.0 to Windows 2000, and you realize there are a number of applications on network client machines that have been on these machines for a while. Some of these programs may still be useful, but they will require upgrading to newer versions. You also have a number of applications that you would like to install that may prove more beneficial to users.

Required Result: Determine what applications need to be removed from network client computers.

Optional Desired Results:

1. Determine what method should be used to automatically remove applications from client machines.

2. Determine a method to automatically apply upgrades and service packs to software that is still being used.

Proposed Solution: Have users assess what applications they use, and which ones they no longer need. Use this information to compile a list of software to remove from the system. Use Add/Remove Programs to deploy and remove applications. Use the Software Installation extension of the Group Policy snap-in to apply upgrades and service packs.

What results are produced from the proposed solution?

A. The proposed solution produces the required result only.

B. The proposed solution produces the required result and only one of the optional results.

C. The proposed solution produces the required result and both of the optional results.

D. The proposed solution does not produce the required result.

LAB QUESTION

Objectives 6.01–6.09

Your network currently runs Windows NT Servers, workstations using Windows 95 and Windows NT Workstation, and Apple Macintosh computers. You are planning to upgrade servers to Windows 2000 Server and some of the workstations to Windows 2000 Professional, but many of the workstations will continue to use the older operating systems. In addition, Apple Macintosh computers will continue to run on the network. None of the servers are running Systems Management Server, and you do not plan to implement it after the upgrade.

1. You are concerned that some applications running on Windows NT Servers will not be compatible with Windows 2000 Server. What resources can you use to check this?

2. After upgrading to Windows 2000, you want some applications designed for Windows 2000 to be available to all computers on the network. What can you use to make these applications available?

3. What tool would you use to detect traffic problems on this network, and what limitation does this tool have?

4. Upon upgrading this network, you want to distribute software using Active Directory. Your plan is to have the software appear as installed and have no shortcuts on the desktop or Start menu. Users can install the application using Add/Remove Programs or by opening a document associated with the application. What will you do?

5. Some users on the network keep moving from computer to computer. You want to control their settings so that the user has the same desktop settings, regardless of the computer they are using. The user should be unable to permanently change these settings. What will you use?

6. You want to manage mapped drives and local drives on computers running Windows 2000 Professional. What WMI enabled tool would you use?

QUICK ANSWER KEY

Objective 6.01
1. A
2. B

Objective 6.02
3. B and C
4. A and C

Objective 6.03
5. B
6. C

Objective 6.04
7. C
8. D

Objective 6.05
9. B
10. A
11. D

Objective 6.06
12. B
13. A, C, and D

Objective 6.07
14. C
15. C

Objective 6.08
16. A
17. C

Objective 6.09
18. C
19. B

IN-DEPTH ANSWERS

6.01: Analyzing the Impact on the Existing Technical Environment

1. ☑ **A.** The proposed solution produces the required result only. A test lab can be used to reveal issues that may arise when upgrading the actual network to Windows 2000. On the test lab network, install Windows NT 4.0 Server and other operating systems used on your network. Try to make the test lab resemble your network as closely as possible.

   ☒ **B, C,** and **D** are incorrect because the proposed solution produces the required result only. The optional requirements were not met because TCP/IP is required on a Windows 2000 network, and not all of the applications should be used on the test lab or on the actual network. Some applications should be retired because they are not being used anymore, whereas other applications are not compatible with Windows 2000 and should be replaced.

2. ☑ **B.** The Security Configuration and Analysis snap-in uses security templates to configure and analyze security settings for each system. It is a Microsoft Management Console snap-in that is used to configure and analyze security, view results, and resolve discrepancies that are exposed by the analysis.

   ☒ **A** is incorrect because the Security Templates snap-in allows you to generate and configure security templates, which are used to control security settings on local systems. **C** is incorrect because Security Configuration Editor is a Windows NT tool that has been replaced by the Security Configuration and Analysis snap-in in Windows 2000. **D** is incorrect because the Security Settings extension snap-in is used to enhance Group Policy editor, allowing the implementation of security processes to impact groups.

6.02: Analyzing the Impact on the Planned Technical Environment

3. ☑ **B** and **C** are correct. Windows 2000 Readiness Analyzer and Microsoft's Web site can provide you with information as to whether software is compatible with Windows 2000.

☒ **A** is incorrect because Microsoft Management Console does not provide the capability to check software compatibility with Windows 2000. **D** is incorrect because there is no such tool as Windows NT Readiness Analyzer.

4. ☑ **A** and **C** are correct. The reason that certain policies are working and others are not might be related to the fact that any new policies that are created are unconfigured by default. Consequently, it is possible that this is causing new policies to be unconfigured and not functioning as you wanted. Each computer running Windows 2000 has a local GPO and may be affected by nonlocal GPOs in the Active Directory. Nonlocal GPOs are linked computers, sites, domains, and organizational units (OUs) in Active Directory.

☒ **B** is incorrect because if the group policies are unconfigured, they cannot affect the local GPO. **D** is incorrect because group policies are used in Windows 2000.

6.03: Analyzing the Technical Support Structure

5. ☑ **B.** The Group Policy snap-in needs to be loaded. Microsoft Management Console with the Group Policy console is used to modify group policies in Windows 2000.

☒ **A** is incorrect because Microsoft Management Console is used with the Group Policy snap-in to modify group policies. **C** is incorrect because the Active Directory Users and Computers snap-in is used to create, delete, modify, move, and set permissions on such objects as users, computers, contacts, groups, printers, shared file objects, and organizational units. It is not used to set group policies. **D** is incorrect because there is no Active Directory User and Group Policy snap-in.

6. ☑ **C.** Terminal Services is a service that can be run on Windows 2000 Servers, allowing users to access Windows 2000 software. Terminal Services Client software provides terminal emulation, allowing users access to applications from a Windows-based terminal, a remote PC, or even a non-Windows device.

   ☒ **A** is incorrect because Terminal Services needs to be running on the Windows 2000 Server. **B** is incorrect because GPO is a short form for Group Policy Object. **D** is incorrect because you can run Terminal Services Client software on a Windows CE device, allowing you to access the Windows 2000 Server.

6.04: Analyzing Existing Network and Systems Management

7. ☑ **C.** The version of Network Monitor that comes with Windows 2000 can capture only packets that are destined for the machine on which Network Monitor is installed. A full version of Network Monitor, available with Systems Management Server, allows you to place your network adapter in "promiscuous mode" so that your computer can capture packets destined for other computers on a network segment.

   ☒ **A** is incorrect because Network Monitor can capture packets for analysis. **B** is incorrect because a version of Network Monitor ships with Windows 2000. **D** is incorrect because Systems Management Server is not shipped with Windows 2000.

8. ☑ **D.** The proposed solution does not produce the required result. The Network Monitor installed on Server2 is not the version that comes with SMS. Therefore, you cannot place your network adapter in "promiscuous mode" so that the packets destined for other computers on a network segment are captured.

   ☒ **A**, **B**, and **C** are incorrect because the proposed solution did not produce the required result. However, the optional results were fulfilled because SMS can be used to create a hardware and software inventory and install the applications remotely.

6.05: Analyzing Planned Network and Systems Management

9. ☑ **B.** Assign the application to a computer. If the application is assigned to a computer, the application is advertised and installed when the computer starts up.

    ☒ **A** is incorrect because when an application is assigned to a user, it is advertised to the user when he or she logs on. This advertisement follows the user, regardless of what computer this person is using. **C** is incorrect because when an application is published to a user, the user must install it using the Add/Remove Programs applet in Control Panel, or by opening a file that is associated with the software. **D** is incorrect because applications are not published to computers.

10. ☑ **A.** Assign the application to the user. This will advertise the application to the user when he or she logs on, regardless of what computer this person is using. The first time the user starts the application, or opens a file associated with the software, the application is installed.

    ☒ **B** is incorrect because if an application is assigned to a computer, the application is advertised and installed when the computer starts up. **C** is incorrect because when an application is published to a user, the user must install it using the Add/Remove Programs applet in Control Panel, or by opening a file that is associated with the software. **D** is incorrect because you do not publish applications to computers.

11. ☑ **D.** Microsoft's Web Administration utility is used to manage servers remotely over the Internet, allowing you to perform administrative tasks on shares, accounts, sessions, servers, and printers. Because it is used through a compatible Web browser, you can perform management tasks from Apple Macintosh computers.

    ☒ **A** is incorrect because Network Monitor is not used for administration of your network. **B** is incorrect because there is no Macintosh Management Console. **C** is incorrect because Microsoft Management Console is for use only on Windows 2000, unless Terminal Services are used.

6.06: Analyzing Business Requirements for Client Computer Desktop Management

12. ☑ **B.** The proposed solution produces the required result and only one of the optional results. Applications can be deployed through Group Policy. If there is software that does not have a package file with the .MSI extension provided by the vendor, then you must create a .ZAP file to distribute the application files. GPOs (Group Policy Objects) can be used to lock down a client computer so that users cannot make changes to their machines. By assigning a policy to prohibit users from making such changes, time is not wasted on trying to discover what settings the user has changed when you are troubleshooting a problem on their machine. It will also prevent users from making inappropriate changes to their backgrounds and other aspects of the desktop.

☒ **A, C**, and **D** are incorrect because the proposed solution produces the required result and only one of the optional results. Windows 2000 has the feature of allowing you to assign the drive space on volumes formatted as NTFS to users or groups, so they are limited to how much of the hard disk space they are allowed to use. However, disk quotas are a Windows 2000 feature for use with NTFS drives and are unavailable on systems running Windows NT, Windows 9x, and Windows 3.x.

13. ☑ **A, C**, and **D** are correct. Disk quota policy applies to all new users as soon as they write to the NTFS volume. The limit will apply to all users on all volumes, regardless of the actual volume size. Thus, it is important to set limit and warning levels so that they match the size of volumes used. If you do not set disk quotas to be enforced, users will be able to exceed the limit you set and continue to write to the volume.

☒ **B** is incorrect because the limit will apply to users with roaming profiles. The limit will apply to all users on all volumes, regardless of the actual volume size. Therefore, users with roaming profiles will be affected by this.

6.07: Analyzing End User Work Needs

14. ☑ **C.** The profile created is not for Terminal Services. To create a profile for a Terminal Services user, you would use the Terminal Services Profile tab on

the property page of the user's account. This is accessed through Active Directory Users and Computers.

☒   **A** is incorrect because the profiles used for Terminal Services are created on the Terminal Services Profile tab. **B** is incorrect because local user profiles are not created using Active Directory Users and Computers. Active Directory Users and Computers is, however, used to create roaming profiles. **D** is incorrect because a standard roaming profile has been created.

15.   ☑   **C.** The Pilot Deployment stage involves deploying the application to a small number of users and computers so that you can see how it actually works on the network.

☒   **A** is incorrect because there is no preliminary planning stage in the deployment process. **B** is incorrect because the Testing and Development stage is the stage in which applications are tested prior to being deployed. **D** is incorrect because the Production Deployment stage involves rolling out the applications to the various users requiring the software.

6.08: Identifying Technical Support Needs for End Users

16.   ☑   **A.** General. The General tab provides information about the server and WMI service, and it allows you to change what user account is used to connect to the service.

☒   **B** is incorrect because the Logging tab allows you to specify the level of logging, maximum size of the log files, and location of the logs. **C** is incorrect because the Security tab allows you to set namespace specific security. **D** is incorrect because the Advanced tab allows you to specify advanced settings in Windows Management on a Windows 2000 or Windows NT computer.

17.   ☑   **C.** Systems Properties is a tool that allows you to view and configure system properties on local and remote computers, including changing settings for the virtual memory paging file on computers.

☒   **A** is incorrect because the WMI Control is used to perform Windows Management configuration tasks. It allows you to set permissions for users and groups, back up the object repository, and control logging of WMI. **B** is incorrect because Services is used to manage services, allowing you to view and configure services, and view other services on which a service is dependent. **D** is incorrect because System Information is a tool used to collect and display information about your system.

6.09: Establishing Required Client Computer Environment

18. ☑ **C.** Add/Remove Programs is an applet available in Control Panel that allows users to manage the software on their computer. It allows you to add, remove, and manage applications on the local computer.

    ☒ **A** is incorrect because there is no Software Installation applet in Control Panel. **B** is incorrect because there is no Windows Installer extension in the Group Policy snap-in. **D** is incorrect because the Windows Installer is not an applet available through Control Panel.

19. ☑ **B.** The proposed solution produces the required result and only one of the optional results. To determine what applications are no longer being used by end users, you can have these users assess what applications they use, and what applications they no longer need. Use this information to compile a list of software to remove from the system. The Software Installation extension of the Group Policy snap-in should be used by administrators to install and manage software and can also be used to apply upgrades and service packs.

    ☒ **A, C**, and **D** are incorrect because the proposed solution produces the required result and only one of the optional results. Add/Remove Programs is not used to automatically remove applications from client machines. It provides a way for users to install, remove, and manage software on their own machines.

A LAB ANSWER

Objectives 6.01–6.09

1.   You can check the compatibility of software using Microsoft's Web site or by running the Windows 2000 Readiness Analyzer program.

2.   Terminal Services can be used to make Windows 2000 applications available to all client computers. The Terminal Server presents a display to the client, including the user interface and results of processing. Using Terminal Services, Windows 2000 can be used on 16- and 32-bit clients. Client machines running Windows 3.*x*, Windows 9*x*, and Windows NT can thereby use a Windows 2000 operating system and applications because their session of Windows 2000 is running on the server and not on the client. They are presented with merely a display of this session.

3.   Network Monitor is a tool used to detect network traffic problems. It captures frames (packets) from the network, which can then be displayed, filtered, saved, or printed. The version that comes with Windows 2000 can capture only packets destined for the server on which Network Monitor is installed.

4.   Publish the application to the user. When an application is published to a user, it does not appear as installed software. There are no shortcuts on the desktop or Start menu. No changes appear in the registry, but the advertised attributes are instead stored in Active Directory. For the application to be installed, the user must use the Add/Remove Programs applet in Control Panel, or open a file that is associated with the software.

5.   Mandatory roaming profiles are roaming profiles that cannot be permanently changed by users. Like roaming user profiles, mandatory roaming profiles are stored on the server and accessed from any desktop.

6.   Logical Drives is a tool for managing mapped drives and local drives on remote and local computers. Using this WMI tool, you can change drive labels, view drive properties, and change security settings on drives.

MCSE
MICROSOFT CERTIFIED SYSTEMS ENGINEER

7

Designing a Directory Service Architecture

TEST YOURSELF OBJECTIVES

A s we have seen from previous chapters, a considerable amount of time is spent analyzing the existing and planned business and IT environments and determining their requirements. The design of your Windows 2000 Active Directory network is driven by this information. Once this research is completed, you are ready to design and implement the Directory Services architecture.

Your design requires consideration of several models. The logical model of an organization is composed of Active Directory components that facilitate the administration of the network. These components include forests, trees, domains, and organizational units (OUs). The physical model is composed of physical components of the network, represented by sites (physical subnets) and domain controllers in Active Directory. The security model of the network involves the technologies and policies that protect the information stored on the network from loss or compromise due to disaster, accident, or attack. Information from all of these models is stored in Active Directory and made available to the network elements that need it.

Forests, trees, domains, and organizational units provide administrative boundaries in Active Directory. Any Windows 2000 network you design will consist of at least one domain, one domain tree, and one forest. A tree consists of one or more domains with contiguous namespaces, and a forest consists of one or more trees. A basic component of a Windows 2000 Active Directory network is a domain, and network utility is enhanced by trust relationships between domains. Although Windows NT networks also use domains and trust relationships, domains and trusts in a Windows 2000 network can be more complex.

TEST YOURSELF OBJECTIVE 7.01

Understanding Forest Characteristics

A forest is a grouping of one or more separate domain trees, and this grouping has a hierarchical structure. When the first domain is created in an Active Directory network, a new domain tree and forest are also created. This initial Active Directory domain is also known as the *forest root*. Although domains in a forest operate independently, the forest enables communication among domains across the entire organization. The domains share transitive, two-way trust relationships with the forest root and with each other. This architecture allows a single logon to be used to access many domains and their resources.

The domain names used in Active Directory are based on the Domain Name System (DNS) naming scheme. It provides user-friendly names that DNS uses to resolve into IP addresses. When dealing with the root domain name, it is important to plan names for domains early, because once the forest root is named, the name cannot be changed without completely reinstalling Active Directory.

Containers are objects in Active Directory that contain other objects. These objects can be user accounts, computers, printers, or other entities in Active Directory. For example, the Configuration container is used to store information about the network's physical topology, sites, and services. Each object belongs to an object class and is described by a collection of attributes. As we discussed in Chapter 5, the definitions of the object classes and attributes that can exist in the forest are stored in the Schema container, which is stored in the Configuration container. There is only one Configuration and Schema container per forest, and they are stored on the first domain controller (DC) created in the forest root domain. If multiple domains are created in the same forest, they will share a common Schema and Configuration container.

Because there is only one Schema container per forest, object class and attribute definitions apply to the entire forest, not just to a single domain. Any modifications to the schema can be made only on the DC that is designated as the schema operations master. By default, this is the first domain controller created in the forest. However, you can designate a different domain controller as the schema operations master. To help prevent excessive schema modification, only members of one group, the Schema Admins group, are authorized to modify the schema.

Since Active Directory contains information on every object in a domain, it can grow to a significant size. This can make finding a particular resource quite slow. To speed the process of locating a resource and allow users access to resources in other domains, a global catalog is used. All domains in a forest share a common global catalog. It is a subset of the Active Directory, containing selected attributes of all objects in the forest. This information enables domain controllers to locate an object anywhere in the forest. A copy of the global catalog is maintained in at least one domain controller (DC) in each domain. Because every DC contains a copy of the AD database, no additional replication is required if additional domain controllers are designated as global catalog servers.

Trust relationships allow users with accounts in one domain to access resources in another domain. Therefore, the user does not need an account in both domains. One domain trusts the other and allows users to access its resources. In Windows NT, all trusts were one-way and explicit. An explicit trust is created manually by an administrator. One-way trusts refer to the fact that although Domain A trusts Domain B, Domain B does not necessarily trust Domain A. By default, all domains in Windows 2000 trust all other domains. Transitive, two-way trusts are automatically created between each domain and its parent, and between the root domains of any domain trees that exist in the forest and the forest root.

When working to understand forest characteristics, you should remember the following points:

- The first Active Directory domain created is the forest root domain.

- The forest root domain contains a Schema container and a Configuration container that are replicated to every other domain in the forest.

- A global catalog consisting of selected attributes of all objects in the forest is maintained on at least one domain controller in each domain to facilitate locating objects throughout the forest.

- By default, all domains in a forest trust all other domains as a result of the two-way transitive trusts created when new domains are created in the forest.

exam
Ⓦatch

A forest is a grouping of domain trees. The domain tree is a collection of domains with a contiguous namespace. Trees in a forest have different naming structures, according to their domains. When a new domain incorporates the forest root's domain into its name, then the new domain is part of the same domain tree as the forest root. When this happens, the domains are said to have a contiguous namespace. When a new domain does not use the domain name of the forest root, this domain is considered part of a different domain tree in the same forest. In this case, the two domain trees do not form a contiguous namespace.

Selecting domain names is an important part of designing Active Directory. In a number of cases, companies may have an Internet presence and a DNS name associated with it. If this is the case, you would use this DNS name as the basis for selecting the root domain name. If additional domains are required, you would make these child domains under the root domain. The root domain would be included in the child domain name. For example, the root domain name might be companyexample.com, and a child domain would be dev.companyexample.com. If a company is using more than one DNS name and wants to use more than one root domain name, then you would select one of the names to be the forest root, and create multiple domain trees.

QUESTIONS

7.01: Understanding Forest Characteristics

1. The following illustration shows the domain tree of the company you work for. The company has recently decided that they would like to change the domain1.com name to a new DNS name they have recently acquired. Which of the following is true?

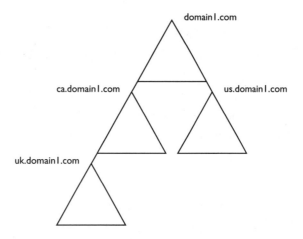

A. The domain1.com name can be changed by changing the name on the first domain controller installed in the forest.

B. The domain1.com name cannot be changed without reinstalling Active Directory.

C. The child domain names must be changed before changing the name of the root domain.

D. When domain1.com is changed, all child domains will automatically change their names.

2. **Current Situation:** Asimov Robotics has a new Windows 2000 Active Directory network. It has two separate domain trees. The first domain in one of these trees is called manufacturing.domain1.com. The manager of manufacturing would like to create a child domain beneath this domain. The Finance Department has also contacted you, and they would like the social security numbers of all employees to appear on the property sheets of user objects. They have stated that they would like additional attributes added later. You feel that you will not have the time to make these changes yourself, and have assigned a member of your team to make the necessary modifications.

   Required Result: Set up your project team member so that this person can make the modifications required by the Finance Department.

   Optional Desired Results:

   1. Create a child domain under the root domain using proper naming conventions.

   2. Have each of these domains trust each other.

   Proposed Solution: Add a member of your team to the Schema Admins group. Have this user make modifications on the schema operations master. Name the child domain domain2.com, and create two explicit one-way trusts between the parent domain and the child domain.

   What results are produced from the proposed solution?

   A. The proposed solution produces the required result only.

   B. The proposed solution produces the required result and only one of the optional results.

   C. The proposed solution produces the required result and both of the optional results.

   D. The proposed solution does not produce the required result.

3. Server1 is the first domain controller created in the forest root domain. It has two child domains that have domain controllers called Server2 and Server3. Which server contains the Schema and Configuration container for the forest, and on which server would you make changes to the schema?

   A. All servers contain a Schema and Configuration container. You can use any server to make changes to the schema.

B. Server1 contains the Schema and Configuration container. You can use any server to make changes to the schema.

C. Server1 contains the Schema and Configuration container and is the only server that can make changes to the schema.

D. Server1 is the only server that can make changes to the schema. All servers contain the Schema and Configuration container.

4. Your organization has three Windows 2000 domains. You know that Active Directory uses a global catalog so that domain controllers can locate objects in the forest. What is the minimum number of global catalog servers that your network will require?

A. One.

B. Two.

C. Three.

D. All domain controllers in the forest will be global catalog servers.

TEST YOURSELF OBJECTIVE 7.02

Designing a Directory Architecture

Before creating the directory architecture, you must develop several plans, including a forest plan, a domain plan, an organizational unit plan, and a site plan. In the simplest design, a single domain is all that is required for an effective directory architecture. Domains are the core unit of logical structure in Active Directory, and they can store millions of objects. They act as administrative boundaries, because administrators in one domain have no authority in other domains unless they are specifically granted authority. Microsoft recommends that, whenever possible, Active Directory should be designed using a single domain. This simplifies administration, as there are no trusts to maintain and less planning is involved. If circumstances dictate a need to create additional domains, domain trees, or even multiple forests, you can build on this simplified design. A forest consists of one or more domain trees. A domain tree is a collection of domains that share a common root domain name. Domain trees are hierarchical, so the domains in a tree are related to each other as parent and child. Every domain except the root domain has a parent and is a child. When a child domain is created, a transitive trust is created by default between parent and child. This means that no additional trusts are necessary, unless special circumstances require it. In the hierarchy of a domain tree, administrative rights do not flow through domains unless specifically granted. By default, administrators in one domain do not have administrative rights in another domain. The exception is when an administrator is a member of the Enterprise Administrators group and has administrative scope in the entire forest.

Just as you should use as few domains as possible, you should also use the minimum number of forests required. Multiple forests mean that your network will have multiple schema, multiple Configuration containers, no transitive trusts between forests, no automatic replication of information between forests, no easy movement of accounts between forests, and no single catalog service that helps users locate all resources in the enterprise. However, these factors may represent the reasons separate forests are required. For example, it may be important to create separate forests if the enterprise is made of separate, autonomous companies. Another reason might be if you want to create a separate test group, where applications and operating systems are tested. You will need as many forests as there are autonomous administrative groups who do not trust each other, or as many forests as there are domains or domain trees that need to have limited trust relationships with other domains or domain trees.

With separate forests, each forest has its own Enterprise Administrators group that has control over domains within that forest, and the only trusts that exist between forests are explicit, external trusts established between a specific domain in one forest and a specific domain in the other. This will be a one-way trust that requires action on the part of an administrator in the trusting domain and an administrator in the trusted domain. An administrator in only one of the forests cannot create the trust. The trust created is also nontransitive. That is, no other domain in the forest containing the trusting domain will trust the trusted domain just because one domain in its forest does. Conversely, the trusting domain does not trust any other domain in the forest containing the trusted domain just because it trusts the trusted domain.

The first domain created on a Windows 2000 network is the forest root and the basis for a namespace. A namespace is a defined space in which a given name can be resolved or matched to some object. Basically, there are two types of naming conventions that can be used in a namespace: organizational and geographical. In an organizational naming convention, names are based on the company and its departmental components or functions. For example, if the forest root were domain1.com, then you would create child domains like sales.domain1.com or finance.domain1.com. As you can see, the child domains are extensions of the forest root name. Geographical naming conventions show the physical location of the domain. For example, if domain1.com had offices in Canada and the United Kingdom, its child domains would use names like ca.domain1.com and uk.domain1.com. You will also need to decide if you want to use the same namespace for the internal network as you use for the external network. If you use the same internal and external namespace, the names used to access your servers from the internal network are the same as those used from outside the network. If two separate namespaces are used, it will delineate the internal network from the external network.

When the forest root domain is created, the default schema is created. The default schema is also called the "base schema" or "base directory information tree" (DIT). It contains almost 200 objects and more than 900 attributes. Active Directory can be extended to include the object classes and attributes required by a new, directory enabled application. Access to the new application will then exist throughout the forest. Extending the schema for the application should be incorporated into the installation process for the application so that it occurs automatically when the application is installed.

The schema can also be modified so that existing object classes and attributes can be customized. Since schema modifications affect the entire forest, only members of the Schema Admins group can modify the schema. It is modified by using the Active Directory Schema snap-in, Active Directory Services Interfaces (ADSI), with a program language such as Microsoft Visual Basic or C/C++, or by using Windows Scripting Host (WSH) in conjunction with the command line tools LDIFDE and CSVDE.

When a new object is created, the object gets an object identifier (OID), which is a globally unique numerical identifier. An OID can be obtained either by contacting the appropriate regional ISO Name Registration Authority or by using the OIDGEN utility available with the Windows 2000 Resource Kit. After obtaining an OID, an appropriate class type must be selected. The three possible class types are abstract, auxiliary, and structural, and each of these has different inheritance characteristics. Object classes are hierarchical in nature, and the location of a class in the hierarchy has an impact on inheritance. When an attempt is made to modify the schema, certain consistency checks and safety checks are performed by Active Directory services to ensure that particular parameters of the objects or attributes being created or modified are unique and valid.

Windows 2000 can be upgraded from Windows NT 3.51 or Windows NT 4.0. To upgrade to Windows 2000 from earlier versions, it is best to upgrade the earlier version to Windows NT 4.0 first, and then perform the upgrade to Windows 2000. When upgrading from Windows NT 4.0, you can perform an in-place upgrade of Windows NT domains to Windows 2000 domains. In doing so, the domain structure remains unchanged, and all accounts and trust relationships are preserved. To do this, select a domain to upgrade first, perform a complete backup of the existing domain information, synchronize BDCs, upgrade the PDC, and upgrade the BDCs. Once all domain controllers are upgraded to Windows 2000, switch to Native mode. As a precaution, it is best to take a BDC offline during the upgrade. If a problem occurs, the upgraded PDC can be removed, and the BDC can be put online and promoted to roll back the upgrade. Once these steps are completed, the upgrade is finished.

Restructuring is the other option. If multiple domains were required due to Windows NT limitations, then a single Windows 2000 domain may be all that is required. To restructure, first create a shell of the Windows 2000 design, and switch it to Native mode. Clone groups and users from the Windows NT domains to the shell, and move resources to the Windows 2000 domain. Once this is done, retire the Windows NT domains. In some cases, you may want to combine in-place upgrades and restructuring. It is possible to perform in-place upgrades of some Windows NT domains and combine other domains into a single Windows 2000 domain for ease of management.

When designing Directory Architecture, remember the following points:

- A domain is an administrative boundary, and administrators in one domain have no authority in other domains unless specifically granted such authority.

- Windows NT domains are upgraded to Windows 2000 by upgrading the Windows NT primary domain controller to a Windows 2000 domain controller.

- Windows 2000 administration is based on a multimaster system in which all domain controllers in a domain contain a writeable copy of the Active Directory database, enabling objects to be created or modified on any domain controller in the domain.

- An organization's structure should be as simple as possible, preferably a single domain, to simplify administration.

- The schema should need to be modified only as a last resort if it is properly planned, tested, and agreed to by all interested parties in your organization.

When upgrading Windows NT domains to Windows 2000 domains, you should keep in mind the differences between the two. As mentioned before, Active Directory supports millions of objects, whereas Windows NT's recommended limit is 40,000 users. Because of this increased support, the multimaster domain structure of Windows NT to accommodate large numbers is no longer required. Because Active Directory uses organizational units for administrative delegation, the Windows NT practice of using resource domains to limit administrative control is also no longer needed. Another change deals with the fact that Windows 2000 does not use the primary domain controller/backup domain controller (PDC/BDC) model of Windows NT. In Windows 2000, a multimaster domain controller model is used to provide automatic fault tolerance. Changes to domain-based information can be saved on any Windows 2000 DC, instead of on only the PDC. Windows 2000 also supports changing the roles of domain controllers on a network. In Windows NT, once a server is a domain controller, the only way to change its role in the network or to move it to another domain is to reinstall the operating system. In Windows 2000, a domain controller can be downgraded to a member server or a stand-alone server. If it is the last domain controller in the domain, it can be moved to another domain and upgraded to a domain controller.

QUESTIONS

7.02: Designing a Directory Architecture

5. **Current Situation:** Asimov Robotics has offices in the United States, Canada, and Asia. The United States offices handle administrative duties, the Canadian offices take care of research, and the Asian offices handle manufacturing. On occasion, administrators from the United States and Canadian offices need access to one another's domains for administrative purposes. To make communication between these sites possible, a new application is being developed. The IT staff has agreed that the developer of this application should have access to modifying the schema, since new objects will be created.

    Required Result: Determine how administrators from the United States domain can manage resources in the Canadian domain, and vice versa.

Optional Desired Results:

1. Name the domains using an organizational naming convention.

2. Allow the developer access to modifying the schema.

Proposed Solution: Make the administrators and the developer wishing to modify the schema members of the Enterprise Administrators group. Name the child domains us.asimovrobotics.com, ca.asimovrobotics.com, and asia.asimovrobotics.com.

What results are produced from the proposed solution?

A. The proposed solution produces the required result only.

B. The proposed solution produces the required result and only one of the optional results.

C. The proposed solution produces the required result and both of the optional results.

D. The proposed solution does not produce the required result.

6. Your company has started a new autonomous company. Occasionally, information will be shared between your company's forest and domain2.com's forest, as shown in the following illustration. How will this be done?

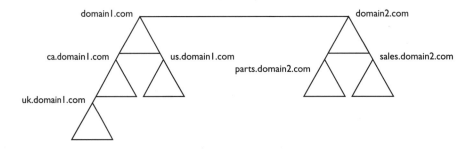

A. The administrator of domain1.com will need to create a one-way trust.

B. The administrator of domain2.com will need to create a one-way trust.

C. Administrators of domains in each forest will need to create the one-way trust.

D. Trusts are automatically established in Windows 2000, so this is not necessary.

Questions 7–9   The next three questions are based upon the scenario that follows. Read the following case study, and then answer the questions. You may refer to this case study as often as needed.

The network administrator for Positronic Robotics and Housewares has just been offered another job. Unfortunately, the time that he will be leaving for this job is just before the network is to be upgraded to Windows 2000 Active Directory. Because a new company is being started by Positronic Robotics and Housewares that is to be autonomous, he has decided that two forests should be created. He determined that they can be made into one forest later, if the new company does not take off. The new company will have a network created from scratch, but Positronic Robotics and Housewares is currently running Windows NT 3.51 and Windows NT 4.0 Servers. In his notes, the network administrator states some concerns about how to upgrade this network. Applications running on this network are critical to business operations, and there is a minimal amount of down time possible. However, members of the Finance and Payroll Departments need new applications that are specifically designed for use with Windows 2000. These applications will take significant training time, so the Training Department would like to have their server and workstations upgraded prior to Active Directory being implemented. You have been hired to reevaluate the network administrator's plans and design and determine if they should continue to be implemented.

7. You are evaluating the former network administrator's forest design. If a single forest is all that is required later, what will you need to do?

   A. Merge the two forests together by using Active Directory Users and Computers.

   B. Merge domains in the two forests together, which will then merge the forests.

   C. Downgrade domain controllers in the unwanted forest to stand-alone servers, then move them to the forest you want to keep, and create new domains.

   D. Multiple forests cannot be made into a single forest without reinstalling Active Directory on both forests.

8. What is the best possible plan for upgrading the network to Windows 2000?

   A. In-place upgrade for the new company being created.

      B. In-place upgrade for the existing company's network.

      C. For the existing company's network, upgrade Windows NT 3.51 computers to Windows 4.0, and then perform an in-place upgrade.

      D. Complete restructuring.

9. When dealing with the requirements of the training department, which of the following is true?

      A. Windows 2000 Server cannot be deployed unless Active Directory is deployed.

      B. Windows 2000 Professional cannot be deployed unless Active Directory is deployed.

      C. Windows 2000 Professional cannot be deployed unless there is an existing Windows 2000 Server.

      D. It is not necessary to deploy Active Directory in order to have Windows 2000 Server and Windows 2000 Professional.

TEST YOURSELF OBJECTIVE 7.03

Analyzing Trust Relationships

Trust relationships are used to allow users access to resources across domain boundaries. Without trust relationships, a user attempting to access a resource in another domain would need an account in that domain. A trust relationship is established between the domain in which a resource exists (the resource domain) and the domain in which a user has an account (the account domain). The trust relationship allows the resource domain to accept authentication of the user in the account domain. With the relationship in place, the resource domain provides access to resources based upon the successful logon to the account domain.

Trusts always involve two domains: a trusted domain and a trusting domain. A trusting domain has resources that users in the trusted domain want to access. In a one-way trust, the trusting domain trusts the trusted domain so that users who have accounts in the trusted domain can access the trusting domain's resources without needing additional authentication. One-way trusts are nontransitive. This means that just because one domain trusts another, that trust is not passed on to other domains that are trusted. In other words, if Domain A trusts Domain B, and Domain B trusts Domain C, then Domain A does not necessarily trust Domain C. If the trusts were transitive, Domain A and Domain C would trust each other automatically. For the domains to trust each other, explicit trusts must be established.

In Windows NT, all trusts are one-way trusts, and they are never created by default. They need to be configured by administrators in each domain that is involved in the trust. To do this, User Manager for Domains is used. One domain must be configured to trust the other domain, and the second domain must be configured to be trusted. The trust is created when each domain is configured. If each domain is to be both trusted and trusting, two separate trusts must be created. In Windows NT, this is what is considered a two-way trust. However, since they are still essentially one-way trusts, they remain nontransitive. This continues to be the case if a trust relationship is created between a Windows 2000 domain and a Windows NT domain, so one-way trusts must be explicitly created between them.

With two-way trusts, both of the domains are trusting and trusted, and in Windows 2000, these two-way trusts are transitive. Two-way, transitive trusts are created by default when domains are created in the same forest. When a forest contains two or more domain trees, the root domain of each domain tree automatically has a two-way trust with the forest root domain. Because every other domain in the forest trusts and is trusted by the forest root domain, every domain in the domain tree trusts and is trusted by every other domain in the forest. Within a domain tree, every domain has a parent-child relationship with other domains in the tree, and each parent-child relationship includes a two-way, transitive trust. Because of this, every domain in a domain tree trusts every other domain in the tree. Although these trusts are created automatically, it is important to recognize that automatic trusts are never created between different forests. If users in a domain in one forest need to access resources in a domain in another forest, an explicit, external trust must be created between the two domains. An external trust is a nontransitive, one-way trust and must be created between the account domain in one forest and the resource domain in the other forest.

When analyzing trust relationships, it is important to remember the following points:

- Only one-way trusts can exist between a Windows 2000 domain and any domain containing Windows NT domain controllers.

- Two-way trusts are always transitive and exist, by default, between pairs of domains in a forest that have a parent-child relationship.

- Only one-way trusts can exist between domains in separate forests.

To avoid confusing trusting and trusted domains, think of the words "Trust Ed" for trusted and "Trust Thing" for trusting. Ed is a user who needs to use a resource (a thing) in another domain. When a trust relationship is in place, the domain with Ed's account is the trusted (Trust Ed) domain. The domain with the resource is the trusting (Trust Thing) domain.

You should also remember that all trusts in Windows NT are one-way and nontransitive, and that a two-way trust in Windows NT is merely two separate one-way trusts. If a trust relationship is to be created between a Windows 2000 domain and a Windows NT domain, a one-way trust must be explicitly created. In Windows 2000, two-way, transitive trusts are used. Two-way, transitive trusts are created by default when domains are created in the same forest. Every domain in a forest trusts and is trusted by the forest root domain. Because of this, every domain in the domain tree trusts and is trusted by every other domain in the forest. Within the tree, every domain has a parent-child relationship with other domains in the tree, and each parent-child relationship includes a two-way, transitive trust. However, if a domain in one forest needs access to resources located in another forest's domain, an explicit, external trust must be created between them. An external trust is a nontransitive, one-way trust.

QUESTIONS

7.03: Analyzing Trust Relationships

10. **Current Situation:** A company's Windows NT environment consists of three domains that have a complete trust relationship. When the network is upgraded to Windows 2000, one of these domains will continue to run Windows NT 4.0 Servers. The company is planning to partner itself with another company that is already running Windows 2000 on its network. A plan needs to be created so that information can be exchanged between domains of the two forests.

    Required Result: Establish a trust between the two forests so that information can be exchanged between the domains of these forests.

Optional Desired Results:

1. Determine how many trust relationships must be established for all domains to trust one another when the network is upgraded to Windows 2000.

2. Determine the type of trusts required for these domains to continue having a complete trust relationship.

Proposed Solution: When Windows 2000 connects to the forest, automatic trusts will be created. Three transitive trusts are all that will be required to establish a complete trust relationship between the Windows 2000 domains and the Windows NT domain.

What results are produced from the proposed solution?

A. The proposed solution produces the required result only.

B. The proposed solution produces the required result and only one of the optional results.

C. The proposed solution produces the required result and both of the optional results.

D. The proposed solution does not produce the required result.

11. You want to establish a trust relationship between a Windows 2000 domain controller running in Mixed mode and a Windows 2000 domain controller running in Native mode. What kind of trust relationship can be created?

A. One-way, transitive trust

B. Two-way, transitive trust

C. One-way, nontransitive trust

D. Two-way, nontransitive trust

12. You have just created a new Windows 2000 Active Directory network for a company. Assuming the defaults are used, which of the following is true? (Choose all that apply.)

A. Every domain in the forest is trusted by the forest root domain.

B. Every forest will trust every other forest.

C. Every domain in the domain tree trusts and is trusted by every other domain in the forest.

D. No domains will be trusted unless the domains are configured to create trust relationships automatically, or unless trusts are manually established.

13. A company's Windows 2000 Active Directory network consists of three domains. As shown in the following illustration, a child domain called DomainD is planned to be added beneath the parent domain, DomainB. You want DomainB and DomainD to completely trust each other. How will you do this?

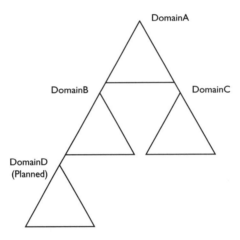

A. Use User Manager for Domains to create two one-way, nontransitive trusts between DomainB and DomainD.

B. Use MMC with the Active Directory Domains and Trusts snap-in to create a two-way, transitive trust between DomainB and DomainD.

C. Use MMC with the Active Directory Domains and Trusts snap-in to create a one-way, transitive trust between DomainB and DomainD.

D. Do nothing. A two-way, transitive trust will be automatically established between the parent and child domains when the child domain is created.

Optimizing Trust Relationships

Although they are not necessary to facilitate the sharing of resources, explicit trusts can be made between domains in the same forest. These are called short-cut trusts or cross-link trusts, and they are created with the Active Directory Domains and Trusts snap-in for MMC. Short-cut trusts are transitive and are used to shorten authentication paths in a forest. For example, a client makes a request to access a resource. This request goes to the domain controller in the user's domain, which determines whether the resource is in the domain. If it is not in the domain, the domain controller will use information about all other domains in the forest and determine a trust path to the resource domain. A trust path is the route the request must travel (from domain-to-domain or from trust-to-trust) until it reaches the resource domain. If a short-cut trust exists, the domain controller will use it to establish the shortest possible trust path. The authentication request is then referred from domain to domain along the trust path until it reaches the resource domain.

Transitive, two-way trust relationships may be considered a security risk. However, trusts do not actually grant access to a resource, they only authenticate the user to the domain containing the resource. The administrators in the domain or organizational unit containing the resource can control access with permissions. Windows 2000 grants everyone access to new files and directories. This is the same as Windows NT. More restrictive permissions must be assigned to control access. If an administrator considers revoking a transitive trust created by default when the domain was created, he or she will find that this is not possible. Transitive trusts that are explicitly created can be revoked using the Active Directory Domains and Trusts snap-in, but the default trusts created when the domains are created cannot be revoked.

When optimizing trust relationships, it is important to remember the following points:

- Short-cut trusts can be created to facilitate sharing of resources between domains in the same forest.

- Within a forest, short-cut trusts are two-way trusts.

- External trusts are always one-way trusts.

exam
⚠️atch

A trust path is the path a request must take from a user's domain to a resource domain. It is the path the request travels from domain to domain along the trusts connecting them. The trust path that the request travels can be long and generate a significant amount of traffic if there are many intermediate domains in the forest between the user's domain and the resource domain. To deal with this problem, short-cut trusts (also called cross-link trusts) can be used to connect the two domains. A short-cut trust is an explicit trust made between domains in the same forest. Rather than sending the request across different trusts linking the entire domain tree, the domain controller will look for the shortest route possible. If a short-cut trust exists between two domains, it will be used instead.

QUESTIONS

7.04: Optimizing Trust Relationships

14. **Current Situation:** Your company has recently deployed a Windows 2000 Active Directory network. It has three domains. A two-way, transitive trust exists between the Admin domain and the Sales domain. Another two-way, transitive trust exists between the Admin domain and the Finance domain. Users in the Sales domain have begun complaining about slow access time to resources in the Finance domain. Managers in the Finance domain have recently created a new folder containing documents relating to promotions. Because of the confidentiality of these documents and the significant use Sales makes of Finance resources, Finance is concerned that Sales employees may gain access to promotions documents if an error has been made setting permissions.

    Required Result: Determine a way to reduce traffic between the Sales and Finance domains.

    Optional Desired Results:

    1. Determine a way to increase the speed of access to resources in the Finance domain for the Sales domain.

    2. Determine a way to keep unauthorized users from accessing the Finance documents.

Proposed Solution: Remove the Everyone groups permissions and use appropriate share and NTFS permissions to control access to the Finance documents. Use User Manager for Domains to create an explicit, one-way trust between the Sales and Finance domains.

What results are produced from the proposed solution?

A. The proposed solution produces the required result only.

B. The proposed solution produces the required result and only one of the optional results.

C. The proposed solution produces the required result and both of the optional results.

D. The proposed solution does not produce the required result.

Questions 15–17   The following diagram shows the trust relationships in a company's domain structure. All domains are running Windows 2000 Servers and Windows 2000 Professional workstations. Based on the information shown in this illustration, answer the following three questions. You may refer to the following illustration as often as you wish:

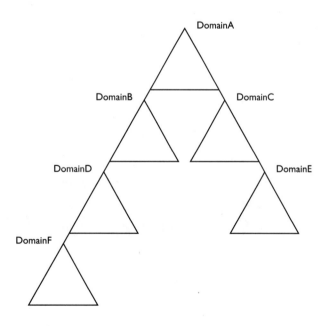

15. You have noticed that there is a significant amount of traffic caused by users in DomainD requesting resources in DomainE. Which of the following will best decrease the traffic caused by requests passing through intermediate domains between the user's domain and the resource domain?

    A. Move all resources in DomainE to DomainD.

    B. Remove trusts linking DomainD and DomainE.

    C. Create a short-cut trust between DomainD and DomainE.

    D. Based on the current design, nothing can be done.

16. When users in DomainF are requesting access to resources in DomainE, what is the trust path that the request must take?

    A. DomainF, DomainD, DomainB, DomainC, DomainE

    B. DomainF, DomainD, DomainC, DomainE

    C. DomainF, DomainD, DomainB, DomainA, DomainC, DomainE

    D. DomainF, DomainE

17. After careful analysis, you determine there is a security risk, in that documents contained in DomainF are too sensitive for many other domains to view. You feel that the trust between DomainD and DomainF that was created when the domains were created is therefore a security risk. What must you do to remove this?

    A. Use MMC with the Active Directory Domains and Trusts snap-in to remove the trust.

    B. Two-way, transitive trusts created when the domain was created cannot be revoked.

    C. Explicitly created trusts created when the domain was created cannot be revoked.

    D. Use User Manager for Domains to remove the trust.

LAB QUESTION

Objectives 7.01–7.04

A friend of yours is network administrator of a Windows 2000 network consisting of three domains. One of the domains has been experiencing problems locating resources in other domains. Because of a slow link connecting this domain to other domains, you are concerned about increased replication traffic caused by the global catalog. The company is planning to partner itself with another company. Each network is to remain autonomous, but will occasionally need to share information between forests. For administrative reasons, additional domains may be added to the company's network.

1. Your friend is concerned about the speed at which queries to objects in Active Directory are processed, but is unsure what to do considering that replication takes place over a slow link. What will you advise the network administrator so that queries of the global catalog are improved?

2. How can administrators in one domain manage other domains?

3. How can information be shared between these forests?

4. As new child domains are created, what trusts will need to be created for information to be shared between the domains of the company's network?

A

QUICK ANSWER KEY

Objective 7.01	
1.	B
2.	A
3.	C
4.	C

Objective 7.02	
5.	A
6.	C
7.	C
8.	D
9.	D

Objective 7.03	
10.	D
11.	C
12.	A and C
13.	D

Objective 7.04	
14.	D
15.	C
16.	C
17.	B

IN-DEPTH ANSWERS

7.01: Understanding Forest Characteristics

1. ☑ **B.** It is important to plan names for domains early, because once the forest root is named, the name cannot be changed without completely reinstalling Active Directory.

    ☒ **A, C,** and **D** are incorrect because the only way to change the root domain name is to reinstall Active Directory.

2. ☑ **A.** The proposed solution produces the required result only. Only members of the Schema Admins group are authorized to modify the schema. Any modifications to the schema can be made only on the DC that is designated as the schema operations master.

    ☒ **B, C,** and **D** are incorrect because the proposed solution produces the required result only. After the root domain has been created, a domain with a higher-level name cannot be created. You cannot create a parent of an existing domain. If the first domain in the domain tree is manufacturing.domain1.com, you cannot later create a child domain named domain2.com. Transitive, two-way trusts are automatically created between each domain and its parent, and between the root domains of any domain trees that exist in the forest and the forest root.

3. ☑ **C.** Server1 is the first domain controller (DC) created in the forest root domain and is thereby the one containing the Configuration and Schema container. There is only one Configuration and Schema container per forest. Any modifications to the schema must be made on the DC that is designated as the schema operations master. By default, this is the first domain controller created in the forest. To help prevent excessive schema modification, only members of one group, the Schema Admins group, are authorized to modify the schema.

    ☒ **A** is incorrect because there is only one Configuration and Schema container per forest, and you can make changes to the schema only from the schema operations master. **B** is incorrect because you can make changes to the Schema only from the schema operations master. **D** is incorrect because there is only one Configuration and Schema container per forest.

4. ☑ **C.** Three. Information used to locate any object in the forest is placed in a global catalog, and a copy of this is maintained in at least one domain controller in each domain.

   ☒ **A, B,** and **D** are incorrect because the minimum number of global catalog servers for this network is three. Only one domain controller in each domain is required to retain a copy of the global catalog. Additional global catalog servers are allowed, but this number is the minimum.

7.02: Designing a Directory Architecture

5. ☑ **A.** The proposed solution produces the required result only. By making administrators from the Canadian and United States domains members of the Enterprise Administrators group, they will have administrative privilege in one another's domain. The Enterprise Administrators group has administrative scope in the entire forest.

   ☒ **B, C,** and **D** are incorrect because the proposed solution produces the required result only. The naming convention used is geographical and not organizational, and only members of the Schema Admins group can modify the schema.

6. ☑ **C.** Administrators of domains in each forest will need to create the one-way trust. The only trusts that exist between forests are explicit, external trusts established between a specific domain in one forest and a specific domain in the other. This will be a one-way trust that requires action on the part of an administrator in the trusting domain and an administrator in the trusted domain. An administrator in only one of the forests cannot create the trust.

   ☒ **A** and **B** are incorrect because administrators from both domains need to be involved in creating the one-way trust. **D** is incorrect because trusts between forests are not automatic.

7. ☑ **C.** When multiple forests are used, it is difficult to undo this and make a single forest. However, it can be done. If you start with multiple forests and later decide that one is all that is required, downgrade domain controllers in the

unwanted forest to stand-alone servers, and then move them to the forest you want to keep, and create new domains.

☒ **A** and **B** are incorrect because you cannot simply merge forests together. **D** is incorrect because multiple forests can be made into a single forest.

8. ☑ **D.** Complete restructuring. The case study states that applications running on this network are critical to business operations, and that there is a minimal amount of down time possible. Complete restructuring will cause the least interference. The Windows 2000 infrastructure can be created, populated with groups and accounts, and thoroughly tested before operations are switched from the Windows NT network to the Windows 2000 network.

☒ **A** is incorrect because the new company does not currently have a network. Therefore, it would be a clean install of Windows 2000 Servers and Professional workstations. **B** is incorrect because it involves a greater degree of interference with current operations, and minimal down time is essential to the upgrade. **C** is incorrect for this same reason. However, it is true that when performing in-place upgrades, it is wise to upgrade all Windows NT 3.51 computers to Windows NT 4.0 before upgrading to Windows 2000. You should also apply the latest service packs.

9. ☑ **D.** It is not necessary to deploy Active Directory in order to have Windows 2000 Server and Windows 2000 Professional. Member servers and workstations can be upgraded to Windows 2000 to take advantage of many of the new features, while still being used with Windows NT domain controllers.

☒ **A** and **B** are incorrect because Windows 2000 Server and Professional can be deployed even if Active Directory has not been deployed. **C** is incorrect because Windows 2000 Professional can be deployed on networks using Windows NT Servers.

7.03: Analyzing Trust Relationships

10. ☑ **D.** The proposed solution does not produce the required result. Automatic trusts are never created between different forests. If users in a domain in one forest need to access resources in a domain in another forest, an explicit, external trust must be created between the two domains. An external trust is a nontransitive, one-way trust, and must be created between the account domain in one forest and the resource domain in the other forest.

☒ **A, B**, and **C** are incorrect because the proposed solution does not produce the required result. If a trust relationship is required between a Windows 2000 domain and a Windows NT domain, a one-way trust must be explicitly created. Because of this fact, two-way trusts can be established between the two Windows 2000 domains, but the Windows NT domain will need two one-way trusts for each Windows 2000 domain with which it wants to have a relationship.

11. ☑ **C.** A Windows 2000 domain controller running in Mixed mode allows Windows 2000 and Windows NT domain controllers to coexist in the same domain. The only kind of trust that can be created between a Mixed mode domain and a Native mode domain is a one-way trust, which is nontransitive.

☒ **A** is incorrect because one-way trusts are nontransitive. **B** is incorrect because a trust between a Mixed mode and a Native mode domain must be a one-way trust. **D** is incorrect because two-way trusts are transitive in Windows 2000.

12. ☑ **A** and **C** are correct. Two-way, transitive trusts are created by default when domains are created in the same forest. Every domain in a forest trusts and is trusted by the forest root domain. Because of this, every domain in the domain tree trusts and is trusted by every other domain in the forest.

☒ **B** is incorrect because forests do not automatically trust one another. If a domain in one forest needs access to resources located in another forest's domain, a one-way, nontransitive trust must be created between them. **D** is incorrect because by default, two-way, transitive trusts are created.

13. ☑ **D.** Do nothing. A two-way, transitive trust will be automatically established between the parent and child domains when the child domain is created. Within the tree, every domain has a parent-child relationship with other domains in the tree, and each parent-child relationship includes a two-way, transitive trust.

☒ **A** is incorrect because this choice outlines how a two-way trust in Windows NT would be created. **B** is incorrect because a two-way, transitive trust will automatically be established when the child domain is created. **C** is incorrect because one-way trusts are nontransitive.

7.04: Optimizing Trust Relationships

14. ☑ **D.** The proposed solution does not produce the required result. Although a short-cut trust would speed access to resources and decrease network traffic, User Manager for Domains is not used in Windows 2000 to create trust relationships. The Active Directory Domains and Trusts snap-in for Microsoft Management Console is used.

    ☒ **A, B,** and **C** are incorrect because the proposed solution does not produce the required result. One of the optional requirements is met because, by removing the Everyone groups permissions and using appropriate share and NTFS permissions to control access, users in the Sales domain will be unable to access the Finance records.

15. ☑ **C.** Create a short-cut trust between DomainD and DomainE. A short-cut trust, also known as a cross-link trust, is an explicit trust made between domains in the same forest. If a short-cut trust exists, the domain controller will use it to establish the shortest possible trust path. The authentication request is then referred from domain to domain along the trust path until it reaches the resource domain.

    ☒ **A** is incorrect because this would create traffic caused by users in DomainE making requests for resources in DomainD. **B** is incorrect because this would prevent users in either domain from using resources in other domains. **D** is incorrect because a short-cut trust can be used to minimize traffic caused by these requests.

16. ☑ **C.** The trust path is the path a request must traverse from the user's domain to the resource domain. In this case, the trust path would be DomainF to DomainD to DomainB to DomainA to DomainC to DomainE.

    ☒ **A, B,** and **D** are incorrect because none of these is the trust path the request must follow from the user's domain to the resource domain.

17. ☑ **B.** Two-way, transitive trusts created by default when the domain was created cannot be revoked.

    ☒ **A** is incorrect because you cannot remove a transitive, two-way trust that was created when the domain was created. **C** is incorrect because explicitly created trusts can be revoked using the Active Directory Domains and Trusts snap-in. However, the trusts created when domains are created are two-way, transitive trusts. **D** is incorrect because User Manager for Domains is not used to revoke trusts.

LAB ANSWER

Objectives 7.01–7.04

1. Although one domain controller in each domain is the minimum used as global catalog servers, you can add additional domain controllers to a domain. Because every DC contains a copy of the AD database, no additional replication is required if additional domain controllers are designated as global catalog servers.

2. By default, administrators in one domain do not have administrative rights in another domain. The exception is when an administrator is a member of the Enterprise Administrators group and has administrative scope in the entire forest.

3. To share information between forests, a one-way trust can be created. If both sides need to share information with the other side, then two one-way trusts can be created. To do this, action is required on the part of an administrator in the trusting domain and an administrator in the trusted domain. An administrator in only one of the forests cannot create the trust. The trust created is nontransitive. No other domain in the forest containing the trusting domain will trust the trusted domain just because one domain in its forest does. Also, the trusting domain does not trust any other domain in the forest containing the trusted domain just because it trusts the trusted domain.

4. None. When the child domain is created, a two-way, transitive trust will be created by default with the parent domain. Within a domain tree, every domain has a parent-child relationship with other domains in the tree, and each parent-child relationship includes a two-way, transitive trust. Because of this, every domain in a domain tree trusts every other domain in the tree.

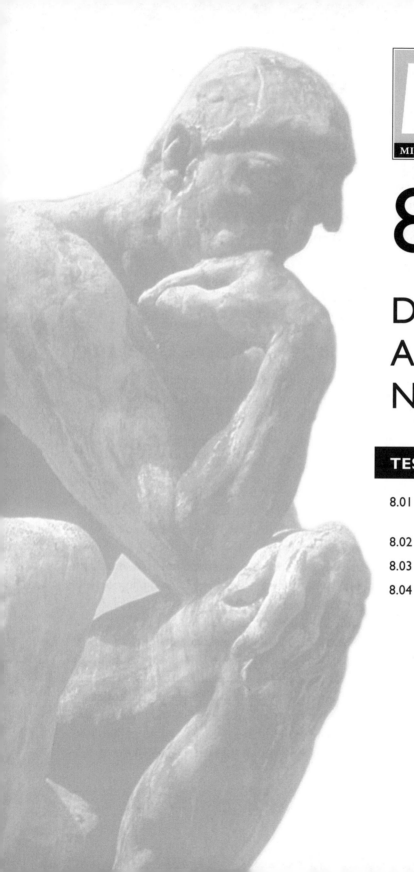

MICROSOFT CERTIFIED SYSTEMS ENGINEER

8

Designing an Active Directory Naming Strategy

When designing an Active Directory naming strategy, it is important to look first at how Active Directory will be used on the network. Will AD be used as an employee database, and is there a need to integrate objects in AD with Microsoft Exchange Server or other applications? You will also need to design a namespace so that domains and resources in your network have valid names. In determining the names to use, you should ensure they agree with naming conventions used in your Active Directory network.

Establishing the Scope of Active Directory

Active Directory scope refers to how AD will be used on the network. Active Directory scope can be molded to match any organization's needs. It can be used as a central employee database, or as a location to which current databases are replicated. By using AD with applications like PeopleSoft, SAP, or Exchange, you can lower administration of user accounts, Exchange mailboxes, or databases used to keep track of employees.

As we have discussed in previous chapters, the schema can be modified so that attributes can be added to AD objects or changed. User accounts can be modified to include employee numbers, social security numbers, email addresses, and so on. Our ability to customize objects makes applications more powerful, as AD will synchronize any changes with all relational databases. For example, suppose Human Resources uses an application to manage employees. When an employee is fired, the application will pass this information to the AD structure to mark the employee as terminated. AD will then remove all records in connected databases related to this person.

It is, however, important to realize that when objects are marked for deletion, they are not deleted automatically. Instead, they are marked as a "tombstone." A tombstone is similar to deleting an item and sending it to the Recycle Bin because the object is not actually gone until it is purged from the Recycle Bin. All tombstones are purged at a set interval known as garbage collection. By default, garbage collection occurs every 12 hours. Like deleted files that are invisible to searches of the hard disk, tombstones are invisible to Lightweight Directory Access Protocol (LDAP) searches of the directory.

The Active Directory Connector (ADC) provides the capability to automate administrative tasks such as creating a new mailbox when a new user is created, tracking its changes, and removing the mailbox if the user is ever removed from the system. ADC is a component that enables communication and synchronization between the Active Directory and the Microsoft Exchange Server 5.5 Directory Service. Microsoft Exchange will not communicate natively with Active Directory, so new data and changes need to be input manually in both directories. To meet this limitation, ADC uses the Lightweight Directory Access Protocol (LDAP) to automatically keep information consistent between the Exchange Server and Active Directory.

ADC allows Active Directory to synchronize in four different ways. Bi-directional synchronization is used so that changes in either directory service are reflected in the other. When information is updated in either directory, both directories will remain current and consistent. ADC also provides selective attribute synchronization so that you can synchronize only the attributes in the directory that you want synchronized. Change synchronization is used so that changes are synchronized at the object level. For example, if 100 objects were updated for 10,000 users, only the 100 objects would be updated. The changes would then be reflected to each user, eliminating excessive bandwidth and time consumption. The fourth method of synchronization, attribute level changes, is used so that when two objects are synchronized, the attributes are compared to determine which will need to be part of synchronization. Rather than updating all attributes, only the ones that need updating are part of synchronization. This makes the synchronization more effective because it eliminates excess bandwidth usage caused by transferring large amounts of data over the network.

When establishing the scope of Active Directory, it is important to remember the following points:

- The Active Directory Connector (ADC) is required to replicate information between the Active Directory and Microsoft Exchange Server 5.5.

- Active Directory can be used as a central location to keep employee records and track their respective changes and updates.

- Tombstones are objects in AD that are marked for deletion.

- Active Directory can synchronize in the following ways: bi-directional synchronization, selective attribute synchronization, change synchronization, and attribute level changes.

exam
ⓦatch

Metadirectory services are integrated into the Directory Services structure of Windows 2000. The metadirectory can contain detailed information about the entire enterprise, including not only physical items, but virtual items as well. Physical items would include workstations, servers, and users. Conceptual items would include departments, organizations, and groups. Digital items include documents, spreadsheets, and images. Finally, geographic items would include locations in the geographic scope of the organization (offices, subsidiaries, and so forth). The metadirectory has a hierarchical structure equivalent to the forest structure in Active Directory, and it uses a namespace. The namespace is comprised of two parts: the metaverse and the connector space. The metaverse is the part of the directory that represents all joined objects, whether they are from connected directories or are unique objects with no connection to external directories. The connector space is the location into which directories are initially imported. Each directory maintains its own area in the connector space.

QUESTIONS

8.01: Establishing the Scope of Active Directory

I. The following illustration shows a breakdown of the metadirectory, which is integrated into the Directory Services structure of Windows 2000. Which components of the metadirectory makes up the namespace? (Choose all that apply.)

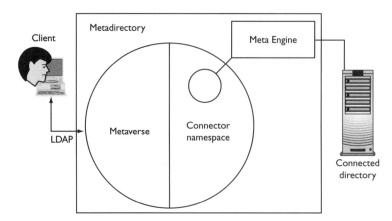

A. Metaverse

B. Connected directory

C. Connector namespace

D. LDAP

2. **Current Situation:** You are attending a meeting with your company's managers and IT staff. The reason for the meeting is to inform managers and administrators of changes with the network, which has just been upgraded to Windows 2000 Active Directory. There are four Windows 2000 Servers, and one of these servers is running Microsoft Exchange Server 5.5. The administrator of the Exchange server mentions that problems have occurred in the past when you have deleted a user account and failed to pass this information along so that the Exchange mailbox is deleted. He is also concerned that when changes are made to users, they will need to be changed in Active Directory and Exchange Directory Services. The Human Resources manager notes that it would be beneficial if user accounts could include employee numbers and social security numbers.

Required Result: Include employee numbers and social security numbers as attributes of user accounts.

Optional Desired Results:

1. Determine how mailboxes will be deleted from Microsoft Exchange Server Directory Service when user accounts in Active Directory are deleted.

2. Determine how changes to accounts in Active Directory can automatically be reflected in Exchange Server Directory Service.

Proposed Solution: Modify the schema so that social security numbers and employee numbers are new attributes of the user object. Explain to the Exchange administrator that the Active Directory Connector will allow communication and synchronization between the Active Directory and the Microsoft Exchange Server 5.5 Directory Service.

What results are produced from the proposed solution?

A. The proposed solution produces the required result only.

B. The proposed solution produces the required result and only one of the optional results.

C. The proposed solution produces the required result and both of the optional results.

D. The proposed solution does not produce the required result.

3. An object is deleted from Active Directory at 9A.M. Later that day, at 6P.M., you realize that this object should not have been deleted. The network uses the default amount of time for purges. Which of the following is true?

A. Once the object is deleted, it cannot be restored.

B. Once the object is deleted, it is marked as a tombstone. It remains marked for eight hours, at which time it is purged. This being the case, you cannot restore the object.

C. Once the object is deleted, it is marked as a tombstone. It remains marked for 12 hours and then it is purged.

D. Once the object is deleted, it is marked as a tombstone. It will not be purged until hard drive space is low.

4. You are explaining the Microsoft metadirectory to a new member of your IT staff. The user asks what types of objects are contained in the metadirectory. What will you say?

A. Physical, conceptual, digital, and geographic.

B. Metaphysical, conceptual, digital, and geographic.

C. Physical, conceptual, analog, and geographic.

D. No objects are contained in the metadirectory.

TEST YOURSELF OBJECTIVE 8.02

Designing the Namespace

When designing an Active Directory namespace, the first step is determining which domain will be the root domain and then assigning its Domain Name System (DNS) name. Names assigned to the child domains will be based on the root domain's name.

This will establish the hierarchy of the forest, since each additional domain will be a child beneath the root domain, or a new tree root. Trees should be used sparingly because too many will be confusing to both end users and administrators. By using as few trees as possible, it will help to organize the domain model so that resources are easier to find, and it will result in fewer names being entered in the proxy client exclusion suffixes listing.

The design of your namespace should be as simple as possible. Domain names should be kept short so that they are easier to remember. They should also be descriptive and distinct so that they will provide a clear understanding of what the resource is. Any names you use should be unique. Duplicate names should be avoided, even if the domains are not physically connected. For example, if your internal network and external network both use the domain name "domain1.com," name resolution problems can result. This may cause log-on errors. Also, a user attempting to access your Web site by this name might get the internal network instead, as the client machine would connect to the first domain answering the locator request.

When creating names, standard DNS characters should be used so that the name is compatible with legacy systems and third party software. RFC 1123 defines the characters used as being any letters from A to Z (upper- or lowercase), any numbers between 0 and 9, and the hyphen character (-). To ensure compatibility with legacy systems, by default, the first part of a Windows 2000 computer's full name (computer name and domain name) is the NetBIOS name. This allows the Windows 9x legacy system and software that is not Active Directory aware to use the resource. When naming servers and resources, avoid names that are too similar, as this may lead to confusion. For example, fs-file.domain1.com and fs-files.domain1.com are similar enough that one may be mistaken for the other.

When designing the namespace, it is important to keep the following points in mind:

- Use trees sparingly to avoid confusion when expanding the directory.
- Use simple, descriptive names when creating the domains so that domain resources can be easily located in the future.
- Follow RFC 1123 guidelines for naming.

Although it is better to use two separate DNS domain names (one for your internal network and one for a Web site), the same registered DNS namespace can be used for both. Two DNS servers can be used: one for the internal network, and one for the external network. The DNS server for the internal network would point to the IP address of the internal domain, whereas the external DNS server would handle internal requests for external resources. If users have access to the Internet, then a firewall should be used to separate the internal namespace from the external namespace, and two separate DNS zones must exist. One zone exists outside the firewall and provides name resolution for public resources. It does not resolve names for internal resources and is not configured to do so. The external zone is then duplicated on the internal DNS so that internal clients can resolve the names of resources in the external zone. If a proxy server is used, it can be configured to treat the DNS name of your network as an internal resource. Proxy clients must be configured to recognize the difference between internal and external resources. This arrangement makes using the same internal and external namespace complicated. It also increases administration, because duplicate zone records for internal and external name resolution need to be maintained.

QUESTIONS

8.02: Designing the Namespace

5. **Current Situation:** A company currently has the domain name domain1.com registered for its Web site. At present, users of the internal network do not have access to the Internet, but this may change in the next year. The company would like to use the same namespace for both the internal and external networks. When Internet access is provided to users, it will be limited, so no firewall or proxy server will be implemented. Two new servers will be added to this namespace. One will be a file server, and the other will be a Web server for the corporate intranet. The file server will be a domain controller, and you need to ensure that the Windows 9*x* legacy system and software that is not Active Directory aware can use the resource.

   Required Result: Determine whether internal and external namespaces should be separate or the same.

Optional Desired Results:

1. Create names for the new domains that use standard Internet characters recommended by RFC 1123.

2. Determine what NetBIOS names will be used by workstations running Windows 95 and Windows 98.

Proposed Solution: Use the same internal and external namespaces, as this will save the money required to register an additional DNS name. Name the new servers file_server.domain1.com and web_server.domain1.com. The NetBIOS names will be file_server and web_server.

What results are produced from the proposed solution?

A. The proposed solution produces the required result only.

B. The proposed solution produces the required result and only one of the optional results.

C. The proposed solution produces the required result and both of the optional results.

D. The proposed solution does not produce the required result.

Questions 6–8   The next three questions are based upon the scenario and illustration that follows. Read the case study, and then answer the questions. You may refer to this case study as often as needed.

A company has hired you and your partner to design a Windows 2000 Active Directory network. Your partner is working on the namespace to be used in this network. When the work on this namespace is complete, you are shown the following diagram:

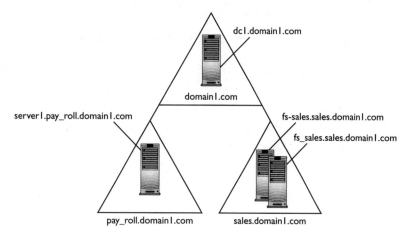

6. What problems exist with the domain names in this design?

    A. Pay_roll.domain1.com is not a valid name.

    B. Sales.domain1.com is not a valid name.

    C. Domain1.com is not a valid name.

    D. All of the names are valid.

7. Looking at the illustration, you see a computer named dc1.domain1.com. You realize that Windows 9x clients will use the NetBIOS name when accessing this resource. Considering this fact, what is the computer name?

    A. dc1

    B. domain1.com

    C. domain1

    D. dc1.com

8. Which of the following servers have problems with their names? (Choose all that apply.)

    A. fs-sales.sales.domain1.com

    B. fs_sales.sales.domain1.com

    C. server1.pay_roll.domain1.com

    D. dc1.domain1.com

TEST YOURSELF OBJECTIVE 8.03

Planning the DNS Strategy

DNS is the Domain Name System. It is a distributed database that provides host to Internet Protocol (IP) address resolution to client machines. Windows 2000 DNS is comprised of three parts: domains, zones, and DNS servers. Domains are top-level DNS names, which we have seen throughout this book in examples such as domain1.com. Below the top-level DNS name, there may be child domains. The child domains are split into zones like sales.domain1.com or finance.domain1.com. These zones are monitored and maintained by Windows 2000 DNS servers. Computers also have a DNS name which consists of two parts: the host name and the primary DNS suffix. These two parts make up the full computer name. For example, if we were to look at a machine with the DNS name server1.domain1.com, server1 would be the DNS host name, and domain1.com would be the DNS suffix.

Because Active Directory relies heavily on DNS, Windows 2000 DNS Server is shipped with Windows 2000 Server. Active Directory integrated DNS has zone data stored as an AD object so that zone data is stored and replicated when AD is replicated. This is what is known as a zone transfer. Because of the increased network traffic of replicating an entire zone, Windows 2000 supports incremental zone transfers (IXFRs). With IXFRs, only changes are replicated so that only updates to the zone table are synchronized. To simplify zone transfers, Windows 2000 DNS notifies other DNS servers of zone changes. The authoritative DNS server notifies secondary DNS servers that a change has been made to the zone, which the secondary server will then replicate. Windows 2000 DNS also supports dynamic updates, allowing hosts to dynamically register their names in the DNS database. DNS servers will not update such hosts unless it has authenticated the update in Active Directory and has the proper permissions to perform a dynamic update.

When Windows 2000 is in Mixed mode, it coexists on the network with legacy Windows NT Servers. In this environment, Windows NT DNS may be used, which does not support Active Directory. The primary DNS server for the domain must support service location resource records, or SRV RR (RFC 2782), to be compatible with Active Directory. Service location resource records are used to locate services on a network using DNS. If SRV RR is not supported, then the Windows 2000 DNS server must be made the primary server with authority over all the DNS names registered by the domain controller.

As mentioned in the previous section, it is also important to use two DNS servers when the domain name is used for both. One DNS server can be used for the internal network and one for the external network. The DNS server used for the internal network points to the IP addresses of resources in the internal domain. The DNS server used for the external network does not handle requests for resources on the internal network, but instead handles requests for external resources.

When planning the DNS strategy, it is important to remember the following points:

- A *full computer name* is comprised of two parts: the DNS host name and the primary DNS suffix.

- In order for a DNS server to be compatible with Active Directory, it must support the service location resource record (SRV RR).

- The server will not perform a dynamic update for the client unless it has authenticated the update in Active Directory and has the proper permissions to perform the dynamic update.

- Incremental zone transfer (IXFR) permits only updates to the zone table to be synchronized.

- In order for a legacy DNS server to work with Active Directory, it must coexist with a Windows 2000 DNS server that is authoritative over the domain.

exam
ⓦatch
You are not limited to having a single DNS server for your entire network. Large companies will often use multiple DNS servers to improve name resolution performance. Although multiple DNS servers can be used on a network, a stand-alone DNS server will generally be used in a domain that has only a single zone to maintain. This is an option for small to midsize organizations that do not generally require multiple domains or locations. Additional DNS servers can be added as the company grows.

QUESTIONS

8.03: Planning the DNS Strategy

9. **Current Situation:** A company has two identical domain names used on the network, both called *domain1.com*. One domain is located on the internal network; the other is located outside of the network. Administrators add host names to DNS manually and have complained about the time spent updating DNS. The help desk has been receiving complaints that users are having difficulty

logging on to the network and accessing required resources. Windows 2000 DNS Server is used on the internal network to resolve names to IP addresses, and when zone transfers are performed, replication is bogging down the network. Users have complained about slow network speed during the times the zone table is synchronized.

Required Result: Resolve the problem users are having logging on to the internal network and accessing its resources.

Optional Desired Results:

1. Improve network performance when zone transfers are performed.

2. Devise a method of adding hosts to the DNS so that they do not need to be added manually.

Proposed Solution: Place a second DNS server on the external network to handle all internal requests to the external domain. Use dynamic updates so that only updates to the zone table are synchronized. Use IXFRs so that hosts dynamically register their names in the DNS database.

What results are produced from the proposed solution?

A. The proposed solution produces the required result only.

B. The proposed solution produces the required result and only one of the optional results.

C. The proposed solution produces the required result and both of the optional results.

D. The proposed solution does not produce the required result.

10. You are analyzing a Windows NT network that will be upgraded to Windows 2000. This network already uses a DNS server. What must be supported for the current DNS server to be compatible with Active Directory?

A. SQL service location resource record

B. Service location resource record

C. Name resolution

D. Linux

11. The illustration below shows some of the elements making up your company's domain, *domain1.com*. The network includes users, servers, and workstations. Which of the following is true about these elements? (Choose all that apply.)

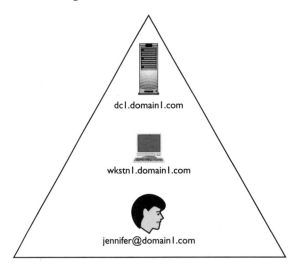

dc1.domain1.com

wkstn1.domain1.com

jennifer@domain1.com

A. jennifer@domain1.com is a full computer name.

B. wkstn1.domain1.com is a full computer name.

C. dc1 is a DNS suffix.

D. domain1.com is a DNS suffix.

12. You want the hosts on your Windows 2000 network to register themselves when a user logs into a network. To do this, you use the dynamic update feature in Windows 2000 DNS. However, after implementing dynamic updates, you notice that some hosts still are not automatically registering their names in the DNS database. Which of the following might be reasons for this? (Choose all that apply.)

A. DNS servers will not update hosts unless the DNS server has authenticated the update in Active Directory.

B. DNS servers will not update hosts unless it has proper permissions to perform a dynamic update.

C. DNS servers will not update hosts because hosts do not have this capability. Hosts cannot register themselves; they can only update static information in the DNS database.

D. Dynamic updates are not used for this purpose.

Understanding Naming Conventions

Naming conventions are standards for naming elements of your network. Naming computers, domains, and forests in your network is not governed by hard and fast rules, but the organization and IT staff should agree on the basis for naming these items. The basis for naming largely refers to the logical structuring of domain names and forests, but the naming conventions may also be influenced by the physical structure. In choosing a naming scheme, the ultimate goal is to ensure resources are easy to find.

A forest is a collection of one or more Windows 2000 domains that are linked with two-way, transitive trusts. Although a forest structure provides communication, each of the domain trees in a forest is separate and completely independent. There are different naming conventions that can be used in forests. Each of the trees in a forest has a different naming structure according to its domains. If the root domain is domain1.com, then domains below this are extensions of that name (e.g., accounting.domain1.com). If another tree had a root domain of otherdomain.com, then its child domains would be based on this name. Together, these two trees could make up a forest.

The child domains used in a forest do not have to follow the naming convention of using the root domain's name in their names, although this does make it easier to identify the child domains. For example, if you had a domain called accountingdomain.com, it might contain child domains accpayable.com or accreceivable.com. In naming a child domain, it is important to keep in mind that the name should make clear the domain's purpose, location, or association to the rest of the tree or forest. Domain names are at the core of Windows 2000 Active Directory design, and any naming scheme should be planned with this in mind.

The grouping of domains and child domains should also be considered so that the resources they contain are similar in nature. The physical location of a domain should not be the determining factor when grouping domains, unless root servers are being used for the purpose of log-on traffic. For example, in a national company, you would not want servers in one part of the country authenticating users at the opposite end of the country. This would bog down the network because servicing logons would congest the network, causing resources to be slow or impossible to access. Although you would physically place servers at each location, the logical structure of your network could have both locations associated with the same root domain.

Organizational units (OUs) are containers that hold users, groups, computers, and other OUs. Organizational units can be nested so that one OU can contain another

OU. An OU is a logical container within a domain model, and it can contain only objects from its parent domain. Unlike with domains, end users do not navigate through OUs. OUs are used to organize objects so that administration is easier. They are the smallest scope to which group policy can be applied and to which authority can be delegated. When you use OUs in combination with ACLs (Access Control Lists), you can grant rights to certain objects, while restricting rights to others. However, OUs should not be mistaken for security models. OUs cannot be made members of a security group. You also cannot grant user permissions to resources because they reside in the OU structure.

When understanding naming conventions, it is important to keep the following points in mind:

- A *forest* is a collection of Active Directory enabled domains.
- Domains within a forest do not have to maintain the same root DNS address.
- An organizational unit (OU) is a container used to maintain the logical structure within a domain model.

exam
Watch

When naming domains, it is important to put thought into the root domain name, as this name will rename static. It will be costly and time consuming, and in some cases impossible, to change the name after the domain structure is in place. Any names used should be simple and descriptive. Users should not be confused by cryptic domain names or find the name difficult to remember. The name should be short, succinct, and not case sensitive. Domain names can be up to 63 characters in length (including periods), and the total length of the fully qualified domain name (FQDN) cannot be longer than 255 characters. Domain controllers are limited to 155 characters for a FQDN.

The domain name must also be unique throughout the DNS namespace so that each subdomain has a unique name within the parent domain. You should use standard Internet characters when creating names so that the name is compatible with legacy systems and third-party software. Windows 2000 supports the DNS characters A to Z, a to z, 0 to 9, and the hyphen (-).

When creating child domains, it is also important to limit the number of domain levels, because having more domain levels will increase administration. Microsoft suggests that DNS host entries should be three or four levels down in the DNS hierarchy and never more than five levels down.

QUESTIONS

8.04: Understanding Naming Conventions

13. **Current Situation:** A company has recently undergone restructuring and has changed its name. The company has offices in Atlanta and New York. Because Active Directory can support millions of objects, both of these locations are part of the same domain. Users in Atlanta log on to and access servers in New York. Recently, users have complained that they are unable to log on the network during peak hours of network traffic. Because of the name change of the company, the CEO has asked whether it would be feasible to change the domain name to match the company's new name. The company's new name is quite lengthy, so the suggested root domain will be 75 characters in length.

    Required Result: Determine a way to improve performance so that users will be able to log on and not experience performance problems.

    Optional Desired Results:

    1. Determine whether the domain name should be changed to match the company name.

    2. Determine whether the suggested root domain is valid.

    Proposed Solution: Associate both locations with the same root domain, and place servers at both locations to provide network authentication. Root domain names can be changed easily by changing the name of the first domain controller in the domain. Domain names cannot be longer than 63 characters in length (including periods), so the suggested root name is not valid.

    What results are produced from the proposed solution?

    A. The proposed solution produces the required result only.

    B. The proposed solution produces the required result and only one of the optional results.

C. The proposed solution produces the required result and both of the optional results.

D. The proposed solution does not produce the required result.

14. You are discussing prospective domain names with members of your IT staff. Based on the following information, which domain names are valid?

A. One proposed root domain name is 63 characters in length (including periods).

B. One name is short, but difficult to remember.

C. One proposed computer name is Server1 plus the domain name, and another proposed computer name is server1 plus the domain name.

D. One full computer name is 255 characters in length (excluding periods).

15. The following illustration shows a network with locations in two cities. These cities are connected via a WAN line. Looking at this illustration, which of the following is true?

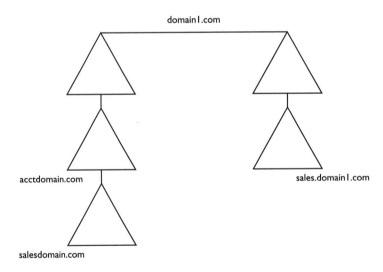

A. Domain1.com is the name of the WAN link.

B. Domain1.com is the root domain of the forest.

C. Sales.domain1.com is the root domain of the forest.

D. Acctdomain.com is the root domain of the forest.

16. You are designing a Windows 2000 Active Directory network. This network will consist of a root domain with several child domains, but you want to limit the DNS hierarchy to minimize administration. What is the maximum number of child domains that Microsoft suggests you should use in your design?

   A. Two

   B. Three

   C. Five

   D. Unlimited

LAB QUESTION

Objectives 8.01–8.05

A company has hired you to design a Windows 2000 Active Directory network. At present, the network uses Windows NT 4.0, with Windows NT DNS Server. Your network has registered the domain name of examplecompany.com. An Internet service provider who has been paid to host the company Web site will use this domain name. In other words, to access the company Web site, users will use the address www.examplecompany.com. Once Windows 2000 is deployed, the company wishes to use the examplecompany.com name for the internal network as well as the external network. The internal network will also have two new child domains, and the names used need to be simple to remember. One child domain will be used for accounting in the internal network, and the other will be used for accounting purposes for Internet sales. One suggested name is AccT.examplecompany.com, and another is acct.examplecompany.com.

1. What is the problem with using the domain name for both the internal and external network?

2. If the same name is used for both the internal and external network, what is the minimum number of DNS servers that should be deployed?

3. What must be done if the Windows NT DNS Server is to coexist on the network with the Windows 2000 DNS Server?

4. What is the problem with the suggested child domain names?

QUICK ANSWER KEY

Objective 8.01

1. **A** and **C**
2. **C**
3. **C**
4. **A**

Objective 8.02

5. **D**
6. **A**
7. **A**
8. **A, B**, and **C**

Objective 8.03

9. **A**
10. **B**
11. **B** and **D**
12. **A** and **B**

Objective 8.04

13. **B**
14. **A**
15. **B**
16. **C**

IN-DEPTH ANSWERS

8.01: Establishing the Scope of Active Directory

1. ☑ **A** and **C** are correct. The namespace is comprised of two parts: the metaverse and the connector space. The metaverse is the part of the directory that represents all joined objects, whether they are from connected directories or are unique objects with no connection to external directories. The connector space is the location into which directories are initially imported. Each directory maintains its own area in the connector space.

   ☒ **B** and **D** are incorrect because the connected directory and LDAP are not part of the namespace. The connected directory is imported into the connector space, and LDAP is the Lightweight Directory Access Protocol, used to access the namespace.

2. ☑ **C.** The proposed solution produces the required result and both of the optional results. By modifying the schema, you can add attributes to the user objects to include employee numbers and social security numbers. Active Directory Connector (ADC) is a component that enables communication and synchronization between the Active Directory and the Microsoft Exchange Server 5.5 Directory Service. Microsoft Exchange will not communicate natively with Active Directory, so new data and changes need to be input manually in both directories, but ADC provides capability for this to happen automatically.

   ☒ **A, B**, and **D** are incorrect, because the proposed solution produces the required result and both of the optional results.

3. ☑ **C.** Objects that have been marked for deletion are not deleted immediately. They are marked as tombstones. Windows 2000 purges them from the directory after a default period of 12 hours.

   ☒ **A** is incorrect because an object can be restored after is has been deleted. **B** is incorrect because the default amount of time before an object marked as a tombstone is purged is 12 hours. **D** is incorrect because there is a time period before objects are permanently purged from the system.

4. ☑ **A.** There are four types of objects in the metadirectory: physical, conceptual, digital, and geographic. Physical items would include workstations, servers, and users. Conceptual items would include departments, organizations, and groups. Digital items include documents, spreadsheets and images. Geographic items would include locations in the geographic scope of the organization (offices, subsidiaries, and so forth).

☒ **B** is incorrect because there are no metaphysical types of objects contained in the metadirectory. **C** is incorrect because there are no analog types of objects in the metadirectory. **D** is incorrect because four types of objects can be contained in the metadirectory.

8.02: Designing the Namespace

5. ☑ **D.** The proposed solution does not produce the required result. Duplicate names should be avoided, even if the domains are not physically connected. Since a firewall will not be implemented, and since there is no proxy server, name resolution problems can result. A user attempting to access the Web site might get the internal network instead. The reason for this is that the client machine would connect to the first domain answering the locator request.

☒ **A, B**, and **C** are incorrect because the proposed solution does not produce the required result. As well, standard Internet characters, defined by RFC 1123, are not used. These are characters including any letters from A to Z (upper or lower case), any numbers between 0 and 9, and the hyphen character (-).

6. ☑ **A.** Pay_roll.domain1.com is not a valid name because it does not use standard Internet characters. As defined by RFC 1123, names should consist of any letters from A to Z (upper or lower case), any numbers between 0 and 9, and the hyphen character (-).

☒ **B** and **C** are incorrect because both of these names are valid. **D** is incorrect because the pay_roll.domain1.com contains an invalid character, namely, the underscore.

7. ☑ **A.** In the name dc1.domain1.com, dc1 is the computer name, and domain1.com is the DNS suffix. To ensure compatibility with legacy systems,

by default, the first part of a server's full computer name is the NetBIOS name. This will allow the Windows 9x legacy system and software that is not Active Directory aware to use the resource.

☒ **B** is incorrect because this is the DNS suffix. **C** is incorrect because this is part of the DNS suffix. **D** is incorrect because this is not part of the name at all.

8. ☑ **A, B,** and **C** are correct. Fs-sales.sales.domain1.com is a problem because it is too similar to fs_sales.sales.domain1.com. This may lead to confusion when users attempt to use this resource or when administrators are managing servers. Fs_sales.sales.domain1.com is not a valid name because an underscore is used in the name. Server1.pay_roll.domain1.com is also not a valid domain name because an underscore was used in the name.

☒ **D** is incorrect because there is nothing wrong with the name dc1.domain1.com.

8.03: Planning the DNS Strategy

9. ☑ **A.** The proposed solution produces the required result only. Placing a second DNS server on the external network to handle all internal requests to the external domain will resolve the problem users are having logging on to the internal network and accessing its resources. One DNS server is used for the internal network and points to the IP addresses of resources in the internal domain. The other DNS server is used for the external network and handles requests for external resources.

☒ **B, C,** and **D** are incorrect because the proposed solution produces the required result only. Because of the increased network traffic of replicating an entire zone, incremental zone transfers (IXFRs) can be used so that only changes are replicated. This means that only updates to the zone table are synchronized. Dynamic updates can be used to allow hosts to dynamically register their names in the DNS database.

10. ☑ **B.** Service location resource records. The primary DNS server for the domain must support service location resource records to be compatible with Active Directory. Service location resource records (SRV RR) are used to locate services on a network using DNS.

☒ **A** is incorrect because there is no such thing as SQL service location resource records. **C** is incorrect because DNS is used for name resolution.

D is incorrect because Linux is an operating system and does not need to be supported for DNS to be compatible with AD.

11. ☑   **B** and **D** are correct. Wkstn1.domain1.com is a full computer name. A full computer name consists of the DNS host name and the primary DNS suffix. Domain1.com is a DNS suffix.

☒   **A** is incorrect because jennifer@domain1.com is not a full computer name. It is an email address or full account name. **C** is incorrect because dc1 is not a DNS suffix; it is the DNS host name.

12. ☑   **A** and **B** are correct. Windows 2000 DNS supports dynamic updates, allowing hosts to dynamically register their names in the DNS database. DNS servers will not update such hosts unless it has authenticated the update in Active Directory and has the proper permissions to perform a dynamic update.

☒   **C** and **D** are incorrect because dynamic updates are used so that hosts can dynamically register their names in the DNS database.

8.04: Understanding Naming Conventions

13. ☑   **B.** The proposed solution produces the required result and only one of the optional results. Because the location of the domain is affecting performance, servers should be placed at each location. The physical location of a domain should not be the determining factor when grouping domains, unless root servers are being used for the purpose of log-on traffic. Although you would physically place servers at each location, the logical structure of your network could have both locations associated with the same root domain.

Domain names cannot be longer than 63 characters in length (including periods), so the suggested root name is not valid. Lengthy domain names would also be difficult for users to remember.

☒   **A**, **C**, and **D** are incorrect because the proposed solution produces the required result and only one of the optional results. Root domain names cannot be changed easily by changing the name of the first domain controller on the network.

14. ☑   **A.** Domain names can be up to 63 characters in length (including periods).

☒ **B** is incorrect because although names should be short, they should also be easy to remember. **C** is incorrect because the names are not case sensitive. **D** is incorrect because the total length of the name cannot be longer than 255 characters.

15. ☑ **B.** Domain1.com is the root domain of the forest.

☒ **A** is incorrect because the WAN line does not have a name in the logical structure. **C** and **D** are incorrect because the root domain of the forest is domain1.com.

16. ☑ **C.** Five. When creating child domains, it is important to limit the number of domain levels, because having more domain levels increases administration. Microsoft suggests that DNS host entries should be three or four levels down in the DNS hierarchy and never more than five levels down.

☒ **A** and **B** are incorrect because these numbers do not represent the maximum number of child domains that are suggested by Microsoft. **D** is incorrect because Microsoft suggests that you should never use more than five levels of child domains.

LAB ANSWER

Objectives 8.01–8.05

1. Duplicate names should be avoided, even if the domains are not physically connected. If your internal network and external network both use the domain name "examplecompany.com," name resolution problems can result. A user attempting to access your Web site by this name might get the internal network instead, since the client machine would connect to the first domain answering the locator request.

2. Two DNS servers could be used: one for the internal network and one for the external network. The DNS server for the internal network would point to the IP address of the internal domain, and the external DNS server would handle internal requests for external resources.

3. The Windows 2000 DNS server must be made the primary server with authority over all the DNS names that will be registered by the domain controller. The primary DNS server for the domain must support service location resource records, or SRV RR (RFC 2782), to be compatible with Active Directory. Service location resource records are used to locate services on a network using DNS. Windows NT DNS does not support SRV RR.

4. Domain names are not case sensitive.

MICROSOFT CERTIFIED SYSTEMS ENGINEER

9

Designing and Planning the Structure of Organizational Units

TEST YOURSELF OBJECTIVES

A s mentioned in previous chapters, organizational units (OUs) are containers that are used within domains. Organizational units lessen the need for multiple domains because OUs can be used to partition an Active Directory domain into manageable units. Organizational units allow you to place users, groups, computers, and other OUs into logical containers and then apply group policies and delegate authority to them. With the use of OUs, the need to create resource domains is reduced, and the ability to administer your network is heightened.

Developing an OU Design Strategy

When developing a design strategy of organizational units, it is important to design OUs to support delegation. Delegating administrative control of objects gives users and groups the ability to manage and administer resources. This allows you to identify specific users to perform common tasks. You can give a user permissions to change properties on a container or to create, modify, or delete objects of a particular type in a specific OU. You can also give the user permissions to modify specific properties on objects of a certain type in a specific container. Organizational units are used to support delegation because it is easier to track permissions at the OU or container level than it is to track permissions at a user level.

It is important that the structure of the OUs is agreed upon before deploying delegation. The first step in planning your design is to investigate how administration is currently performed. Centralized administration was common to the Windows NT architecture because there was no way to delegate administration without third-party products. If administration is centralized, it will ensure that delegation is not currently used and will provide information as to why delegation may not be desired for use in Active Directory. If delegation is used, and if there are multiple sites, you should consider whether there is proper bandwidth to continue using centralized administration.

If administration is decentralized, you will be able to build on this structure when creating OUs. In decentralized administration, local administrators or power users may be utilized at different locations to perform common administrative tasks. By analyzing this arrangement, you will be able to see how well delegation is working, whether administration should continue to be decentralized, and what elements of administration should be changed. You may find out that the current roles of

Information Technology (IT) staff should be modified and that Windows NT domains have been implemented for the purpose of decentralized administration. In such cases, you may determine that certain domains are no longer needed. Organizational units can be used to replace certain domains, and administration can then be delegated back to the same administrators, with more control over what tasks they perform.

When designing OUs, you will need to look at what administrative features are available for Active Directory and how they will apply to a proposed structure. Group policies are used to control and define users, groups, and computers, and they can be set at the site, domain, and OU level. Group policies can be forced down the hierarchy so that changes are not allowed, or they can be filtered from higher hierarchical policies. As we saw in Chapter 6, organizational units can also use group policies to assign or publish software. Another useful feature of Windows 2000 is IntelliMirror, which provides management features that are implemented using OUs. One such feature is Remote Installation Services (RIS) that allows an administrator to set up client computers remotely.

Once it is decided what features will be implemented, an administrative model should then be designed. Organizational units are designed around organizational and/ or geographical boundaries. An excellent design tool is the company's organizational chart, since this will indicate organizational, and possibly geographical, boundaries. Geographical structures are least likely to change, so the first level of OUs should be based on them. The next levels will depend on how the current administrative model is designed and on what plans exist for future administration. OUs may be used to manage organizational boundaries, such as lines-of-businesses, business units, or departments, and they may be built around resources such as servers, printers, or workstations.

Organizational units can be nested so that one OU is contained within another. This creates a hierarchical architecture. When nesting is used, properties of the parent container, such as security or group policies, flow down the hierarchy. This is called *inheritance*, because child containers inherit the properties of the parent containers. Although OUs can be nested to a maximum of 62 deep, and group policies to a maximum of 32 deep, neither should be nested to this extent. Nesting too deeply can cause latency with the authentication process, as well as confusion as to where a particular object inherited its properties. Organizational units can also stand alone without being nested in a hierarchy, thus creating a flatter hierarchical structure. This allows the OU to have no dependencies on other OUs.

When developing a design strategy for organizational units, it is important to remember the following points:

- Design OUs to support delegation.
- OUs can be designed around organizational boundaries and geographical boundaries. OUs are also designed to group resources together by type, such as printers or servers.
- OUs can be nested to create a hierarchy.
- Geographical OUs are the OU structures least likely to change.
- Do not nest OUs too deeply. This can cause latency problems with authenticating and can cause confusion.

exam
Ⓦatch

When planning your design, you should try to keep the hierarchy of organizational units as shallow as possible, and remember that OUs should represent business structures that are not subject to change. You will also need to determine what model will be used for classifying OUs. A business function model bases OUs on business functions in the company. The top level of OUs will relate to business divisions, whereas the second level will correspond to functional divisions within the business divisions. For example, the top level OU might be SALES, and the second level might include DOMESTIC and INTERNATIONAL. Another model that can be used is geographical, wherein OUs are based on locations. The top level would correspond to a broad geographical location, and the second level would correspond to office locations. For example, the top level OU might be EAST, and the second level might include Atlanta and New York. A combination model of both business function and geographical OUs could also be used. In such a structure, the top level OUs would correspond to locations (e.g., CANADA), and the second level OUs would represent functional divisions in the business (e.g., SALES).

QUESTIONS

9.01: Developing an OU Design Strategy

Questions 1–3 The next three questions are based upon the scenario and illustration that follows. Read the following case study, and then answer the questions. You may refer to this case study and illustration as often as needed.

Asimov Robotics and Housewares has recently deployed a Windows 2000 network but has been having problems since it was deployed. The network administrator states that he had some difficulty designing the organizational unit structure. They have asked you to look at the OU structure and give your opinions on how it has been designed. After opening Active Directory Users and Computers, you see the following screen:

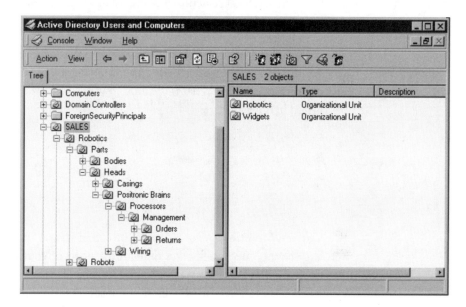

1. What type of model is being used in the OU design of this company?

    A. Geographical

    B. Business function

    C. A combination of business function and geographical

    D. Flat structure

2. When users in the Orders Department of Processor sales attempt to log on, they find it takes considerable time. During peak hours, some users find they

cannot log on during their first attempt. Which of the following may be causing this?

A. Organizational units have not been nested deeply enough. This is causing latency in the authentication process.

B. Organizational units are nested too deeply. This is causing latency in the authentication process.

C. Organizational units have exceeded the nesting limit.

D. A hierarchical structure is being used. Organizational units are not designed to support this structure, and it is causing latency.

3. As seen in the current OU structure, the organization of the company is complex. For this reason, the network administrator who designed the structure nested organizational units. What is the limit to which organizational units can be nested in this structure?

A. 26 deep

B. 32 deep

C. 62 deep

D. Unlimited

4. **Current Situation:** A company has offices in several cities, spread across a large county. Because it takes time for members of your IT staff to drive from office to office, you would like to give specific users at each location the ability to manage certain groups of users and resources. Although the company is currently running Windows NT 4.0 Servers and Workstations, it is preparing to upgrade to Windows 2000. In the past, it has taken a significant amount of time to install software on client computers. Most of the time spent by IT staff deals with installing the software, but time is also spent determining which users should get which programs. Once it is established who gets which program, IT staff members must seek out the computers and users to begin the match-up process. Each of these issues needs to be resolved when upgrading to Windows 2000.

Required Result: Devise a way for specific users to manage users and resources in their office.

Optional Desired Results:

1. Devise a method of setting up software on remote computers without having to visit each client.

2. Implement a procedure for controlling what programs will appear on a user's desktop and Start menu.

Proposed Solution: Place user accounts and resources into organizational units, and then use Group Policy to give users and groups the ability to manage and administer these resources. Use Group Policy to control what programs will appear on a user's desktop and Start menu. Use IntelliMirror with OUs so that the Remote Installation Services can be used to set up client computers remotely.

What results are produced from the proposed solution?

A. The proposed solution produces the required result only.

B. The proposed solution produces the required result and only one of the optional results.

C. The proposed solution produces the required result and both of the optional results.

D. The proposed solution does not produce the required result.

TEST YOURSELF OBJECTIVE 9.02

Understanding Security

The objects in Active Directory are protected through authentication and access control. Access control allows you to manage access to an object as a whole, or to specific attributes. For example, you could allow users in Human Resources to modify user objects, or to modify only their names and addresses. However, to provide for such granular administration of objects, the proper permissions must be assigned.

Security principals are objects that can be used for assigning permissions, and they include users, groups, and computers, but not OUs. An OU or container is used to organize directory objects. Although objects in AD have a distinguishable name, the name of an object can be changed. To identify an object, two unique identifiers are used internally: a security identifier (SID) and a globally unique identifier (GUID). A SID identifies a security principal in a domain. The first part of a SID is a unique domain identifier, whereas the second part of a SID is created with uniqueness for a particular domain. This part of the SID is called the relative identifier (RID). As in Windows NT 4.0, the SID cannot be used outside the domain. When an object is moved from one domain to another, it is given a new SID. The only boundary for a GUID is a Windows 2000 forest. A GUID is a 128-bit number that is guaranteed to be unique, regardless of how many domains exist in a tree or forest.

Every object in Active Directory has a security descriptor, which describes who owns the object and what Access Control Lists (ACLs) it contains. An ACL is a list of who has permission to an object, and what that permission is. The granular permissions in ACL are called Access Control Entries (ACEs). When a process attempts to access a resource, the SID is compared to the resource's ACL. If the SID matches the entry in the ACL, the process is allowed to use the resource.

In Active Directory, every object has an owner. By default, the user who creates the object is made its owner, giving him or her full control over it. If you do not have access to a particular object you created, ownership allows you to grant yourself access. By default, ownership will always include the administrator and members of the administrator's domain local group. When a user belongs to the administrator's domain local group, in effect they have full control. Even if they were denied, they could reestablish their own permissions.

The object type determines the permissions that can be selected, and the permissions you can select vary between different object types. You can allow or deny permissions. Denied permissions will always take precedence, even if permission is otherwise granted through other groups.

Inheritance refers to the fact that a child object will retain the characteristics or properties of a parent object. This applies to Active Directory as well as group policies. Organizational units are the smallest scope to which Group Policy settings can be assigned. Group Policy settings enable you to control access and use of resources for organizational units and any child objects they contain. This includes users, groups, computers, and other organizational units. Group policies will be discussed in greater detail in the next chapter. The permissions flow down through the hierarchy so that a child object inherits the permissions applied to an OU or parent object.

Inheritance can be blocked so that settings are not applied beyond the point where the inheritance block is set. This allows you to create different security structures at lower levels of the hierarchy. By unchecking the Allow Inheritable Permissions from Parent to Propagate to This Object check box on an object's properties, you will block inheritance. This means that any child objects will not inherit permissions.

When dealing with security in the organizational unit process, you should remember the following points:

- Security principals are objects that can be used for assigning permissions.
- Access Control Lists (ACLs) are lists that are attached to objects to reflect who has access to that object and what type of access they have.
- Ownership of an object is given by default to the creator of the object.
- Permissions are inherited from parent object by default. Inheritance can be blocked at an object level.

e x a m

Watch

Although the object type determines permissions, there are standard permissions that are available for most objects. Full Control is a permission that allows you to take ownership of and change permissions on an object. When this permission is selected, all other standard permissions are also allowed to this user. The Read permission allows you to view permissions, ownership, objects, and their attributes. Write is used to change an object's attributes. Change All Child Objects allows a user to add any type of child object to an OU. Delete All Child Objects allows a user to remove any type of child object from an OU.

Assigning permissions to an object is done through Active Directory Users and Computers. By bringing up the Properties of an object, you can set permissions on the Security tab. If the Security tab does not appear, you should check that Advanced Features has been selected on the View menu. In setting these permissions, it is important to remember that at least one user has Full Control. If no user has Full Control, the object may be inaccessible. Even an administrator will be unable to access the object, unless ownership of it is changed.

QUESTIONS

9.02: Understanding Security in the OU Process

5. You have decided to assign permissions to an object, as shown in the following illustration. Upon checking the permissions to the object, you find that the

Allow Inheritable Permissions from Parent to Propagate to This Object check box is checked. Which of the following is true? (Choose all that apply.)

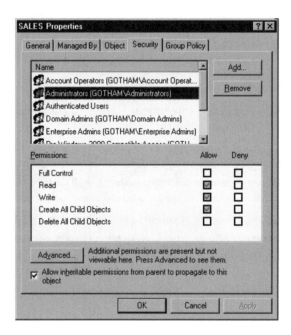

A. Because the Allow Inheritable Permissions from Parent to Propagate to This Object check box is checked, the object will not inherit permissions from the parent object.

B. Because the Allow Inheritable Permissions from Parent to Propagate to This Object check box is checked, the object will inherit permissions from the parent object.

C. When permissions are changed, any existing child objects will inherit permissions from the parent container.

D. When permissions are changed, any existing child objects will not inherit permissions from the parent container.

6. **Current Situation:** A user tells you that he has changed permissions on an object he created. To ensure security, he changed every user's and group's permissions to the object to Read and Write. Now the user cannot modify permissions on the object. When you attempt to look at the permissions on the Security tab of the

object's Properties, you find this tab does not appear. The user also complains that he does not have access to a printer. The user states that his user account is allowed permissions to the printer object, but he is a member of a group that has been denied permissions.

Required Result: Enable the user to have access to the Printers container.

Optional Desired Results:

1. Determine why the Security tab of Active Directory Users and Computers does not appear.

2. Change security on the object so that the user can modify permissions on the object.

Proposed Solution: Remove the user from the group that has been denied permissions to the printer object. Select Advanced Features from the View menu of Active Directory Users and Computers. This will allow the Security tab to appear in the object's Properties. When it appears, set the permissions so that the user will have Full Control of the object.

What results are produced from the proposed solution?

A. The proposed solution produces the required result only.

B. The proposed solution produces the required result and only one of the optional results.

C. The proposed solution produces the required result and both of the optional results.

D. The proposed solution does not produce the required result.

7. A process attempts to access a resource on your network. Which of the following will occur?

A. The SID will be compared to the resource's Access Control List (ACL). If the SID matches the entry in the ACL, then the process is allowed to use the resource.

B. The RID will be compared to the SID. If the RID matches the entry in the SID, then the process is allowed to use the resource.

C. The ACE will be compared to the ACL. If the ACE matches the entry in the ACL, then the process is allowed to use the resource.

D. None of the above. Unique identifiers are not used in Windows 2000.

8. You are preparing to assign standard permissions to an Active Directory object. Which of the following permissions would be the minimum in order to allow a user to view ownership of an object?

A. Full Control

B. Read

C. Write

D. Read and Write

TEST YOURSELF OBJECTIVE 9.03

Delegating Administration

The purpose of delegating administration is to decentralize administration. It allows users and groups to administer resources that are familiar and logical to them, and it reduces the network administrator's burden of having to manage them. Consequently, the total cost of ownership (TCO) is reduced.

When planning for delegation, it is important to determine what needs to be delegated. Based on the OU structure, you will need to analyze whether there is a need to delegate some, all, or none of the OUs. This analysis is essential because not all organizational units may have been created for delegation. Some may have been created for group policies or logical groupings based on the company's organizational model. You will also need to determine on an OU-by-OU level what administration will occur. By delegating administration, you are acknowledging that IT staff will not be handling administration throughout the enterprise. Therefore, it is important to determine administrative boundaries. In other words, you will need to determine what part of the OU structure users will manage, and what level of administration these users will have for controlling access.

When delegating administration, it is important to remember the following points:

■ Delegating administration can help to reduce the cost of administering groups of resources by giving that responsibility to other resources.

■ The first step in designing delegation is to determine at what level delegation needs to begin.

■ In Windows NT you could not delegate administrative control without the use of third-party products.

Windows 2000 boasts vast improvements compared to Windows NT regarding delegation of administration. Windows NT had a limited ability for administration. To delegate administration, you could potentially give excessive rights to users, because Windows NT did not allow assigning permissions at a granular level. To introduce a hierarchy to a Windows NT design and assign permissions granularly, third-party software was needed. The only other alternative was to use multiple domains. This increased the complexity of the network, as different trust relationships had to be used. These choices opened up holes in security, added additional costs for administration, or created undue complexity.

QUESTIONS

9.03: Delegating Administration

9. As shown in the following illustration, a company's Atlanta domain consists of a number of departments that are organized as organizational units. The domain administrator would like users in the Finance Department to control the Finance organizational unit. The administrator would also like these users to control Payroll, ACCT, ACCTPAY, and ACCTREV. Too much control over OUs in the domain is unacceptable. At what level will this control be given?

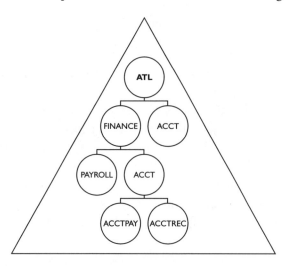

A. Delegate administration at the ATL level.

      B. Delegate administration at the FINANCE level.

      C. Delegate administration at the ACCT level.

      D. Delegate administration at the ACCTPAY level.

10. Several users in Human Resources need to administer a new organizational unit. How will you achieve this result?

      A. Place users in the OU.

      B. Create a group and give it administrative rights to the OU.

      C. Create a group and place users that need to administer the OU in that group.

      D. Create a group, place users that need to administer the OU in that group, and give the group administrative rights to the OU.

11. You are analyzing whether to implement delegation of administration on your Windows 2000 Active Directory network. Which of the following will you take into account during this analysis?

      A. Delegation will reduce total cost of ownership.

      B. Third-party software will be required to implement delegation of administration.

      C. Multiple domains will need to be implemented.

      D. The network will become more complex, since different trust relationships will need to be used.

12. **Current Situation:** A domain called XYZ contains a large number of organizational units. There has been significant time spent dealing with the Human Resources Department OU. The HR OU contains PERSONNEL, TEMPS, and BENEFITS OUs. PERSONNEL handles hiring and firing of employees, TEMPS handles temporary employees and co-op students, and BENEFITS handles medical and other benefit claims. The manager of Human Resources is adept with Active Directory, and has offered to administer the entire domain. This would cut down on your administrative duties with this domain, allowing you to focus on other domains and network duties. Although the manager is familiar with Human Resources needs and resources, he is unfamiliar with other resources in the domain. You are concerned that by giving administrative control at a particular level, you will be unable to control

the same resources the manager controls. Also, there are some organizational units you do not want the Human Resources manager to control.

Required Result: Determine at what level the manager of Human Resources should be delegated administrative control.

Optional Desired Results:

1. Determine whether delegating control at this level will affect your administrative control of the domain.

2. Devise a way to block the Human Resources manager from controlling specific OUs.

Proposed Solution: Delegate administrative control at the XYZ level of the domain. The domain administrator will still be able to control resources at this level and below, however, the manager of HR will also have administrative control. Block inheritance at the OUs you do not want the manager to control.

What results are produced from the proposed solution?

A. The proposed solution produces the required result only.

B. The proposed solution produces the required result and only one of the optional results.

C. The proposed solution produces the required result and both of the optional results.

D. The proposed solution does not produce the required result.

TEST YOURSELF OBJECTIVE 9.04

Delegating Control

There are two methods of delegating administrative control in Active Directory: the Delegation of Control Wizard, and implementing delegation manually. The Delegation of Control Wizard is a program that takes you step-by-step through the process of delegating administrative control, and it has predefined roles that include the basic functions of delegation.

The Delegation of Control Wizard has six common tasks that can be delegated. The Create, Delete, and Manage User Accounts task gives an object full control over all user class objects, including permission to create and delete user class objects. The Reset Passwords on User Accounts task gives the right to reset the password for other user class objects. Read All User Information gives the object only the right to read all properties for other user class objects. Create, Delete, and Manage Groups gives full control over all group class objects, including permission to create and delete group class objects. The Modify the Membership of a Group task gives the right to read and write members to group class objects. Finally, the Manage Group Policy Links task gives the right to read and write Group Policy rights and links. In addition to these predefined tasks, customized tasks can be created and delegated through the wizard.

The wizard, however, lets you allow permissions only for delegation. To deny permissions, delegation must be done manually. To manually delegate administrative control, you assign permissions to an object. As we saw earlier in this chapter, you can modify the access control through the Properties of an object.

When delegating control, it is important to keep the following points in mind:

■ Delegated permissions can be controlled at a granular level.

■ The Delegation of Control Wizard is a useful tool to start delegation because it provides some default and basic roles that are normally delegated.

■ You cannot use the Delegation of Control Wizard to deny permissions.

It is important to remember that the Delegation of Control Wizard is used only to allow permissions. This is for good reason. If permissions are set correctly, permissions should not need to be denied. Denied permissions indicate mistakes made when assigning group membership. If you do need to deny permission, you will need to assign this manually.

QUESTIONS

9.04: Delegating Control

13. You want to delegate control of printer objects to a user. The user will be responsible for creating and deleting printer objects. Using Delegation of

Control Wizard, shown in the following illustration, how would you assign this common task?

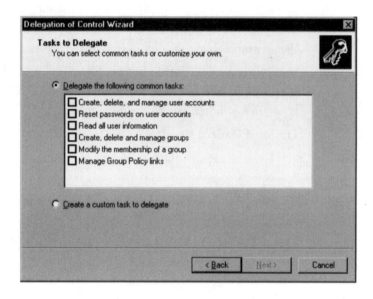

A. Assign the Create, Delete, and Manage User Accounts task.

B. Assign the Create, Delete, and Manage Groups task.

C. Assign the Modify the Membership of a Group task.

D. Create a custom task.

14. You are analyzing delegation for organizational units in a domain. While studying permissions assigned to objects, you find that a particular permission should be denied to a problem user. Which of the following will you do?

A. Run the Delegation of Control Wizard and deny the user permission to the object.

B. Manually remove the permission from the object so that it is unavailable to all users. This is done through Active Directory Users and Computers, by selecting the permission and deleting it.

C. Manually deny the permission through the Properties of the object.

D. Manually deny the permission through the Delegation of Control Wizard.

15. **Current Situation:** You have decided to delegate administrative control to a group of users. You want to associate one group of users with a new object and give them the right to read all properties for other user class objects, as well as the right to set it up so that when the user logs on with a default password, the user must change it immediately. You want to assign to another more experienced user the task of having full control over all user class objects.

    Required Result: Give the object full control over all user class objects, and assign this common task to the more experienced user.

    Optional Desired Results:

    1. Give the object only the right to read all properties for other user class objects.

    2. Give the object the right to reset the password of other user class objects.

    Proposed Solution: For the more experienced user, assign the common task of Create, Delete, and Manage User Accounts. For the less experienced user, assign the common tasks of Reset Passwords on User Accounts and Read all User Information.

    What results are produced from the proposed solution?

    A. The proposed solution produces the required result only.

    B. The proposed solution produces the required result and only one of the optional results.

    C. The proposed solution produces the required result and both of the optional results.

    D. The proposed solution does not produce the required result.

16. Which of the following tasks would you delegate to give the right to read and write Group Policy rights and links? (Choose all that apply.)

    A. Modify the Membership of a Group

    B. Manage Group Policy Links

    C. Manage Group Policy Rights

    D. Create, Delete, and Manage Groups

LAB QUESTION

Objectives 9.01–9.04

A company has offices in Atlanta, Richmond, and New York. Each of the locations is running Windows NT 4.0 and is connected with slow links. For administrative reasons, there are three domains in Atlanta, one in Richmond, and four in New York. Once the network has been upgraded to Windows 2000 Active Directory, you plan to use organizational units to organize objects and assign permissions.

1. Upon upgrading to Windows 2000, what type of administration should be used (centralized or decentralized) and why?

2. What can be done to decrease the number of domains after upgrading to Windows 2000?

3. After upgrading your network to Active Directory, you decided to assign permissions to an object. When you bring up the object's Properties, you find that the Security tab is not appearing. Why?

4. What methods are available for delegating administration in Active Directory?

QUICK ANSWER KEY

Objective 9.01	
1.	B
2.	B
3.	C
4.	D

Objective 9.02	
5.	B and C
6.	B
7.	A
8.	B

Objective 9.03	
9.	B
10.	D
11.	A
12.	D

Objective 9.04	
13.	D
14.	C
15.	C
16.	B and D

IN-DEPTH ANSWERS

9.01: Developing an OU Design Strategy

1. ☑ **B.** Business function. Looking at the structure of OUs in the illustration, you can see that only functions of the company are used. Each level of OUs is divided into business functions.

 ☒ **A** and **C** are incorrect because no geographical locations are used in the OU structure. **D** is incorrect because a hierarchical structure is used in the OU design, meaning OUs are nested within one another.

2. ☑ **B.** Organizational units are nested too deeply. Nesting too deeply can cause latency with the authentication process. Each OU must be processed, and the deep nesting is thus slowing the log on.

 ☒ **A** is incorrect because the more deeply organizational units are nested, the longer it takes to process them. **C** is incorrect because OUs can be nested 62 deep, and the illustration shows nowhere near this level of nesting. **D** is incorrect because OUs do support a hierarchical structure with OUs nested within one another.

3. ☑ **C.** Organizational units can be nested 62 deep. This means that you can have a maximum of 62 OUs nested within one another.

 ☒ **A**, **B**, and **D** are incorrect because OUs can be nested 62 deep. Option B, a limit of 32 deep, is the maximum number of group policies that can be nested.

4. ☑ **D.** The proposed solution does not produce the required result. Delegation is used to give users and groups the ability to perform common administrative tasks and manage resources.

 ☒ **A**, **B**, and **C** are incorrect because the proposed solution does not produce the required result. The optional results, however, have been fulfilled. Group policies can be used to control the behavior of a user's desktop, such as controlling what programs appear on the desktop and Start menu. IntelliMirror provides management features such as Remote Installation Services (RIS) that are implemented with OUs, allowing you to set up software on remote computers without having to visit each client.

9.02: Understanding Security in the OU Process

5. ☑ **B** and **C** are correct. Because Allow Inheritable Permissions from Parent to Propagate to This Object is checked, the object will inherit permissions from the parent object. All existing child objects will also inherit these permissions.

   ☒ **A** is incorrect because if this check box is checked, the object will inherit permissions from the parent object. **D** is incorrect because when permissions are changed, any existing child objects will inherit permissions from the parent container.

6. ☑ **B.** The proposed solution produces the required result and only one of the optional results. Denied permissions will always take precedence, even if it is otherwise granted through other groups. Therefore, you would either remove the user from the group that is denied permissions, or allow permissions to the group. The Security tab of an object's Properties is used to modify permissions. For this tab to appear, you must select Advanced Features from the View menu of Active Directory Users and Computers.

   ☒ **A**, **C**, and **D** are incorrect because the proposed solution produces the required result and only one of the optional results. If no user has Full Control, the object may be inaccessible. Even an administrator will be unable to access the object, unless ownership of it is changed.

7. ☑ **A.** When a process attempts to access a resource, the security identifier (SID) is compared to the resource's Access Control List (ACL). If the SID matches the entry in the ACL, then the process is allowed to use the resource.

   ☒ **B** is incorrect because this would result in a comparison of the SID with itself. The first part of a SID is a unique domain identifier, whereas the second part of a SID is created with uniqueness for a particular domain. This part of the SID is called the relative identifier (RID). **C** is also incorrect because this involves a comparison of the Access Control List (ACL) with itself. An ACL is a list of who has permission to an object, and what that permission is. The granular permissions in ACL are called Access Control Entries (ACEs). **D** is incorrect because unique identifiers are used in Windows 2000.

8. ☑ **B.** Read. The Read permission allows the user to view permissions, ownership, objects, and their attributes.

☒   **A** is incorrect because Full Control is a permission that allows the user to take ownership and change permissions on an object. When this permission is selected, all other standard permissions are also allowed to the user. **C** is incorrect because write is used to change an object's attributes. **D** is incorrect because a combination of Read and Write would not be the minimum permissions required to view ownership.

9.03: Delegating Administration

9. ☑   **B.** Delegate administration at the FINANCE level. Inheritance will allow lower organizational units also to be administered by this group of users.

☒   **A** is incorrect because it gives users too much administrative control. **C** is incorrect because this would not allow users administrative control over the FINANCE OU. **D** is incorrect because this would not give users control over the parent OUs and the ACCTREV OU.

10. ☑   **D.** By placing users in a group, you can change administrative control for the entire group, rather than for individual users. Users that will administer the OU are added to the group, and the group is given administrative rights to the OU.

☒   **A** is incorrect because the users have not been given administrative rights to the OU; they have only been placed in that container. **B** is incorrect because no users have been placed in the group. **C** is incorrect because the group has not been delegated administrative control of the object.

11. ☑   **A.** Total cost of ownership (TCO) is reduced. Delegation of administration allows users and groups to administer resources that are familiar and logical to them, and it reduces the network administrator's burden of having to manage them.

☒   **B** is incorrect because third-party software is not required. **C** is incorrect because multiple domains are not required to implement delegation of administration. **D** is incorrect because different trust relationships are not required.

12. ☑   **D.** The proposed solution does not produce the required result. Administrative control should be delegated only to users who find the resources they manage familiar and logical. The manager is unfamiliar with the needs,

tasks, and resources of particular OUs, as well as the users who use them, because they are unrelated to his department.

☒ **A**, **B**, and **C** are incorrect because the proposed solution does not produce the required result. Each of the optional requirements is met. The domain administrator will still be able to control resources at this level and below, but the manager of Human Resources will also have administrative control. The manager will lose permissions on the OUs where inheritance is blocked and on any child OUs they contain.

9.04: Delegating Control

13. ☑ **D.** Create a custom task. By selecting this option and clicking Next, you can select an AD object type to indicate the scope of the task to be delegated and then assign permissions.

☒ **A** is incorrect because the Create, Delete, and Manage User Accounts task gives an object full control over all user class objects, not just printer objects. **B** is incorrect because the Create, Delete, and Manage Groups gives full control over all group class objects, including permission to create and delete group class objects. **C** is incorrect because the Modify the Membership of a Group task gives the right to read and write members to the group class objects.

14. ☑ **C.** To deny permission on an object, you must manually deny it. To do this, modify the access control in the Properties of the object.

☒ **A** is incorrect because the Delegation of Control Wizard does not allow you to deny permissions. **B** is incorrect because you cannot remove permissions by deleting them in Active Directory Users and Computers. **D** is incorrect because the Delegation of Control Wizard cannot deny permissions.

15. ☑ **C.** The proposed solution produces the required result and both of the optional results. The Create, Delete, and Manage User Accounts task gives an object full control over all user class objects. Read All User Information gives the object only the right to read all properties for other user class objects. Reset Passwords on User Accounts gives the right to reset the password for other user class objects. When an object has this right he can reset the password to the default. Then when the user logs on with that default password, the user must change it immediately.

☒ **A**, **B**, and **D** are incorrect because the proposed solution produces the required result and both of the optional results.

16. ☑ **B** and **D** are correct. Create, Delete, and Manage Groups gives full control over all group class objects. Manage Group Policy Links gives the right to read and write group policy rights and links.

☒ **A** is incorrect because the Modify the Membership of a Group task gives the right to read and write members to the group class objects. **C** is incorrect because there is no Manage Group Policy Rights task.

LAB ANSWER

Objectives 9.01–9.04

1. Decentralized. Because each site is connected with a slow link, it will be difficult to administer the entire network centrally. By delegating administration, users and groups at each location will be able to manage resources.

2. Windows NT domains have been implemented for the purpose of decentralized administration and may no longer be needed. Organizational units can be used to replace certain domains, and administration can then be delegated back to the same administrators, with more control over what tasks they perform.

3. The Security tab will not appear unless the Advanced Features is selected on the View menu of Active Directory Users and Computers. Without this tab, you will not be able to assign permissions.

4. You can delegate administrative control manually or by using the Delegation of Administration Wizard.

10

Working with Group Policy Objects

Group policies are collections of user and computer configuration settings. They allow you to set guidelines for collections of system users and computers, both to individual desktop systems and to servers. These settings can be linked in Active Directory to sites, domains, organizational units (OUs), and computers. They are used to control the desktop configuration for groups and for individual users, and they are created using Group Policy Objects (GPOs), which are collections of group policy settings.

Even if it is not part of a network, every Windows 2000 computer has a local GPO. The local GPO is stored on the computer and is the least influential type of GPO, because others that are Active Directory based may override it. These AD based GPOs are called nonlocal GPOs. To use them, a Windows 2000 domain controller must be installed, and the user's computer must be on the network. Nonlocal GPOs are linked to sites, domains, or OUs in the Active Directory, and they can be applied to users and computers. The GPOs are cumulative, so they have a snowball effect. As GPOs are applied to a user or computer in this hierarchical fashion, the settings from each level are added together.

TEST YOURSELF OBJECTIVE 10.01

Planning Groups

The group policy settings contained in a GPO are used to determine the user's desktop environment. They allow you to perform such tasks as limiting access to specific Control Panel options, configuring desktop settings, auditing log-on validation attempts, and executing start-up scripts. GPOs provide the capability to centralize network administration. Because group policies are integrated within Active Directory, you can control user and computer settings across the network. It is therefore important that GPOs be well planned, documented, and executed, or they may become more of a problem than a solution. It is a tradeoff between control and convenience. The more measures are implemented to control users and computers, the less users are able to do. It is important that you do not put so many constraints on a user or computer that it becomes difficult or impossible for them to do their jobs.

There are two types of Group Policy settings: user settings and computer settings. The user configuration settings are applied to users when they log on the computer. Because the policies are applied to the user, it does not matter which computer the person logs on to. Computer configuration settings are applied to computers when the operating system starts. It does not matter which user logs on the computer.

Both computer configuration settings and user configuration settings are broken into three sections: Software settings, Windows settings, and Administrative templates. By default, the Software settings contain only software installation settings, which are used to specify how applications are installed and managed. Windows settings contain Scripts and Security settings. There are two types of scripts that can be used in this container: startup/shutdown (which runs the script when the computer starts or shuts down) and logon/logoff (which runs when a user logs on or off). Security settings are used to configure the security levels associated with the local GPO and nonlocal GPOs. Administrative templates contain any registry-based settings. These settings include Network settings (for Offline Files and Network and Dial-up Connections), System (for controlling Group Policy and log-on and log-off operations), and Windows Components (such as Internet Explorer, Windows Explorer, NetMeeting, Task Scheduler, Windows Installer, and even Microsoft Management Console).

Microsoft Management Console with the Group Policy snap-in is used to specify group policy settings. When this snap-in is started, all of the group policy extensions are loaded, allowing you to create custom consoles and modify the behavior of MMC. There are two modes that can be used in MMC with the Group Policy snap-in: User mode and Author mode. Author mode allows you to add and remove snap-ins, create new windows, navigate the entire console tree, and adjust all of the available MMC options. The User mode allows you to work within the snap-in selections that exist in the MMC. There are three levels to the User mode, which are considered modes unto themselves: limited access, single window; limited access, multiple window; and full access. In User mode full access, users have access to all windows management functions for MMC and full access to the context tree. Users do not have the ability to add and remove snap-ins or change console file options. Save commands are unavailable in this mode, because changes that do not affect snap-in relationships are saved automatically. In User mode limited access multiple window, users cannot open new windows or access areas of the console tree that were not visible when the console file was saved. Multiple child windows are allowed, but users cannot close them. The restrictions set on full access user mode also apply. In User mode limited access single window, all the restrictions set on User mode limited access multiple window apply, except that there is a single window. Controls for working with multiple windows are not available in this mode.

When planning groups, it is important to remember the following points:

- GPOs enable network administrators to centralize the administration of their networks.

- Group policies are created and managed through the use of a MMC snap-in.

- With GPOs we are able to do the following: centrally manage installation, removal, and updates of applications; configure the user desktop, applications, and system services through registry-based settings; set critical security settings that can be established by host, domain, or network; locate user Home folders in various areas throughout the network; and create custom scripts that can be executed during startup, shutdown, logon, or logoff.

- The User mode allows us to work within the snap-in selections that exist in the MMC. User mode is broken into three separate modes: limited access, single window; limited access, multiple window; and full access.

- The Author mode allows us to add snap-ins and adjust all of the available MMC options.

exam
ⓦatch
There are two types of scripts that can be used in the Windows settings container of User Configuration settings and Computer Configuration settings: startup/shutdown and logon/logoff. Startup/shutdown runs the script when the computer starts or shuts down, whereas logon/logoff runs when a user logs on or off. Any ActiveX scripting language can be used to create these scripts. The scripts execute from top to bottom in the hierarchy, and the order of execution can be controlled through the Properties dialog box. Windows 2000 executes the start-up script before the log-on script, and it executes the shut-down script after the log-off script. The timeout limit for processing scripts is 600 seconds (10 minutes), so if the script takes longer than this to process, this default timeout value will need to be adjusted. This is done through a software policy.

QUESTIONS

10.01: Planning Groups

1. You have just become the new network administrator of a Windows 2000 network. When users who are members of the Finance organizational unit log on to the network, a script runs that modifies the behavior of their desktops. You do not want this script to run, but upon checking group policies associated

with the OU, you find that no group policy is running this script. What is causing this script to run?

A. GPOs are cumulative, so there is probably a legacy GPO from a previous Windows NT installation that is being run. Check the SAM database.

B. GPOs are noncumulative. Since there is no script being run through the GPO associated with the Finance OU, then there must be a script being run on the machines these users are logging in to.

C. GPOs are cumulative, so there are probably nonlocal GPOs on the user's computer that are being applied.

D. GPOs are cumulative, so there are probably GPOs associated above or below the Finance OU that are being applied.

2. **Current Situation:** You have recently upgraded your single domain network to Windows 2000, and you have decided to use group policy settings to control user and computer configurations. Using GPOs, you want to modify log-on and log-off operations for all network users, and you want to control offline files. You have also decided to control the installation of a new program used by members of the Sales OU.

Required Result: Control log-on and log-off operations of network users by applying the GPO at the domain level.

Optional Desired Results:

1. Modify software installation settings for the program used by the Sales OU.

2. Control network settings for offline files.

Proposed Solution: Modify software installation settings in the Windows settings. Modify log-on and log-off operations through Administrative templates. Control network settings for offline files through the Software settings.

What results are produced from the proposed solution?

A. The proposed solution produces the required result only.

B. The proposed solution produces the required result and only one of the optional results.

C. The proposed solution produces the required result and both of the optional results.

D. The proposed solution does not produce the required result.

3. You have decided to create scripts using an ActiveX scripting language. In deciding how these scripts will run, which of the following should you be aware of?

   A. Log-on scripts will run before a start-up script.

   B. ActiveX scripting languages cannot be executed through a GPO.

   C. Shut-down scripts will run before a log-off script.

   D. Log-on scripts will run after a start-up script.

4. You have written a script to run when the user logs on to a Windows 2000 machine. Each time the user logs on, however, the script runs part of the way through and then stops. You open the properties and see what appears in the illustration below. How will you fix this problem? (Choose all that apply.)

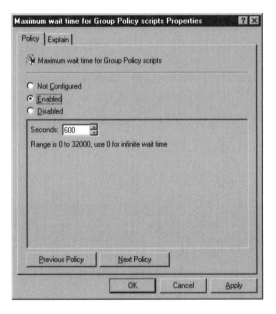

   A. Decrease the value.

   B. Increase the value.

   C. Keep the value the same.

   D. Change the value to 0.

Planning Group Policy Object Management

Identifying business needs is where planning GPO management starts. The planning process will require meetings with individual groups and identification of specific needs. During this planning, you will need to look at the benefits of groups and organizational units to simplifying the creation and maintenance of GPOs. A group is a collection of users, computers, contacts, and other groups. Groups can be used as security or as email distribution collections. Distribution groups are used only for email, whereas security groups are used both to grant access to resources and as email distribution lists. Organizational units are logical containers into which you can place users, groups, computers, and other organizational units. Organizational units allow you to refine the process of applying policies. Some policies can be applied only at the domain or individual system level, but not at the OU level. Also, through linking, one OU can use policies from another OU, but an OU from one domain cannot be used in another domain.

Group Policy Objects are created on the basis of the settings they contain. There are three common designs that can be used when planning GPOs: single policy type, multiple policy type, and dedicated policy type. Single policy types are used to apply a single type of setting, such as those dealing with security. With the single policy type design, a single policy is created for software, another policy for security, and so forth. Read/write access is then given to users who administer the GPO. Multiple policy types are used to apply multiple types of settings, such as those dealing with security and scripts. A dedicated policy type is devoted to settings for either computer configuration or a user configuration. Computer configuration settings are placed in one GPO, and user configuration settings are placed in a separate GPO.

GPO design can be either layered or monolithic. With a layered strategy, as few GPOs as possible are used to contain specific settings. When changes are required, a minimal number of GPOs need modification. A base GPO is created at the domain level, containing basic settings for all users and computers. Additional GPOs are created below this, containing group-specific settings. With this type of structure, there are longer log-on times for users. With a monolithic design, one GPO, or as few as necessary, is used for any user or computer. All policies for a site, domain, or OU are contained in one GPO. Although this makes administration more difficult, it results in shorter log-on times.

Change management is an important part of planning GPO management. Not only members of your project team should be kept up to date on one another's progress, but you should also involve all levels of end users. It is important to interact with other members of IT staff so that you can fully understand the services your network provides. You will also need to work with end users when planning GPOs in order to fully identify specific needs. These needs are then cross-referenced to specific user and computer policies. This will allow you to identify the groups of users that policies will be planned for, as well as geographic locations which will be used in planning computer groups and organizational units (OUs).

Group policies can be used with Windows Installer Packages to deploy software to groups and computers throughout your network. The packages are stored as files with the .MSI extension, and they allow you to change registry settings, add Windows components, modify short-cut configurations, install Windows services, and change file-type configurations. To deploy an application that does not have an .MSI file provided by the vendor, you could create a .ZAP file. A .ZAP file is a text-based file that is similar to the unattended text files of the original Windows NT operating system. Using these files, you can use group policies to introduce all applications, patches, and updates.

Policies are applied in the following order: local GPOs, site GPOs, domain GPOs, and OU GPOs. Local GPOs are stored on the local computer, and every Windows 2000 computer has one. Site GPOs are GPOs that are linked to the site, and processing of these is synchronous. The administrator specifies the order in which site GPOs are processed. Domain GPOs are multiple domain linked GPOs. Like site GPOs, they are processed synchronously, with the administrator specifying the order of processing. OU GPOs are GPOs linked to OUs, and they are processed starting with the parent OU, followed by child OUs. GPOs linked to the OU containing the user or computer are processed last. If more than one GPO is linked to an OU, they are processed synchronously with the administrator specifying the order.

When planning Group Policy Object management, it is important to remember the following points:

- Some of the steps involved in policy planning are as follows: define the needs of your organization or company; use groups and organizational units to simplify the creation and maintenance of GPOs; identify multilevel effects of the implementation of GPOs; and plan for change management.

■ The planning process will require meetings with individual groups (these will probably become your global group configurations) and identification of specific needs.

■ A group is a collection of users, computers, contacts, and other groups. Groups can be used as security or as email distribution collections. Distribution groups are used only for email. Security groups are used both to grant access to resources and as email distribution lists.

■ Organizational units are logical containers into which you can place users, groups, computers, and other organizational units. An organizational unit can contain objects only from its parent domain. It is the smallest scope to which you can apply a Group Policy or delegate authority.

■ We must know in detail the order in which policies are applied. This order is as follows: (1) The local GPO; (2) Site GPOs; (3) Domain GPOs.

■ The OU GPOs are applied starting with the parent OU and proceeding through child OUs. If there are multiple GPOs for a site, domain, or OU, the administrator can specify the order of application.

exam
ⓦatch   *Although there is a default order to processing Group Policy settings, it is important to remember the exceptions to this order. If a computer is not part of a network or is a member of a workgroup, then only the local GPO is processed. If a GPO that is linked to a site, domain, or OU is set to No Override, then none of its settings can be overridden. If more than one GPO in the hierarchy is set to No Override, then the highest GPO takes precedence. Block Policy Inheritance is applied directly to a site, domain, or OU to block policies inherited from other sites, domains, OUs, or higher in the AD hierarchy. If No Override is set, then inherited settings cannot be blocked. Finally, the loopback setting is often used in highly controlled environments. When enabled, the loopback setting can be configured to Replace or Merge. Replace is used to replace the GPO list with a list already obtained when the computer started. Merge combines the GPO list obtained at startup with the GPO list obtained when the user logged on.*

QUESTIONS

10.02: Planning Group Policy Object Management

5. You are concerned that policy settings are overwriting other settings for a particular user. The computer this user is working on is part of a workgroup that is separate from the domain. The computer has recently been upgraded to Windows 2000. In troubleshooting this problem, you need to know in what order policies are applied. Which of the following is true?

   A. The local GPO is applied first, so it may be overwritten by the GPOs linked to the site, domain, or OUs.

   B. The local GPO is applied last, so it may be overwriting nonlocal GPOs.

   C. Windows 2000 computers do not have a local GPO. Only nonlocal GPOs are used on a Windows 2000 Active Directory network.

   D. Only the local GPO is processed because it is a member of a workgroup.

6. You have decided to create a single GPO for all user configuration settings, and another GPO for all computer configuration settings. What policy type are you planning to create?

   A. Single policy type

   B. Multiple policy type

   C. Dedicated policy type

   D. Monopolic policy type

7. **Current Situation:** You are network administrator for a college campus. This is a demanding environment that requires controlling user and computer settings. Unfortunately, the IT Department is severely understaffed. You have

decided to ease administrative workload by deploying software to groups and computers throughout your network, but no files were supplied by the vendor to be used with Windows Installer. To keep in contact with users and control access, you would like to create a group to grant access to resources and act as email distribution lists. Also, when students log on to the network, you want to control their settings. You would like the GPO list obtained at startup to be merged with the GPO list obtained when the user logs on.

Required Result: Create a file that will be used to deploy software to groups and computers throughout the network.

Optional Desired Results:

1. Control the environment so that the GPO list obtained when the computer starts is merged with the GPO list obtained when the user logs on.

2. Implement a method to grant groups of users access to resources and act as email distribution lists.

Proposed Solution: Create a .ZAP file to deploy the software. Use the loopback setting and configure it to Merge so that the GPO list obtained at startup is merged with the GPO list obtained when the user logs on. Create a security group to grant access to resources and act as email distribution lists.

What results are produced from the proposed solution?

A. The proposed solution produces the required result only.

B. The proposed solution produces the required result and only one of the optional results.

C. The proposed solution produces the required result and both of the optional results.

D. The proposed solution does not produce the required result.

8. You have set Block Policy Inheritance directly to an OU to block policies inherited from sites, domains, or OUs that are higher in the AD hierarchy. It has come to your attention that policies are not being blocked. You check the

properties of the site and view the information shown in the following illustration. What is wrong?

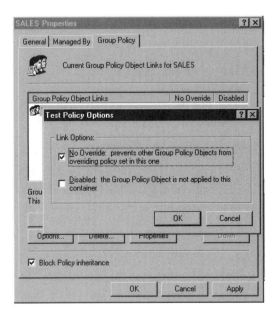

A. Block Policy Inheritance is not set.

B. Block Policy Inheritance is set.

C. No Override is set.

D. No Override is not set.

TEST YOURSELF OBJECTIVE 10.03

Understanding Computer Policies

Computer policies are group policies that are used to apply computer configuration settings. They allow control of networks via computers within representative groups. Because the policies are applied to computers, these settings are applied regardless of who logs on to the machine. The settings are applied when the operating system starts.

As mentioned earlier, computer policies are broken into three sections: Software settings, Windows settings, and Administrative templates. We discussed how these sections relate to computer configuration settings. The settings allow administrators to set and enforce password log-on policies, write custom start-up and shut-down scripts, activate specific Kerberos policy, and utilize Administrative templates that allow for ease of configuration that will affect system, network, and printer use. You can also set up detailed audit policies that can be viewed later through the security log. The implementation of computer-based GPOs should take into consideration the type of system that will be impacted: workstation, server controller, or terminal server.

In understanding computer policies, it is important to remember the following points:

■ Computer policies are the GPOs that allow control of our networks as they relate to computers within representative groups.

■ Computer policies allow network administrators to gain control of their network resources based on individual PCs or groups of PCs.

■ Group policies for computers are broken into three sections: Software settings, Windows settings, and Administrative templates.

■ With computer policies, network administrators are able to do the following: set and enforce password log-on policies (only once per domain); write custom start-up and shut-down scripts; activate specific Kerberos policy (only once per domain); and set up detailed audit policies.

exam
Ⓦatㄷh

It is important that you be familiar with computer and user configuration settings available through group policy. Some settings may seem like they should be user configuration settings, but they are actually computer configuration settings. Computer configuration settings allow you to control user interface settings, such as the ability to use the Run command on the start menu or the bitmap used as the desktop background. It is also vital that you remember that these policies are applied to the computer, regardless of who logs on to the machine.

QUESTIONS

10.03: Understanding Computer Policies

9. You are planning to use computer policies to manage computers on your network. Which of the following can be controlled and managed through computer policies? (Choose all that apply.)

    A. Internet Explorer Maintenance

    B. Folder Redirection

    C. Activation of specific Kerberos policy

    D. Setting detailed audit policies

10. You are creating a group policy to configure the computer configuration settings. When a user sits at the computer this policy applies to, turns it on, and logs on, what will happen?

    A. The computer configuration settings will be applied when the operating system starts.

    B. The computer configuration settings will be applied when the user logs on the computer.

    C. The computer configuration settings will be applied when the user shuts down the computer. The settings will take effect the next time the user logs on.

    D. The computer configuration settings will not be applied because only user configuration settings can be applied to a computer.

11. **Current Situation:** Users have been downloading programs from the Internet at home and then bringing them in to work. They start these

applications through the Run command on the Start menu, which has resulted in several viruses being activated. You want to control the user interface so that this command no longer appears on the Start menu. You also want to enable group policy settings so that you can view the events at a later time. There are a number of other policies you plan to implement. After you have created a plan, a coworker criticizes it, stating that you did not consider that the GPOs you will create would impact other computer systems, such as terminal servers.

Required Result: Use group policy to control the user interface so that the Run command is no longer available.

Optional Desired Results:

1. Determine where events logged through auditing will be viewed at a later time.

2. Determine whether your plan will need to be revised to consider different computer types.

Proposed Solution: Modify user configuration settings so that the Run command on the Start menu is not available. View events logged through auditing using the security log. All computers are impacted in the same way by computer policies, so there is no need to revise your plan.

What results are produced from the proposed solution?

A. The proposed solution produces the required result only.

B. The proposed solution produces the required result and only one of the optional results.

C. The proposed solution produces the required result and both of the optional results.

D. The proposed solution does not produce the required result.

12. As shown in the following illustration, you have decided to set disk quota limits for all volumes on a Windows 2000 server. You add a new user and perform a

test to see if the new quotas work. Later that day, you find that existing users are not affected by the disk quota limits. What is the problem?

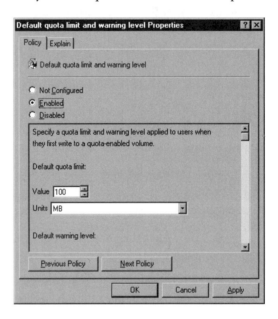

A. The users need to log on to the network for disk quotas to take effect.

B. The users are saving to a different NTFS volume on this server than the one to which this policy was applied.

C. The default quota limit has already been reached by the users.

D. This policy will be applied only to new users, not current ones.

TEST YOURSELF OBJECTIVE 10.04

Planning Policy Management for Users

User policies are group policies that are used to apply user configuration settings. They allow control of networks via users within representative groups. Because the policies are applied to users, these settings are applied regardless of what machine a user logs on to. The settings are applied when the user logs on the machine.

We saw earlier in this chapter that there are a number of settings that are common to both users and computers; however, there are a number of settings that are only for user configuration. User policies are broken into three sections: Software settings, Windows settings, and Administrative templates. The Administrative Template settings available for user configuration are registry-based GPO settings that allow you to control a user's Start menu, taskbar, desktop, and Control Panel. The Start Menu & Taskbar settings control the Windows Start menu and taskbar of a user, whereas the Desktop settings are used to control the behavior of the Windows desktop. Control Panel settings are used to control what applets in the Control Panel are available to the user.

There are additional Windows settings available for user configuration. These additional group policy settings consist of Internet Explorer Maintenance, Remote Installation Services, and Folder Redirection. Internet Explorer Maintenance is used to manage and customize IE on Windows 2000 computers. Folder Redirection is used to redirect folders. Folders like My Documents, Application Data, Desktop, and Start menu can be redirected from the default profile location to a centralized location on the network where they can be managed. Remote Installation Services is used to control installation of software on remote machines and can also be used to deploy software packages.

By distributing software through group policy, network processes are centralized in an automated, controlled manner. A primary benefit of this is that the network's total cost of ownership is reduced. When deploying software through group policy, packages are created which include all of the necessary files to fully install an application. Software can be distributed either by assigning applications to users or computers, or by publishing them to users.

When planning policy management for users, you should keep the following points in mind:

- When implementing a distribution process, the network administrator will create what is known as a package.
- A package will include all of the necessary files to fully install an application. Software applications can be either published or assigned.
- Packages can be assigned to a computer or a user.
- Publishing a software package causes the software to appear in the Add/Remove Programs applet, not in the Start menu.

■   When software is published to a user, the application will be available the next
time the user logs on to Windows 2000 Professional.

*Applications can be published or assigned to users. Packages to be assigned to
users are made available for installation using the Windows Installer package.
When software is assigned to a user, the application will be available the next
time the user logs on. Publishing software packages results in the software
appearing in the Add/Remove Programs applet, not in the Start menu. The
package can then be installed either through Add/Remove Programs, or by
attempting to launch an associated file type. A disadvantage of publishing
packages, as opposed to assigning them, is that once an application is deleted,
it will not be automatically reinstalled. Publishing an application places more of
the responsibility of software management on the user than does assigning.*

*When an application is assigned to a computer, the application is advertised
and installed when the computer starts up or when it is safe to do so. It is
important that there be no competing processes when installation occurs.*

QUESTIONS

10.04: Planning Policy Management for Users

Questions 13–15   The next three questions are based upon the scenario that
follows. Read the following case study, and then answer the questions. You
may refer to this case study and illustration as often as needed.

You have recently upgraded your network to Windows 2000 Active Directory.
To control the behavior of users' desktops, you have decided to implement
GPOs. You plan to publish software to users so that the software appears in the
Add/Remove Programs applet. To configure group policy, you open Microsoft

Management Console with the Group Policy snap-in, as shown in the illustration below.

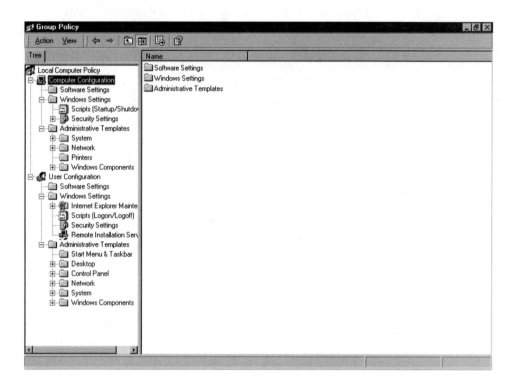

13. After installing an application that has been published to a user, the user decides he does not need it anymore and deletes it. Later he calls you, stating that he realizes he still needs the application, and he asks how he can reinstall it. How can the user reinstall the application?

A. Launch a file associated with the application.

B. Start the application by selecting it from the Start menu.

C. Reinstall the application through the Add/Remove Programs applet.

D. Do nothing; the application will automatically reinstall the next time the user logs on.

14. As shown in the previous illustration, user policies are broken into three sections: Software settings, Windows settings, and Administrative templates. In which of these sections would you modify registry-based GPO settings to control a user's Start menu, taskbar, desktop, and Control Panel?

    A. Software settings.

    B. Windows settings.

    C. Administrative template.

    D. None. You can control this only through computer policies.

15. When user policy settings are configured, when will they be applied?

    A. When the computer starts

    B. When the user logs on a specific computer

    C. When the user logs on any computer in the company

    D. When the user logs off any computer in the company

16. **Current Situation:** The Human Resources, Finance, and Administration Departments of your company have contacted you regarding installation of software. After some discussion with the managers of these departments, you have decided to deploy software using group policy. For the Human Resources Department, all users will need to use the software. Users in this department are not experienced with installing programs themselves. For the Finance Department, only certain users will require the applications, and these users are familiar with installing software themselves. The software for Administration is being used to evaluate employees. It should be available only on computers in that department so that there is some supervision of what is being entered. It should not matter who logs on these computers in the Administration Department.

    Required Result: Make the software available for installation the next time users in Human Resources log on. The method should make installation as easy as possible.

    Optional Desired Results:

    1. Make the Finance software available for installation by the users themselves.

2.   Devise a method so that the Administration software is available only to
     computers in that department.

Proposed Solution: Assign applications to users in the Human Resources OU.
Publish software to users in the Finance OU and the Administration OU.

What results are produced from the proposed solution?

A.   The proposed solution produces the required result only.

B.   The proposed solution produces the required result and only one of the
     optional results.

C.   The proposed solution produces the required result and both of the
     optional results.

D.   The proposed solution does not produce the required result.

LAB QUESTION

Objectives 10.01–10.04

You are planning GPOs for use with the Active Directory network. You decide to use MMC with the Group Policy snap-in to create group policies that will be applied to users and computers. One of a number of policies you want to create will deal with customizing IE on Windows 2000 computers. Another policy will control installation of software on remote machines. You want to set group policy to the mode that will allow you to add snap-ins and adjust all of the available MMC options. In planning a GPO, you decide to create a single policy for each type of setting.

1. What mode will you use for MMC with the Group Policy snap-in to work as stated above?

2. What policy type are you planning to use?

3. What type of access should you give the users who administer the GPO?

4. Where would you configure the settings to modify and customize IE on Windows 2000 computers?

5. Where would you configure settings to control installation of software on machines?

A QUICK ANSWER KEY

Objective 10.01

1. D
2. A
3. D
4. B and D

Objective 10.02

5. D
6. C
7. C
8. C

Objective 10.03

9. C and D
10. A
11. D
12. D

Objective 10.04

13. C
14. C
15. C
16. B

IN-DEPTH ANSWERS

10.01: Planning Groups

1. ☑ **D.** GPOs are cumulative, so there are probably GPOs associated above or below the Finance OU that are being applied. GPOs are applied to a user or computer in a hierarchical fashion, which means that the settings from each level are added together.

    ☒ **A** is incorrect because GPOs were not used in Windows NT and are not stored in the SAM database. **B** is incorrect because GPOs are cumulative. **C** is incorrect because the local GPO is stored on a Windows 2000 machine, whereas nonlocal GPOs are stored in Active Directory.

2. ☑ **A.** The proposed solution produces the required result only. You can modify log-on and log-off operations through the System container in Administrative templates. By applying this GPO at the domain level, all users in this single domain network will be affected by the policy.

    ☒ **B, C,** and **D** are incorrect because the proposed solution produces the required result only. Software installation settings are controlled through Software settings, and network settings for offline files are controlled through Administrative templates.

3. ☑ **D.** Log-on scripts will run after start-up scripts. Log-on scripts run when the user logs on, whereas start-up scripts run when the operating system initializes.

    ☒ **A** is incorrect because start-up scripts will run before log-on scripts. **B** is incorrect because any ActiveX scripting language can be used. **C** is incorrect because log-off scripts will run before shut-down scripts.

4. ☑ **B** and **D** are correct. This problem indicates that the timeout value is being reached. To solve the problem, you must increase the wait time for group policy scripts. The default value is 600, but it can be increased up to a value of 32000 to provide additional time for the script to process. Changing the value to 0 will set an infinite wait time so that the script will never time out.

    ☒ **A** is incorrect because this would give less time to process the script. **C** is incorrect because keeping the same value would not solve the problem.

10.02: Planning Group Policy Object Management

5. ☑ **D.** If a computer is not part of a network or is a member of a workgroup, then only the local GPO is processed.

   ☒ **A** is incorrect because the other GPOs would not overwrite the local GPO, since it is part of a workgroup. **B** is incorrect because the local GPO would not overwrite nonlocal GPOs, since the nonlocal GPOs are processed after the local GPO. **C** is incorrect because every Windows 2000 computer has a local GPO.

6. ☑ **C.** Dedicated policy type. This type of policy attempts to include all user configuration settings in one group policy, and all computer configuration settings in another separate policy.

   ☒ **A** is incorrect because single policy types are used to apply a single type of setting, such as those dealing with security. With the single policy type, a single policy is created for software, another for security, and so forth. **B** is incorrect because multiple policy types are used to apply multiple types of settings, such as those dealing with security and scripts. **D** is incorrect because there is no such thing as a monopolic policy type.

7. ☑ **C.** The proposed solution produces the required result and both of the optional results. Security groups are used both to grant access to resources and as email distribution lists. The loopback setting is useful in controlled environments and can be configured to Merge in order to combine the GPO list obtained at startup with the GPO list obtained when the user logs on. To deploy an application that does not have a .MSI file provided by the vendor, a .ZAP file must be created.

   ☒ **A**, **B**, and **D** are incorrect because the proposed solution produces the required result and both of the optional results.

8. ☑ **C.** No Override is set. The No Override setting prevents other GPOs from overriding policies set to sites, domains, and OUs. Block Policy Inheritance is applied directly to a site, domain, or OU to block policies inherited from other sites, domains, OUs, or higher in the AD hierarchy. However, if No Override is set, inherited settings cannot be blocked.

   ☒ **A** and **B** are incorrect because Block Policy Inheritance is set, so this is not causing the problem. **D** is incorrect because No Override is set.

10.03: Understanding Computer Policies

9. ☑ **C** and **D** are correct. Computer configuration settings can be used to set detailed audit policies and Activate specific Kerberos policy.

   ☒ **A** and **B** are incorrect because Internet Explorer Maintenance and Folder Redirection are available only through user configuration settings.

10. ☑ **A.** Computer configuration settings are applied to computers when the operating system starts. It does not matter which user logs on the computer.

   ☒ **B** is incorrect because user configuration settings, not computer configuration settings, are applied to users when they log on the computer. **C** is incorrect for this same reason. It is also incorrect because settings are not applied when the computer shuts down. **D** is incorrect because computer configuration settings are applied to the computer.

11. ☑ **D.** The proposed solution does not produce the required result. Although user interface settings are being affected, the Run command is a computer configuration setting, not a user configuration setting.

   ☒ **A, B**, and **C** are incorrect because the proposed solution does not produce the required result. When auditing is enabled through Group Policy settings, the events are displayed in the security log. The implementation of computer-based GPOs should take into consideration the type of system that will be impacted: workstation, server controller, or terminal server.

12. ☑ **D.** The Default Quota Limit and Warning Level applies to new users as they write to the volume, but it does not affect disk quota limits for current users or customized settings for individual users.

   ☒ **A** is incorrect because this policy will affect only new users as they write to the volume. It will not affect current users. **B** is incorrect because this policy applies to all NTFS volumes on the server. **C** is incorrect because this policy does not affect current users.

10.04: Planning Policy Management for Users

13. ☑ **C.** Reinstall the application through the Add/Remove Programs applet. When a software package is published, it will appear in the Add/Remove

Programs applet. After the application is assigned, if it is deleted, it will not be automatically reinstalled.

☒ **A** is incorrect because an application that has been published to a user will not be reinstalled automatically by launching a file that is associated with the application. **B** is incorrect because when an application is published to a user, it appears in Add/Remove Programs, not in the Start menu. **D** is incorrect because the application will not automatically be reinstalled.

14. ☑ **C.** Administrative template settings allow you to configure registry-based GPO settings. This allows you to control a user's Start menu, taskbar, desktop, and Control Panel.

☒ **A** and **B** are incorrect because neither of these is used to control registry-based settings. **D** is incorrect because you can control registry-based GPO settings through the Administrative template settings.

15. ☑ **C.** When the user logs on. The user configuration settings are applied to users when they log on the computer. It does not matter which computer they log on to.

☒ **A** is incorrect because computer configuration settings, not user settings, are applied to computers when the operating system starts. **B** is incorrect because the policies are applied to the user; it does not matter which computer the person logs on to. **D** is incorrect because the user configuration settings are applied when the user logs on, not when he or she logs off.

16. ☑ **B.** The proposed solution produces the required result and only one of the optional results. Applications can be published or assigned to users. When assigned to a user, the application is made available the next time he or she logs on. It is made available for installation using the Windows Installer package. When published to a user, the software appears in the Add/Remove Programs applet. It can be installed either through Add/Remove Programs or by attempting to launch an associated file type.

☒ **A, C,** and **D** are incorrect because the proposed solution produces the required result and only one of the optional results. The needs described for the Administration department indicate that applications should be assigned to computers, not users. When applications are assigned to computers, it does not matter which user logs on the computer. The application will be available to all users of that computer.

LAB ANSWER

Objectives 10.01–10.04

1. Author mode. The Author mode allows you to add snap-ins and adjust all of the available MMC options. The other mode available is User mode, which allows you to work within the snap-in selections that exist in the MMC.

2. Single policy type. Single policy types are used to apply a single type of setting, such as those dealing with security. With single policy types, a single policy is created for software, another for security, and so forth.

3. Read/write access is required by any users who will administer the GPO.

4. In the Windows settings of User Configuration settings, you would use Internet Explorer Maintenance to manage and customize IE on Windows 2000 computers.

5. In the Windows Settings of User Configuration settings, you would use Remote Installation Services to control installation of software on remote machines. This can also be used to deploy software packages.

MCSE

MICROSOFT CERTIFIED SYSTEMS ENGINEER

11

Designing a Directory Service Architecture

TEST YOURSELF OBJECTIVES

A s we have seen in previous chapters, Active Directory represents the logical structure of an enterprise network, allowing you to organize the structure along departmental or hierarchical lines. However, sites are representative of the physical aspects of the network and are independent of the logical Active Directory structure. A site is one or more domain controllers (DCs) and other computers located on a TCP/IP subnet. A site will generally follow the boundaries of physical network segments. However, sites may be comprised of multiple subnets and contain computers from multiple domains.

Since sites provide a physical representation, site design relies on proper planning in terms of your network architecture design. The architecture will affect server response times, optimization of log-on validations, and Active Directory replication. Site designs can be changed without the knowledge of users, so a good design is vital to your Active Directory implementation.

Designing an Active Directory Site Topology

Designing Active Directory site topology includes identifying the physical locations that are part of the network, defining sites from those locations, and determining how the network is segmented into TCP/IP subnets. Generally, sites will map to subnets that form a LAN structure. Sites relate to the physical characteristics of a network, rather than logical aspects, and generally have the same boundaries as a local area network. Because they are not limited by logical structures imposed by AD, sites can contain domain controllers from multiple domains. DCs for a single domain can exist on many different sites depending on the physical and logical requirements of a company.

It is important that sites are well connected. Subnets comprising sites should have fast, inexpensive, and reliable connections. Microsoft recommends the network connections be at least 512 Kbps, with 128 Kbps or higher of available bandwidth. The need for this speed relates to the primary tasks that sites perform: authentication and replication.

Authentication occurs when a user logs on to a Windows 2000 domain. A domain controller is sought out to validate the username and password. Windows 2000 will always look first in the site containing the client computer in order to keep intersite network communications to a minimum. This makes the log-on procedure as fast as possible by ensuring it is carried out by a computer with fast connections to the client.

Replication is a process whereby changes to information in AD are replicated to other domain controllers. DCs in the same site will replicate changed information to each other quickly and automatically. Replication can be configured to occur at certain times and in such a manner that changes only, rather than the entire Active Directory, are replicated to domain controllers outside of the site. Administrators can also set up multiple redundant links to ensure replication will take place in the event of a failure. Replication can occur between DCs in the same site, which is called "intrasite replication," or between DCs in different sites, which is called "intersite replication." Intersite replication, either through IP or Simple Mail Transfer Protocol (SMTP), supports data compression to minimize impact on WAN communications. Intrasite replication does not support compression.

Another advantage to using sites is employing Active Directory services like the Windows 2000 Distributed File System (DFS). DFS allows file shares that are spread across the network on different computers to appear in a single directory tree. This makes file and folder objects distributed across a number of servers appear as if they are stored in one common location. Such Active Directory services can be made site-aware, and they will allow client computers to access files from different servers when they connect to different sites, removing any necessity to connect to a specified universal naming convention (UNC) sharename over slow WAN links.

Site structures are also useful when deploying Windows 2000 Professional clients using Remote Installation Services (RIS). RIS operates by a client computer with either a remote-boot ROM or a RIS boot disk requesting an IP address through the Dynamic Host Configuration Protocol (DHCP) service. RIS servers will offer their own IP addresses as part of the log-on process, and those in the same site will be accepted in preference.

When designing an Active Directory site topology, it is important to remember the following points:

- A site consists of at least one DC and other computers linked by fast, inexpensive, and reliable connections, and it is typically a LAN topology.

- Sites should be associated with at least one physical subnet.

- Sites are not restrained by the logical structure of Active Directory, and they can cut across groups and organizational units.

exam
ⓦatch

In designing an Active Directory topology, it is important to remember that sites are associated with at least one physical subnet. A subnet can be looked at as a mini-network because it is a portion of a network and generally a physically separate network segment. A subnet shares a network address with the rest of the network but is distinguished as being separate by a subnet number. This information is used by computers to find a domain controller in the same site. Computers are assigned to sites based on their location in one or more subnets which groups them based on their proximity to one another. This allows client computers to find DCs in the same site so they can be quickly authenticated. It is also used during replication to find the fastest route between DCs.

QUESTIONS

11.01: Designing an Active Directory Site Topology

Questions 1–3 The following three questions are based on the scenario that follows. You may refer to this scenario as often as necessary.

You are designing a Windows 2000 Active Directory network for a company that is located in a large city. The business is spread across three buildings. Each building is currently a different subnet, and you have already decided to keep this the same when designing subnets. Each subnet will become a site, and there is one domain controller at each site. Building A is connected to Building B with a 10-Mbps line, whereas Building B is connected to Building C with a 512-Kbps connection. Building C is connected to Building A with a 128-Kbps connection.

1. There is some concern about the current speed of connectivity between these buildings, but keeping costs down to a minimum is essential. What is the minimum speed required for fast connections between the sites so that communication between sites is effective?

   A. 64 Kbps.

   B. 512 Kbps.

   C. 10 Mbps.

   D. Any speed will work effectively.

2. What features are available to decrease network traffic during replication between domain controllers within the same site? (Choose all that apply.)

   A. Data compression

   B. Scheduling

   C. Incremental replication of Active Directory

   D. Full replication of Active Directory

3. There are some performance concerns regarding how users will be able to log on to the network over these slow connections. IT staff is also concerned about redundancy. When a client computer attempts to log on to the domain but the only DC in the site is down, how will your design deal with this?

   A. The only way to address redundancy issues would be to put multiple domain controllers in each site.

   B. The domain controller on the client's site will pass the request along the fastest connection to a domain controller on another site.

   C. The client will seek out the first domain controller it finds. If the domain controller on its site is down, it will seek out a domain controller on another site.

   D. By default, a client computer will authenticate to domain controllers on other sites first. This provides the fastest access to resources in other sites.

TEST YOURSELF OBJECTIVE 11.02

Defining Site Boundaries

When defining site boundaries, it is important to identify all locations where computers will be connecting. Since sites are associated with subnets, networks with existing subnets will often use them to define site boundaries. As well, since sites define sets of domain controllers, if a location requires a domain controller, it will generally become a site. This does not mean that you should allow the existing infrastructure to unduly influence your design. You should consider the impact existing subnets will have on the new design and whether existing subnets should continue to be used, merged, or dissolved.

Site boundaries should be kept inside fast connections. As mentioned in the previous section, computers within a site should have fast and permanent connections. It is advisable that these connections be 10 Mbps or higher, but the minimum that Microsoft recommends is 512 Kbps. It is important to remember that if there is no domain controller for a site, users will have to log on over WAN links. This means that the WAN link will require the bandwidth necessary to handle this traffic. In any situation, you will need to consider how the location is going to be connected to the network and what the speed of this connection will be. You will need to estimate the number of users who will be at the location and the impact of their logging on and accessing a (global catalog) GC server over slow links.

domain controllers (DCs) need to be able to authenticate users quickly, so sites should include at least one DC for every domain, with users located in that site. Although it is not a requirement for each site to have its own DC, it is advisable in many cases. If sites are connected to a DC via a slow WAN link, then logons will take a considerable amount of time, and if the link goes down, then users will be unable to log on at all. Multiple domain controllers should also be considered for fault tolerance. Although adding multiple domains will increase overhead, since more data will need to be replicated, it will allow users to log on to a DC in their own site even if one DC fails. If the domain controllers are within the same site boundary, they will replicate through intrasite replication, which needs no configuration by administrators.

Generally, a global catalog (GC) server should also be included in each site, since it is used to locate and use objects in Active Directory. Performance can suffer to an unacceptable level if GC queries are performed over slow WAN links. If it is implemented in a single domain, configuring all DCs as GC servers will make no difference to replication traffic. This is because the global catalog is a subset of the Active Directory, which DCs replicate. This being the case, DCs should also be configured as GC servers.

When defining site boundaries, you should always keep the following points in mind:

- Site boundaries should normally be kept inside fast connections with plenty of bandwidth and should not include slow WAN links.

- All DCs inside the same site boundary will replicate through intrasite replication which needs no configuration by administrators.

- Avoid placing several sites on a single LAN; this can increase the bandwidth usage and requires a greater investment in terms of servers and support.

Microsoft recommends that network connections be at least 512 Kbps, with 128 Kbps or higher of available bandwidth. However, when planning sites and site boundaries, it is important to view these as guidelines rather than hard and fast rules. If a small number of users are connected by a very fast, permanent connection, such as a T1 connection, users would not normally encounter problems with bandwidth. In such a case, each location may not need to be planned as a separate site so that users are authenticated by a local server or in order for them to use a local GC server.

It is also important to realize that a computer can belong to only one site. A computer with multiple network cards may have IP addresses relating to different sites, but the computer can belong to only one site.

QUESTIONS

11.02: Defining Site Boundaries

4. A company is upgrading to Windows 2000 Active Directory. The planned network will consist of two sites, shown in the following illustration. One site will have two domain controllers, and the other will have one domain controller. Each of these will also act as a global catalog server. Based on this information and the information in the illustration, what problems exist with the plan?

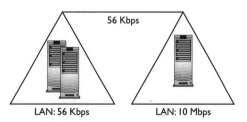

A. Sites making up a network need an equal number of domain controllers. The plan should have one domain controller in each site.

B. Each site can have only one global catalog server.

    C. Network connections for the WAN link and one of the LANs is too slow.

    D. There can be only one site per network.

5. You are configuring sites. On the network, there is a computer with multiple network cards. One card has an IP address relating to one site, and the other card has an IP address relating to another site. How many sites can this computer belong to?

    A. One.

    B. Two.

    C. Neither of the two sites.

    D. There is no limit to how many sites a computer can belong to.

6. **Current Situation:** A company has offices in several cities located in the same county. Recently, it has opened a new office in the same city as an existing site. This new office has a small staff and will be connected using an ISDN connection. New servers have been purchased which will run Windows 2000 Server. It has not been decided where these servers will be placed.

    Required Result: Determine how sites should be planned with the inclusion of the new office.

    Optional Desired Results:

    1. Determine the placement of the new domain controller.

    2. Determine the placement of a global catalog server.

    Proposed Solution: Make the office part of a nearby site so that users can authenticate by using domain controllers located at that site. Place the new server computer at the nearby site. Set this server up as a domain controller and global catalog server so that users can authenticate and browse the GC.

    What results are produced from the proposed solution?

    A. The proposed solution produces the required result only.

    B. The proposed solution produces the required result and only one of the optional results.

    C. The proposed solution produces the required result and both of the optional results.

    D. The proposed solution does not produce the required result.

Designing a Replication Strategy

As you will remember from previous chapters, replication is the sharing of information between domain controllers. All domain controllers in a domain are equal in Windows 2000 networks and require a complete read/write copy of the Active Directory. When a change is made to AD, the changes are replicated to other DCs so that each copy of the Active Directory is up to date. Sites help to define how and when replication occurs in a domain, because the site defines the physical topology.

Depending on the type of servers involved, three types of information may be replicated: schema, configuration, and domain information. Schema information relates to objects and the attributes that can be held in Active Directory. Configuration information defines the logical structure of the domain tree or forest. Domain information defines the objects in the domain. The schema and configuration information is replicated to all DCs in a domain tree or forest, whereas domain information is replicated to all global catalog servers on a domain specific basis.

Replication can take place between DCs in the same site (intrasite replication) and in different sites (intersite replication). For intrasite replication, Active Directory runs a process called the Knowledge Consistency Checker (KCC). The KCC generates a logical, two-way ring topology to replicate information and provide fault tolerance if a DC goes down. New connection objects can be added manually and replication can be forced, but the KCC can automatically perform this task and optimize replication. It periodically monitors the topology to check for efficiency and will automatically reconfigure it if a DC is removed or added. For large sites with a significant number of DCs, problems could result by replication cycles being created that take too long to move around the ring. To resolve this, the KCC creates additional connections between DCs so that it should never take an update more than three hops to reach every DC from the originating server.

Although replication within a site is automatic and requires no configuration, this is not the case with intersite replication. With intersite replication, a strategy is required to optimize replication. This strategy must take into consideration the amount of replication traffic generated and minimize its impact on the network. This is a tradeoff between making data as up to date as possible and increasing traffic. To control intersite replication, administrators can designate times that replication will take place, set frequency of replication update checks, and determine the network transport and connection to use.

For data to be replicated between sites, a link needs to be established between the sites. Site links allow computers in different sites to connect to one another and exchange replicated information, and these links are created by members of the Enterprise Admins group using Active Directory Sites and Services. The attributes of the site link allow you to control the frequency of replication, schedule when links are available for replication, and set the preferred order in which links are to be used.

When Active Directory is installed on the first domain controller of a site, the Active Directory Installation Wizard creates a default site object in the IP container called DEFAULTIPSITELINK. This object can be renamed and configured to suit your needs, and additional site links can be created separately. By default, these links are available for replication at any time, but their availability can be controlled. The frequency with which AD uses a connection to check for updates can also be controlled. The default value is 180 minutes, but you can set any frequency between 15 minutes and 10,080 minutes (i.e., seven days). If a connection is unavailable when a replication cycle comes due, replication will not take place.

Costs can be associated with links, but the actual figures are unimportant. The default value associated with a link is 100, but any link with a lower cost will be tried first. The costs associated should be assigned based on their actual bandwidth cost. For example, a dial-up connection or ISDN line should have a higher cost than a T1 line. Active Directory will always take the path associated with the smallest cost, as long as that path is available.

Replication can be configured to use either IP or SMTP. IP can be used for both intersite and intrasite replication, but SMTP is used only for replication across site links. SMTP is an asynchronous protocol and typically ignores schedules, so if the link is using SMTP replication, availability should not be configured.

Site links between more than two sites can be transitive if they are using the same transport protocol. Transitive transport is enabled or disabled using the Bridge All Site Links check box on the Properties sheet for the transport protocol (IP or SMTP). By default, all site links are bridged, creating a transitive trust between all site links, and enabling replication information to cross all the available links. In a fully routed network, no further configuration would be required, since all site links using the same transport would be included in the transitive bridge. If the network does not have IP routes between all sites, or if additional control is needed over replication traffic, the Bridge All Site Links check box can be cleared and site link bridges can be configured manually.

A single domain controller in a site can be designated as a bridgehead server, thereby becoming a single point of contact for replication to and from other sites. Ordinarily, all domain controllers are used in replicating information, but bridgehead servers allow replication between sites to be carried out by specific servers, which then use intrasite replication to keep the other servers in the site up to date. The first domain controller created in a site is the bridgehead server, but other servers can be configured to perform this role. Just as different transport protocols can have different bridgehead servers, IP and SMTP transports will not necessarily use the same DC as a bridgehead.

More than one DC can be designated as a preferred bridgehead server, but only one will be active at any given time. If intersite replication becomes due and the preferred bridgehead server is not available, the KCC will automatically designate another DC from the list of specified servers to be the bridgehead. If no preferred bridgehead server is available, it will designate another DC from the site. The designated server will be chosen by examining the globally unique identifiers (GUIDs) of all the available servers and selecting the one with the lowest number.

When designing a replication strategy, it is important to remember the following points:

- Intersite replication is one of the biggest consumers of bandwidth, so schedule replication availability for off-peak hours, if possible.

- You can choose which transport protocol to use for intersite replication, IP or SMTP. You should configure a CA server if you use SMTP.

- You can bridge all of the site links in the domain using the Bridge All Site Links check box in the transport protocol Properties sheet, or you can exercise more control over bridging by creating site link bridges.

exam
Watch

Directory replication is different from directory synchronization. Synchronization occurs when data needs to be replicated between different versions of directory services. In these cases, a software layer that is trusted by both versions is required to act as an agent between the two. A typical instance of synchronization would take place between Windows 2000 Active Directory and Novell's Directory Service, NDS. Directory replication takes place between Windows 2000 domain controllers. It requires identical schemas to be present and occurs after changes are made to Active Directory. In Windows 2000, multimaster replication is used. All domain controllers are equal, and there are no primary domain controllers or backup domain controllers as seen in Windows NT. All DCs replicate information on one another, and any contradictory information is reconciled by the use of Update Sequence Numbers (USNs). USNs are maintained by every server and used by DCs to determine which updates to replicate to other domain controllers. When two updates conflict, they are resolved by a stamp that contains the version number of the object or attribute, the time, and the GUID of the DC that did the originating write.

QUESTIONS

11.03: Designing a Replication Strategy

7. You have several sites on your network. One site link uses a T1 connection, and the other uses an ISDN connection. The link using the T1 connection has a cost of 100 associated with it. Upon checking the costs associated with the other link, you find what is shown in the following illustration. When replication occurs, which link will be used over the other?

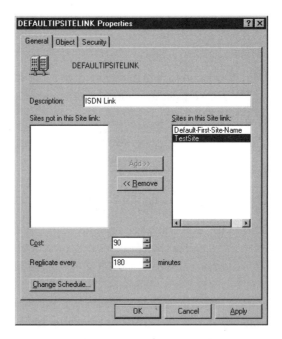

A. The T1 link.

B. The ISDN link.

C. Neither.

D. Both will be used equally.

8. **Current Situation:** A domain contains several sites, and you want to implement replication between all of them. To do this, you need to decide on the transport protocol that will be used for replication. You ask a new member of the IT staff to create a site link between two of these sites. This user is only a member of the Users group and has not been given additional access. When the user attempts creating the site link, he finds he cannot.

   Required Result: Determine why the user cannot configure site links.

   Optional Desired Results:

   1. Implement Active Directory replication between all sites.

   2. Decide on a transport protocol to be used for replication across site links.

   Proposed Solution: Add the user to the Enterprise Admins group and have him use Active Directory Sites and Services to create the site link. Configure site links involving all of the sites, and ensure that the Bridge All Site Links option is selected in the Transport Properties sheet. Select IP as the transport protocol to be used across site links.

   What results are produced from the proposed solution?

   A. The proposed solution produces the required result only.

   B. The proposed solution produces the required result and only one of the optional results.

   C. The proposed solution produces the required result and both of the optional results.

   D. The proposed solution does not produce the required result.

TEST YOURSELF OBJECTIVE 11.04

Defining a Schema Modification Policy

The schema is a repository for object classes and object attributes making up Active Directory. It is a list of definitions which define the kind of objects and object attributes that can be stored in AD. In other words, the schema defines what attributes an object must contain and may contain. Although the default schema will have enough object classes and attributes to suit the needs of most networks, it can be extended. If a user is a member of the Schema Admins group, Microsoft Management Console (MMC) can be used to create, modify, or deactivate object classes or attributes. Such changes to the schema can also be done programmatically by running a script through the Active Directory Services Interface (ADSI). Schema Admins is a Universal group located in the root domain of the forest, and by default, only the Administrator account from the root domain is a member of this group. If an application is Active Directory aware and installed by a member of the Schema Admins group, the application can create object classes and attributes during installation.

Modifications to the schema will affect every DC throughout the enterprise. The entire forest has only one schema, and changes are replicated to every tree and domain within it. Since schema information is hierarchical, and since classes and auxiliary classes use attribute inheritance, changing a class may impact other classes. Some changes are irreversible because classes and attributes cannot be removed from the schema, but must be disabled. Once a class type is deactivated, objects of that class type cannot be created until it is reactivated. Consequently, it is important that changes not be made arbitrarily and that no changes be made without making sure of the readiness for the proposed changes. It is also important that one person be designated to modify a class at any given time. If two people attempt to modify the schema at the same time, inconsistencies can be generated.

Whereas replication of Active Directory uses a multimaster model, modification of the schema requires a single-master model to prevent conflicts. Only one domain controller in an enterprise, called a schema operations master, can performs updates at any given time. This is called a Flexible Single Master Operation (FSMO), which automatically overrides normal multimaster operations by providing a single, authoritative point and effectively locking out any other means of making changes. By default, the first domain controller installed is the schema operations master, but other DCs can be designated to take over this role. Also by default, write access (and therefore, modifications) to the schema is disabled on all DCs, including the DC that is first installed and becomes the schema operations master.

There are three types of classes in the schema: structural, abstract, and auxiliary. Structural classes are objects that can be created only by administrators. Abstract classes cannot be created, but other class objects can be derived from them. Auxiliary classes also can't be created, but other class objects can include them in their definitions in order to inherit attributes from more than one other class. In most cases, new object classes will be structural. The object will have a unique OID, either granted by an external authority, or created for use solely within your own enterprise by running the OIDGEN utility.

When creating new class objects with new attributes, you should create the attribute objects first. Any attributes that you want to add to a new class must already exist in the schema. Some attributes are mandatory and must be included in a class definition object. Existing attribute-definition objects can be modified, unless they have a system-only designation. System-only attributes are recognizable by having their system-only attribute set to *true*.

When defining a schema modification policy, it is important to remember the following:

■ Schema modifications will impact the entire forest and cannot be reversed.

■ You cannot modify the schema without first installing the appropriate tools. To modify schema you must be a member of the Schema Admins universal group.

■ Restrict membership of the Schema Admins group. Remove members from it except when schema modification is taking place, and ensure that the DCs, including the operations master, are not normally configured to allow schema replication to be carried out.

exam
Ⓦatch

When changes are made to the schema, modifications will not be immediately visible. Active Directory holds a copy of the entire schema in memory. This is called a schema cache. Although this is an exact replica most of the time, the cache will wait five minutes before reloading after a modification. This means that for five minutes after a schema modification, the cache will hold an out-of-date copy. An immediate update of the cache can be forced so that a new copy will build in memory. However, this should not be done more than once during a schema modification session, because a copy of the old cache will remain in memory to service threads of existing processes. The old cache remains in memory until the processes are finished and the threads are killed.

QUESTIONS

11.04: Defining a Schema Modification Policy

9. A user is installing an Active Directory aware application, but the application does not create new object classes or attributes. You check the group membership

of the user and find what is shown in the following illustration. What is most likely the problem?

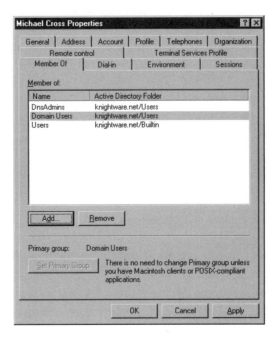

A. The user is a member of the DnsAdmins group.

B. The user is not a member of the Schema Admins group.

C. The user is not a member of the Domain Admins group.

D. Applications cannot modify the schema.

10. **Current Situation:** A user has created a new object class with attributes but has made mistakes in the attributes of the class. The name of this class is ClassA. Since other users in the domain are already using it, the user wants to know whether the class will affect other sites. To fix the attributes that have problems, you assign people to modify the class. You later have second thoughts and decide to do the work yourself. In reviewing the schema, you notice there is an object class created earlier for a project that is now complete; therefore, this class is no longer needed. The name of this class is ClassB.

Required Result: Determine how far reaching the effects of ClassA will be and who in the network may be able to access the class.

Optional Desired Results:

1. Remove ClassB from use, so the object class is no longer available.

2. Determine the effect of two users modifying the same class.

Proposed Solution: ClassA will be available to all sites across the network. Delete ClassB from the schema. When two users modify the same class, a read-only copy of the class will be available to the second user who accesses the class for modification.

What results are produced from the proposed solution?

A. The proposed solution produces the required result only.

B. The proposed solution produces the required result and only one of the optional results.

C. The proposed solution produces the required result and both of the optional results.

D. The proposed solution does not produce the required result.

11. You want to make modifications to the schema so that new object classes are created. Which of the following can be used to modify the schema? (Choose all that apply.)

A. Microsoft Management Console

B. Scripts

C. Schema Operations Master application in Control Panel

D. Active Directory aware applications

TEST YOURSELF OBJECTIVE 11.05

Designing an Active Directory Implementation Plan

Many enterprises will not have implemented a directory services infrastructure, so a good AD implementation plan is a must to the success of a Windows 2000 project. This design will reflect the organization and will differ from business to business. As we discussed in the first chapters of this book, before beginning an implementation plan, you will need to investigate various aspects of the organization. Reporting and geographical structures are vital elements to consider in deciding on the complexity of the domain structure within Active Directory. In looking at this information, you will need to determine if any changes are planned in the future. You will also need to look at the existing IT infrastructure, such as operating platform and the bandwidth and speed of wide area links, and current delegation of network administration and security. Once you have documented the business objectives, proposed technical innovations can then be mapped to the objectives.

In designing your plan, you will need to determine how many domains will be used. A medium or large organization may require multiple domains, whereas smaller businesses will probably require only one. It is important that IT staff not work alone when making decisions and planning AD implementation. Questions of organization, responsibility, reporting, and corporate hierarchy are often best answered by senior management.

Since it is likely that you will be upgrading to Windows 2000 from a previous network operating system, it is vital to consider the existing IT infrastructure in your plan. The constraints of the existing platform may have placed restrictions on the network that may not be relevant once Windows 2000 is deployed. You should also consider whether the company has an Internet presence, because the business may want to use the root domain name to match the domain name used for the Web site. Additionally, you should find out whether the company shares links with other organizations, such as an extranet. A different name should be used for the root domain if a distinction is to be made between the internal and external resources.

Documentation should also be produced detailing the current physical structure of the network, including servers and their locations, links between physical sites and the hardware and protocols they use, and available bandwidth. This documentation should include information on the speeds of all local and wide area connections, the actual and potential number of users at each site, and baseline and peak bandwidth requirements. You should also analyze growth, including the potential growth available with the current technology and infrastructure, as well as the growth envisaged by management.

Testing should play a part in your Active Directory implementation plan so that you can test both the physical and logical aspects of the network. Microsoft's recommended strategy is to divide testing into two stages. The first stage occurs in a controlled lab environment, whereas the second is a pilot project in the actual network. The lab environment can take several forms. One method is to implement testing across the network at a number of locations so that sites and subnets can be tested to determine correct IP addressing, site-subnet mapping, and testing speeds of various intersite connections. At the end of the lab phase, you should have an Active Directory configuration that satisfies the requirements of the original business plan in both logical and physical respects. The pilot project generally consists of two phases. The first phase involves tuning the deployment plan to deal with any risks involved in the project, and the second phase is actual deployment.

It is important to remember that a Windows 2000 domain can operate in two modes: Mixed and Native. Mixed mode allows both Windows 2000 and Windows NT servers to operate as DCs in the domain. In Mixed mode, the Windows NT Administration tools will still be able to manage the domain. However, a number of Windows 2000 features will not be enabled. In Native mode, all domain controllers are running Windows 2000 Server, and all Windows 2000 services are enabled.

When designing an Active Directory implementation plan, it is important that you remember the following points:

■ Start with a documented list of business objectives, and map proposed technical innovations to each one.

■ Be aware of the organization's reporting and geographical divisions. Remember that the rules imposed by Windows NT may not apply to Active Directory.

■ Domains are independent administrative and security boundaries. Organizational units exist inside a domain and are easier to administer. Choose which model will best suit each implementation.

exam
ⓦatch
Many of the constraints imposed by previous infrastructures may not be relevant upon upgrading to Windows 2000 Active Directory, so you should not let them unduly influence your design and plan to implement AD. One example is the size limitations of the SAM database in Windows NT, which may have required adding additional domains, thereby dividing the enterprise along domain lines. Another example is an enterprise where Windows NT was previously introduced alongside existing Novell NetWare servers. In order to adhere to existing standards, Windows NT servers may have been configured to run NWLink as the only protocol to allow communication with the NetWare IPX/SPX protocol. Windows 2000 Active Directory is based on IP and Dynamic DNS, and therefore TCP/IP should be the main protocol in use on any Windows 2000 network.

QUESTIONS

11.05: Designing an Active Directory Implementation Plan

12. As shown in the following illustration, the company you are network administrator for has three domains running Windows NT 4.0 Servers. Novell NetWare is also used on the network, so the only protocol used is NWLink. You are preparing to upgrade this network to Windows 2000. Based on this information and on the information provided in the illustration, which of the following factors will you need to consider in your Active Directory implementation plan?

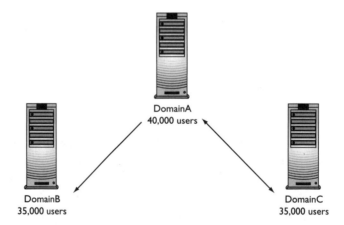

DomainA
40,000 users

DomainB
35,000 users

DomainC
35,000 users

A. Because three domains are used, three domains must continue to be used in upgrading to Windows 2000.

B. Because of projected growth, three domains should be used; otherwise, there will be more users in each domain than the network can support.

C. NWLink must be used after the upgrade because Novell NetWare is used on part of the network. No other protocol can be supported.

D. Because Active Directory relies heavily on TCP/IP, this protocol should be used on the network.

13. **Current Situation:** A large company is headed by a board of directors and has hired you to upgrade their current Windows NT environment to Windows 2000. Members of the board have minimal knowledge of the current infrastructure and very little understanding of how to use computers in general. Despite this, they tell you that they have heard good things about Windows 2000 and would like all servers upgraded to Windows 2000 Server. Workstations will be a mixture of Windows NT Workstations and Windows 2000 Professional machines. The company has a registered domain name and is wondering if this name can be used for the Windows 2000 network, as well as the Web site. The Web site is hosted by an Internet service provider and few users have Internet access in the company.

Required Result: Determine what mode Windows 2000 will use.

Optional Desired Results:

1. Determine to what degree the board of directors will make decisions about the new Windows 2000 Active Directory structure.

2. Decide whether the registered domain name can be used for the internal network.

Proposed Solution: Because there are Windows NT machines on the network, Windows 2000 can use only mixed mode. Since members of the board are not familiar with the current infrastructure, decisions on the AD implementation plan should be made by only IT staff. Because the domain name is already being used by the Web site, the company will have to use a different name.

What results are produced from the proposed solution?

A. The proposed solution produces the required result only.

B. The proposed solution produces the required result and only one of the optional results.

C. The proposed solution produces the required result and both of the optional results.

D. The proposed solution does not produce the required result.

LAB QUESTION

Objectives 11.01–11.05

A company has three offices that are part of a Windows NT network. Each of these offices is a different subnet and is currently connected with ISDN connections. There have been few problems with the existing design. The offices are in different cities and have a large number of users at each location. The company is planning to upgrade all computers to Windows 2000 so that they can take advantage of Active Directory and other features. Unless only one site is implemented, the sites will have domain controllers with various processors and memory capacity. They have hired you to plan the new site structure.

1. How many sites should this network have?

2. What connectivity problems exist with the current infrastructure which will limit the design of the sites?

3. After upgrading to Windows 2000 Active Directory, where will the first site object be located?

4. When configuring intersite replication, you want specific servers to be used. How will this be done?

5. You have asked a member of the IT Staff to install Microsoft Exchange 2000 on a machine. This application is Active Directory aware. The user must be a member of what group for this application to make schema modifications?

A QUICK ANSWER KEY

Objective 11.01

1. **B**
2. **B** and **C**
3. **C**

Objective 11.02

4. **C**
5. **A**
6. **D**

Objective 11.03

7. **B**
8. **C**

Objective 11.04

9. **B**
10. **A**
11. **A, B,** and **D**

Objective 11.05

12. **D**
13. **D**

IN-DEPTH ANSWERS

11.01: Designing an Active Directory Site Topology

1. ☑ **B.** Microsoft recommends that network connections be at least 512 Kbps with 128 Kbps or higher of available bandwidth.

   ☒ **A** is incorrect because this is too slow a link. **C** is incorrect because this is not the minimum. **D** is incorrect because speeds below 512 Kbps will be too slow.

2. ☑ **B** and **C** are correct. Windows 2000 supports scheduling and incremental replication so that changes to information in AD are replicated effectively to other domain controllers. Replication can be configured to occur at certain times and in such a manner that changes only, rather than the entire Active Directory, are replicated to domain controllers outside of the site. Incremental replication is replication of changes, rather than the full Active Directory.

   ☒ **A** is incorrect because data compression is available only for replication between sites. Intrasite replication does not support compression. **D** is incorrect because full replication of AD would increase network traffic.

3. ☑ **C.** The client will seek out the first domain controller it finds. If the domain controller on its site is down, it will seek out a domain controller on another site.

   ☒ **A** is incorrect because clients will authenticate to domain controllers in other sites if the DC on their site is down. **B** is incorrect because the client will seek out a DC on another site. This answer is impossible because there is only one DC per site, and the question states that the DC on the user's site is down. Consequently, it could not pass on a request. **D** is incorrect because Windows 2000 will always look first in the site containing the client computer in order to keep intersite network communications to a minimum.

11.02: Defining Site Boundaries

4. ☑ **C.** Network connections for the WAN link and one of the LANs is too slow. The network connections should be at least 512 Kbps, with 128 Kbps or higher of available bandwidth.

   ☒ **A** is incorrect because a site can have more than a single domain controller. **B** is incorrect because each site can have more than one global catalog server. **D** is incorrect because there can be more than one site per network.

5. ☑ **A.** One. A computer can belong to only one site. A computer with multiple network cards may have IP addresses relating to different sites, but the computer can belong to only one site.

   ☒ **B, C,** and **D** are incorrect because a computer can belong to only one site.

6. ☑ **D.** The proposed solution does not produce the required result. Sites need to be connected using fast connections. ISDN operates at speeds up to 128 Kbps, and the minimum recommended by Microsoft is 512 Kbps; therefore, the connection between the offices is not suitable.

   ☒ **A, B,** and **C** are incorrect because the proposed solution does not produce the required result. However, the new Windows 2000 Server should be placed in the new site and set up as a domain controller and global catalog server.

11.03: Designing a Replication Strategy

7. ☑ **B.** The ISDN link has a lower cost associated with it, so it will be used in preference over other site links. Active Directory will always take the path associated with the smallest cost, as long as that path is available. The default value associated with a link is 100, but any link with a lower cost will be tried first. The costs associated should be assigned based on their actual bandwidth cost.

   ☒ **A** is incorrect because the T1 link has a higher cost associated with it. **C** is incorrect because the link with the lowest cost will be used first. **D** is incorrect because both will not be used equally. The link with the lower cost will be used first, if it is available.

8. ☑ **C.** The proposed solution produces the required result and both of the optional results. Members of the Enterprise Admins group can create sites and

site links using Active Directory Sites and Services. These links will need to be configured and the Bridge All Site Links option must be selected in the Transport Properties sheet. Replication can be configured to use either IP or SMTP. IP can be used for both intersite and intrasite replication, whereas SMTP is used only for replication across site links.

☒   **A**, **B**, and **D** are incorrect because the proposed solution produces the required result and both of the optional results.

11.04: Defining a Schema Modification Policy

9. ☑   **B.** The user is not a member of the Schema Admins group. If an application is Active Directory aware and installed by a member of the Schema Admins group, the application can create object classes and attributes during installation.

☒   **A** is incorrect because membership in other groups would not affect the fact that the user needs to be a member of the Schema Admins group for the application to modify the schema. **C** is incorrect because the user needs to be a member of the Schema Admins group. **D** is incorrect because Active Directory aware applications can modify the schema.

10. ☑   **A.** The proposed solution produces the required result only. The entire forest has only one schema, and changes are replicated to every tree and domain within it.

☒   **B**, **C**, and **D** are incorrect because the proposed solution produces the required result only. Classes and attributes cannot be removed from the schema. They must be disabled if they are no longer wanted. If two users modify the same object class, inconsistencies may result.

11. ☑   **A**, **B**, and **D** are correct. Microsoft Management Console (MMC) can be used to create, modify, or deactivate object classes or attributes. Such changes to the schema can also be done programmatically by running a script through the Active Directory Services Interface (ADSI). If an application is Active Directory aware, it can also make modifications to the schema if the person installing it is a member of the Schema Admins group.

☒   **C** is incorrect because there is no schema operations master application in Control Panel.

11.05: Designing an Active Directory Implementation Plan

12. ☑ **D.** Active Directory relies on TCP/IP, so it should be implemented on the network. TCP/IP can be used in addition to other protocols.

☒ **A** is incorrect because the domains could be merged. **B** is incorrect because there is no 40,000-user limitation in Windows 2000. **C** is incorrect because NWLink is not the only protocol that can be used. A mixture of different protocols can be used.

13. ☑ **D.** The proposed solution does not produce the required result. Because only Windows 2000 Servers will be used on the network, Windows 2000 can run in native mode. Your team should work with decision-makers in the organization, since they can answer questions regarding organization, responsibility, reporting, and corporate hierarchy. This information can then be used to create an Active Directory structure. Also, the internal network can use the domain name currently used by the Web site.

☒ **A**, **B**, and **C** are incorrect because the proposed solution does not produce the required result.

LAB ANSWER

Objectives 11.01–11.05

1. Three. There are three offices that are different subnets and have a large number of users. There is also a slow connection between each subnet. It is best to create one site for each subnet so that there are no slow connections within the site.

2. The ISDN lines. Sites should be connected using fast, inexpensive links. The ISDN line does not qualify as fast connectivity.

3. When Active Directory is installed on the first domain controller of a site, the Active Directory Installation Wizard will create a default site object in the IP container called DEFAULTIPSITELINK.

4. The most powerful servers should be designated as bridgehead servers, and the Bridge All Site Links should be cleared. This will make specific servers bridgehead servers.

5. Schema Admins. Active Directory aware applications like Microsoft Exchange 2000 make modifications to the schema, but they cannot do so unless the user installing is a member of the Schema Admins group.

MICROSOFT CERTIFIED SYSTEMS ENGINEER

12

Designing
Service
Locations

TEST YOURSELF OBJECTIVES

A ctive Directory depends on the placement of several different types of servers on a network, each of which provides important services. The first is the Domain Name System (DNS), which provides name resolution. A DNS server must be available before Active Directory can be installed, because without it, AD would be unable to locate servers and resources on the TCP/IP network. Once AD is installed, a global catalog (GC) server is needed so that users can locate objects in the forest or, in Native mode, in domains, to log on.

You will remember from previous chapters that Windows 2000 networks use a multimaster or peer model, in which all domain controllers (DCs) share responsibilities on the network. This is different from Windows NT, which used a single master model and relied on primary domain controllers (PDCs) and a number of backup domain controllers (BDCs). Changes could be made only on a PDC, which replicated these changes to BDCs. In a Windows 2000 network, each DC contains a read-write copy of the Active Directory database, and changes to Active Directory can be made on any DC. However, in the multimaster model there is significant potential for two administrators making changes to the same object. To avoid conflicting updates, certain operations use a single master model. These are called Flexible Single-Master Operations (FSMO, pronounced *fizmo*).

There are five types of servers called FSMO servers, or operation masters, in Active Directory, which handle additional roles beyond those of ordinary servers. They are the schema master, PDC emulator, domain-naming master, infrastructure master, and relative identifier (RID) master. These operation masters are created when AD is installed and prevent conflicts when critical operations are performed. Domain changes and modifications to the schema affect the entire forest, so there is one DC in the forest that is designated as a domain-naming master and one designated as a schema master. The domain-naming master is the only DC that can be used to add or remove domains or modify the domain namespace, whereas the schema master is the only DC that can be used to modify the schema. The infrastructure master, relative identifier (RID) master, and PDC emulator control domainwide changes, so there is only one for each domain.

Designing the Placement of Operation Masters

When Active Directory is installed on the first DC on your network, the domain that is created becomes the forest root. Being the first DC of the network, this DC also performs the five FSMO roles: the schema master and domain-naming master for the forest, and the PDC emulator, RID master, and infrastructure master for the forest root domain. These roles can be transferred to other DCs added to the network, but for smaller networks this may be unnecessary. If additional domains are added to the forest, the first DC in each new domain will become the PDC emulator, RID master, and infrastructure master for the new domain. If the network uses both Windows 2000 and Windows NT domain controllers, only the Windows 2000 DCs can hold the operation master roles.

The schema master is an operation master that controls updates and modifications to the schema. It is the only domain controller in the forest on which these updates can be made. By default, it is located in the forest root. When an update to the schema is complete, the update is replicated to all domain controllers in the forest. There is normally no reason to change the default placement of the schema master.

The domain-naming master is used to add and remove domains, and it ensures that changes to the domain namespace are unique. It is used to avoid naming conflicts when new domains are added to the forest and is the only DC that manages domain names throughout the forest. The same DC should always perform the roles of schema master and domain-naming master and may be dedicated to performing only those functions. For the domain-naming master to function properly, this operation master must also be a global catalog server.

The PDC emulator is an operation master that provides services on a Windows 2000 Native mode or Mixed mode network. In Mixed mode, the PDC emulator provides the services of a primary domain controller to down-level clients (BDCs and computers without Windows 2000 client software). In a Windows NT domain, changes are made to the PDC and replicated to BDCs so that each BDC has an updated, read-only copy of the directory database. Also, Windows NT servers report their shared resources to a master browser. Windows NT clients use the master browser to obtain a browse list and locate resources. Finally, if clients in a Windows NT domain need to change their passwords, the changes can be made only to a PDC, since it has the only read-write copy of the directory database. After the PDC is upgraded to Windows 2000, these down-level clients still require the existence of the PDC. The PDC emulator updates BDCs, acts as the domain master browser when the Windows NT browser service is enabled, and allows down-level clients to update their passwords.

In Native mode, the PDC emulator still provides a function in the Windows 2000 network. When all BDCs and client computers have been upgraded to Windows 2000, the PDC becomes the final authority for authentication. When a password change is made, the change will take time to replicate to every DC in a domain but will be replicated immediately to the PDC emulator. If a DC cannot authenticate a user because of an invalid password, the password may be invalid because it has not been replicated to the originating DC yet. In such a case, authentication is referred to the PDC emulator, which checks whether the password is valid or not.

The relative identifier master is responsible for allocating sequences of RIDs to DCs in a domain. When a user, group, or computer object is created, the DC on which it is created assigns a unique security identifier (SID). The SID has two parts: a domain ID that is the same for all objects in a domain, and a RID that is unique to each domain. The RID master issues each DC a pool of RID numbers so that DCs can issue unique SIDs. As soon as a DC has used 450 of the 500 RID numbers issued to it, the DC contacts the RID master for another pool of numbers.

The infrastructure master updates the group-to-user references when members of groups are renamed or changed. Groups can contain members from other domains, and a reference to a user in another domain contains a globally unique identifier (GUID), SID, and the distinguished name (DN) of the user. If a user is moved from one domain to another, the GUID will never change, but the SID and DN will change. The infrastructure master updates the SID and DN for cross-domain object references. Unless there is only one DC in a domain, the infrastructure master role should not be held by a DC that is also the global catalog server, since it contains information on objects from all domains. However, this operation master should be well connected to a global catalog server in the same site. If the infrastructure master runs on a global catalog server, it will not be able to detect cross-domain conflicts or find data that is out of date.

If a DC that is acting as an operation master needs to go offline, the role of an operation master can be transferred to another DC. To transfer this role to another DC, you need to be a member of the appropriate group. To change the schema master, you need to be a member of the Schema Admins group, whereas changing the domain-naming master requires being a member of the Enterprise Admins group. To change the RID master, infrastructure master, or PDC emulator, you need to be a member of the Domain Admins group.

Management of operation masters can be done through MMC snap-ins. The schema master role is managed using the Active Directory Schema snap-in, whereas the domain-naming master is managed using the Active Directory Domains and Trusts snap-in. The three domain-wide roles are transferred or seized using Active Directory Users and Computers. A more powerful tool for managing operation masters is the NTDSUTIL.EXE. NTDSUTIL does not require the Windows interface, since it is a command-line utility that allows you to manage FSMO roles.

When designing the placement of operation masters, it is important to remember the following:

- There is only one schema master and one domain-naming master per forest.

- There is one PDC emulator, one RID master, and one infrastructure master per domain.

- An administrator with the appropriate permissions can easily transfer an operation master role to another DC. By default, the groups granted the appropriate permissions to perform such a transfer are Schema Admins for the schema master, Enterprise Admins for the domain-naming master, and Domain Admins for the three domain-wide operation masters.

- If it is necessary to seize the schema master role, the domain-naming master role, or the RID master role, the DC that originally held each of these roles should never be allowed back online.

exam
ⓦatch

In most cases, the temporary loss of an operation master will not have a drastic effect on the network. Seizing a role and transferring it to another DC is a drastic step and should normally be done only if the original operation master is not expected to go back online. An exception is the PDC emulator. If the DC holding the PDC emulator role is to be taken offline, the role should be transferred to another DC first. If it cannot be repaired and brought back online quickly, the role should be seized and transferred to another DC. When the original PDC emulator comes back online, the role should be transferred back to it. The same applies to the infrastructure master. If it is offline for an extended period, its role can be seized and transferred. When the original DC goes back online, the role should be transferred back to the original holder. The same is not true for the other operation masters, in which cases the role should not be transferred back to the original holder.

QUESTIONS

12.01: Designing the Placement of Operation Masters

1. You are planning to upgrade a network running Windows NT 4.0 to Windows 2000. You create the following diagram to show how operation masters will be placed on the network. What problems exist in the diagram?

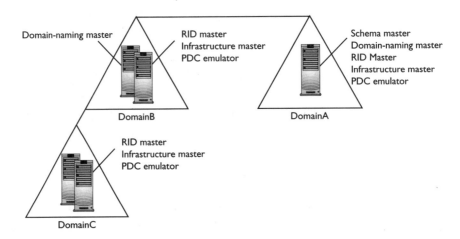

A. There cannot be more than one domain-naming master in a forest.

B. There must be one domain-naming master per domain.

C. There cannot be more than one RID master, infrastructure master, and PDC emulator in a forest.

D. The RID master, infrastructure master, and PDC emulator cannot exist in the same domain.

2. **Current Situation:** You are designing a Windows 2000 network for a company. The network currently uses Windows NT 4.0 Servers, and these will continue to be used on the network after new servers running Windows 2000 are added.

Two domains are currently used, and an additional domain will be added after upgrading to Windows 2000. Although Domain1 will use only Windows 2000 Servers, Domain2 will use the existing PDC and several Windows 2000 servers. Domain1 consists of Canadian employees, and Domain2 consists of American employees. Human Resources would like a field added to the user object's properties so that a field appears to input the Social Insurance Number for Domain1 users and the Social Security Number for Domain2 users.

Required Result: Determine which servers will be operation masters.

Optional Desired Results:

1. Determine the extent to which changes to the schema will affect the network.

2. Determine which operation master will be used to add a new domain.

Proposed Solution: The Windows 2000 Server in Domain1 and the Windows NT Server in Domain2 will be operation masters. Changes to the schema on Domain1's schema master will impact only Domain1, whereas changes to the schema on Domain2's schema master will impact only Domain2. The domain-naming master will be used to add a new domain.

What results are produced from the proposed solution?

A. The proposed solution produces the required result only.

B. The proposed solution produces the required result and only one of the optional results.

C. The proposed solution produces the required result and both of the optional results.

D. The proposed solution does not produce the required result.

3. You have decided to transfer the infrastructure master to another domain controller. Which of the following will you use to do this?

   A. MMC with the Active Directory Schema snap-in

   B. MMC with the Active Directory Domains and Trusts snap-in

   C. NTDSUTIL with the Active Directory Sites and Services snap-in

   D. MMC with Active Directory Users and Computers

4. You have decided to add a new domain to a Windows 2000 network running in Native mode. Which of the following operation masters will be used to create the new domain?

A. Infrastructure master

B. RID master

C. Domain-naming master

D. PDC emulator

TEST YOURSELF OBJECTIVE 12.02

Designing the Placement of Global Catalog Servers

The global catalog (GC) contains a replica of every Active Directory object and a subset of object attributes that are commonly used in search operations. Because there is only a subset of attributes, it is much faster to search the GC than it would be to search the entire Active Directory. Although searching the global catalog is faster, if a search of the GC fails to locate an object, then the Active Directory is searched.

The global catalog is also necessary for logging on to a Windows 2000 domain that is operating in Native mode. The GC is the only repository of information on objects throughout the forest, and it contains information on universal groups. Universal groups contain members from various domains in a forest, and the GC is used to determine membership in this group. If no GC is available, then membership in the group cannot be verified. If this occurs, then it cannot be established whether the user should be allowed or denied access to a resource. In such a case, the user is not allowed to log on the domain unless the user is a member of the Domain Admins group. If the user has an account on the local computer and is not a member of the Domain Admins group, he or she can log on that machine but will be unable to log on the domain.

The GC is maintained on a DC that is designated as a global catalog server. This server stores a complete replica of the domain in which it is located, and a partial replica of other domains. When Active Directory is installed on the first DC in the forest root, the GC is created automatically and the DC becomes the global catalog server. As new domains and sites are created, Windows 2000 designates additional GC servers. Administrators can also create additional GCs using Active Directory Sites and Services.

GC servers are based on sites, not domains, and by default there is one GC server in each site. If multiple domains are in the same site, each domain does not need its own GC server since one GC server will have attributes of objects from all domains. Multiple GC servers will improve the speed of queries to the global catalog, but it is important to realize that in a multiple domain environment, too many GC servers can increase replication traffic. In a single domain environment, this performance issue does not apply because every DC already contains a full replica of Active Directory.

Consideration should be given to the operation master running on a domain controller when a global catalog server is created. In creating GC servers in domains with multiple domain controllers, it is important that the DC acting as the infrastructure master is not made a GC server. This would inhibit the capability of the infrastructure master to resolve all cross-domain references. However, the domain-naming master should be running on a GC server. The domain-naming master is used to create new domains, and it ensures the names of these domains are unique in the forest. By running this operation master on a GC server, the uniqueness of domain names is ensured.

When designing the placement of global catalog servers, you should remember the following points:

- The DC holding the infrastructure master role should never be enabled as a GC.

- A DC that is a GC contains a full replica of its domain and a partial replica of all other domains in the forest.

- Users other than members of the Domain Admins group can log on only to their local computer in a Native mode Windows 2000 domain if a GC is not available.

- A GC is needed in every domain or in every site because a DC can contact a GC in any domain, but a GC in every site can enhance operations.

exam
Watch

The objects and attributes in the global catalog are modified through the schema. A member of the Schema Admins group can select in which object class attributes will be included in the global catalog and have the ability to add additional attributes or remove default ones. If too many attributes are added to the GC, the performance of global catalog searches and replication is impacted. Additional attributes being added to the GC will slow searches. Since changes will need to be replicated to all GC servers, additional attributes will increase the size of the GC, thereby increasing replication traffic.

QUESTIONS

12.02: Designing the Placement of Global Catalog Servers

Questions 5–7 The following three questions are based on the following scenario. You may refer to this scenario as often as necessary.

A company has created a new network that uses Windows 2000 Servers and Windows 2000 Professional Workstations. The network has two domains. Domain1 has a global catalog server, but Domain2 does not. Human Resources would like the ability to search the global catalog by a user's employee number. While you are working on this problem, the link between these domains goes down. A user who is a member of the Domain Admins group attempts logging on Domain1 from Domain2, but finds he cannot. He can, however, log on the local computer. Another user who is a member of the Domain Admins group successfully logs on the domain.

5. Why can one user log on the domain, but the other user cannot?

   A. Each domain needs its own GC. Unless there is a GC in the domain, no users can log on the network unless they are members of the Domain Admins group.

   B. The fact that the user can log on the local computer shows that the user can log on the network. Consequently, the user is mistaken and has actually logged on.

   C. No users in either domain can log on the network because the GC is used to log on all users.

   D. The GC is used to determine membership in the universal group. Since the link to the GC is down, membership in this group cannot be verified.

6. You decide to create additional global catalog servers on domain controllers on the network. Which of the following will you use to create these GC servers on existing domain controllers?

    A. Microsoft Management Console with the Active Directory Users and Computers snap-in.

    B. Microsoft Management Console with the Active Directory Sites and Services snap-in.

    C. Nothing can be used. Global catalog servers are created automatically when new sites are created. Unless new sites are created, no GC servers can be created.

    D. Nothing can be used. The global catalog server is created automatically on the first DC in the forest root. No additional GC servers can be created.

7. On what server would you add this attribute that allows members of Human Resources to search the global catalog by an employee number?

    A. global catalog server

    B. Schema master

    C. RID master

    D. Any domain controller

8. **Current Situation:** A company has a Windows 2000 network with two domains located in a single site. Currently there is only one global catalog server, but you have decided to add additional GC servers to the network.

    Required Result: Determine the minimum number of global catalog servers required by the network.

    Optional Desired Results:

    1. Determine which operation master should be run on a global catalog server.

    2. Determine which operation master should not be run on a global catalog server.

    Proposed Solution: Only one global catalog server is required, but additional GC servers can be created. Create the global catalog server on the domain controller that is performing the role of infrastructure master. Avoid creating the global catalog server on the domain controller that is performing the role of domain-naming master.

What results are produced from the proposed solution?

A. The proposed solution produces the required result only.

B. The proposed solution produces the required result and only one of the optional results.

C. The proposed solution produces the required result and both of the optional results.

D. The proposed solution does not produce the required result.

TEST YOURSELF OBJECTIVE 12.03

Designing the Placement of Domain Controllers

A domain controller is distinguished in Windows 2000 by having a replica of the domain directory, which is the local domain database, and it is used to manage user access to the network. All user logons, authentication, and access to resources and directory searches are accomplished through a DC. Each DC contains a full read-write copy of Active Directory so that objects can be created, deleted, or modified on any DC in a domain. Windows 2000 uses a multimaster model, which makes all DCs peers. As peers, each DC is required to replicate any changes made to Active Directory to other DCs. A subset of these changes is also replicated to all global catalog servers in the forest.

Every domain on a Windows 2000 network requires a domain controller, but additional DCs should be placed in domains for fault tolerance. If a domain has a single DC and it fails, users will not be able to log on and be authenticated. In a single domain network, if the DC is damaged and cannot go online again, all domain information will need to be rebuilt. Multiple DCs are also appropriate for performance reasons, such as when the server is supporting a large number of users.

Network performance can be affected by the placement of DCs on the network. In most cases, each site should have at least one domain controller. A site's DC can support users in another site, but there will be degraded performance if there is insufficient bandwidth between these sites. Because changes to Active Directory and a subset of AD are replicated to other DCs, this replication traffic can also have a significant effect on network performance. As the number of DCs increases, so does the replication traffic. If replication occurs over a slow WAN link, it is important to consider placing DCs at each end of the link, scheduling replication to occur during off-peak hours, or both.

Domain controllers are created using the Active Directory Installation Wizard on a member server, which installs Active Directory on that server. Windows 2000 automatically sets up with other DCs to keep the Active Directory database current, and additional functions can be assigned to the DC. This includes assigning the DC different roles, as discussed earlier in this chapter.

When designing the placement of domain controllers, you should remember the following points:

- If possible, a DC should be placed in each site.
- All Windows 2000 DCs contain a writeable copy of the Active Directory database; therefore, objects can be created, deleted, or modified on any DC in the domain.
- If there is only one DC in a domain and that DC fails, the domain is lost.
- A server can be a DC for only one domain. Therefore, if a site contains three domains, three separate DCs are required.

exam

Watch

A Windows 2000 domain controller can handle significantly more users than a Windows NT server. In Windows NT networks, it is recommended that a BDC be installed for every 3,000 users, but no such recommendations exist for Windows 2000 networks. A single Windows 2000 DC can handle thousands of users, so you should consider factors like the number of logons and the amount of server activity when determining how many DCs to place on your network. If there are a number of users separated from the DC by a slow link, you should seriously consider placing a DC on each side of the link. The Active Directory Sizer tool can be used to determine the number of DCs, GCs, and bridgehead servers required in a site, as well as the capacity required of DCs. Based on information you provide about your network, it will recommend the placement of servers and predict the size of AD.

QUESTIONS

12.03: Designing the Placement of Domain Controllers

9. As shown in the following illustration, a company's network consists of a single domain with two sites. Site A is in Atlanta, and Site B is in Toronto. All users in each site start work at the same time, and all of them use the network. Site A has 5,000 users, and Site B has 4,000 users. Users in Site B are complaining that it is taking too much time to log on the network and access resources. How will you remedy this problem?

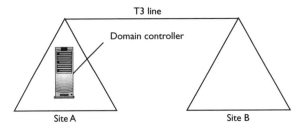

A. Place additional domain controllers within Site A.

B. Place additional domain controllers within Site B.

C. Because of the number of users in each site, additional domain controllers must be placed in both sites. One Windows 2000 DC must exist for every 3,000 users.

D. Upgrade the link between the sites so that there is a fast link between them.

10. A Windows 2000 network consists of three domains. One domain is in New York, one is in Atlanta, and the third is in Redmond. New York has 2,000 users, Atlanta has 3,000 users, and Redmond has 5,000 users. According to this

information, what is the minimum number of domain controllers needed for each of these sites?

A. New York requires one DC, Atlanta requires one DC, and Redmond requires two DCs.

B. New York, Atlanta, and Redmond require one DC each.

C. New York, Atlanta, and Redmond require two DCs each.

D. One DC is required to service all three of these locations.

11. **Current Situation:** A Windows 2000 single domain network, using the minimum number of domain controllers required, consists of three sites. One site is in New York, one is in Atlanta, and the third is in Redmond. The domain controller goes down. Upon investigating the problem, you find that the server is irrecoverable, and you will not be able to bring it back online.

Required Result: Restore the domain information so that users can access the resources provided through the DC.

Optional Desired Results:

1. Determine what impact the loss of this DC will have on users.

2. Determine how the problems can be avoided in the future.

Proposed Solution: Domain information will not be lost because each DC holds a full read-write copy of Active Directory. Users will be able to log on to DCs in other sites and will not be greatly impacted by the loss of this server. Use multiple DCs to provide fault tolerance in the future.

What results are produced from the proposed solution?

A. The proposed solution produces the required result only.

B. The proposed solution produces the required result and only one of the optional results.

C. The proposed solution produces the required result and both of the optional results.

D. The proposed solution does not produce the required result.

12. Two sites in a single domain are connected via a slow WAN link. Each site has its own domain controller. Users in Site A are complaining that it is taking a considerable amount of time to use resources located across the WAN. You talk

to the network administrator in Site B and find that he has received similar complaints. You decide to add additional domain controllers at each side of the link. What effect will this have?

A. It will improve the speed at which users are able to access resources across the WAN.

B. Additional DCs will improve authentication and the speed at which users will be able to access resources.

C. It will degrade performance because replication between DCs in Site A and replication between DCs in Site B will use considerable bandwidth.

D. It will degrade performance because replication between Site A and Site B will use considerable bandwidth.

TEST YOURSELF OBJECTIVE 12.04

Designing the Placement of DNS Servers

The Domain Naming System (DNS) is used to resolve DNS names to IP addresses, and vice versa, allowing users to enter a name of a computer on the network rather than remembering a series of numbers making up the IP address for that particular host. Active Directory relies on DNS for this reason and stores information about domain controllers on DNS servers. Windows 2000 clients can query the DNS server to locate a particular DC.

To locate domain controllers, Windows 2000 uses service (SRV) resource records (RRs). Resource records are entries in a zone database that associate DNS names to information about a network resource. The SRV RR identifies which servers provide a particular service. For example, if a client needed a server to validate a log-on request, it would contact a DNS server to obtain a list of servers that provides this service. If the client cannot find a DNS server, it will be unable to log on and access network resources.

When upgrading a network to Windows 2000, it is important to determine whether existing DNS servers support SRV RRs. DNS servers that do not support them can remain on the network to resolve queries for other resources, but there must be at least one DNS server on the network that supports SRV RRs. To install Active Directory on the first Windows 2000 Server in a forest, a DNS server that supports SRV RRs must already be running on the network or be installed as part of AD installation.

DNS uses a primary DNS server and one or more secondary DNS servers. The primary DNS server is used to store a zone file containing name-to-IP address mappings, which it loads into memory when it boots up. A zone is a subtree of the DNS database, which can consist of a domain, or a domain with subdomains. It allows that portion of the DNS database to be administered as a separate entity on a DNS server. The primary DNS server is authoritative for the zone because it is used to update the zone file. When a secondary DNS server starts on the network, it connects to the primary DNS server and requests a zone transfer. A zone transfer occurs when the DNS database is replicated to secondary DNS servers, which then load the DNS database into memory. Clients can then query either the primary or secondary DNS servers for name resolution. If a primary DNS server goes offline and cannot be recovered, a secondary DNS server can then be promoted.

Zone transfers between primary and secondary DNS servers will increase network traffic between sites. The extent of this increase depends on the number of secondary name servers and the volume of updates. To deal with this issue, incremental zone transfers can be used so that only changes are replicated, as opposed to replicating the entire database. In an incremental zone transfer, individual records are transferred instead of the entire DNS database.

DNS database information can also be integrated into Active Directory. When AD integration is used, primary and secondary DNS servers are unnecessary, since the DNS zone file is stored in AD and replicated to all DCs when AD is replicated. DCs can thus resolve name lookup requests, and because each DC now holds a read-write copy of DNS, DCs can be authoritative and write to the DNS zone. This allows every DC to act as a DNS server. If AD integration is used, DNS replication is eliminated because zone information will be replicated with AD. Despite this apparent improvement, AD replication will be affected because the size and frequency of replication will increase as changes are made.

Windows 2000 DNS supports the dynamic updating of DNS records as defined in RFC 2136. This allows hosts to provide information to dynamically update DNS records. A DHCP server, which dynamically assigns IP addresses, or the client receiving the IP address can update DNS records when IP address changes occur. Implementations of DNS prior to RFC 2136 required administrators to manually update records that were stored in a static database.

Because DNS is needed to find DCs on a Windows 2000 network, it is important that they be placed so they are accessible to clients. If a site has no DNS server and connects to another site to access DNS, it is important that the link between these sites be reliable. Since users will be unable to find DCs without DNS, it is recommended that each site have its own DNS server. If AD integration is used, a domain controller should be placed in each site. This is because zone files are stored in the Active Directory on each DC, allowing it to perform name resolution.

A DNS server that is overloaded with queries or is not immediately available will degrade network performance. Multiple DNS servers can be used to deal with this problem—a primary name server is used in a site with numerous clients, and secondary name servers are used at other sites. To provide load balancing, clients can be configured to query a local DNS server and then query name servers in other sites. A disadvantage to this arrangement is that all changes to the zone must be done on the primary master name server.

When designing the placement of DNS servers, you should remember the following points:

- DNS must be available in order to install Active Directory on a Windows 2000 server.

- A DNS server must support service location resource records and dynamic updating of DNS records in order to support Active Directory.

- If a Windows 2000 DNS server is used on a Windows 2000 network, the DNS server can be integrated into Active Directory, which effectively makes every DC a DNS server.

- Windows 2000 DNS servers can perform incremental zone transfers in which individual records are replicated rather than the entire DNS database.

exam
ⓦatch
Although Windows 2000 DNS supports SRV RRs, it is important to remember that other DNS servers may not. Windows 2000 requires that DNS servers support the service resource records (SRV RRs) defined in RFC 2052, which are used by Windows 2000 Active Directory to locate DCs. Because of this requirement, there must be one or more DNS servers on a Windows 2000 network that supports SRV RRs. If there is not, the Active Directory Installation Wizard will give you the option of automatically installing DNS or manually setting up a DNS server.

You should also remember that although the Windows Internet Name Service (WINS) used in Windows NT is supported, it is not necessary for name resolution in Windows 2000. WINS was used on NT networks to resolve NetBIOS names to IP addresses.

QUESTIONS

12.04: Designing the Placement of DNS Servers

13. To provide name resolution, your network currently uses a Unix-based DNS server and a Windows NT server, neither of which supports SRV RRs. After upgrading existing Windows NT servers to Windows 2000, you plan to also use Windows 2000 DNS for name resolution so that these servers will work with the existing DNS servers on the network. One Windows 2000 server will act as a primary DNS server, and another Windows 2000 server will act as a secondary DNS server. On which of these servers would changes be made to the zone file so that Windows 2000 Professional clients can successfully find Windows 2000 domain controllers?

    A. The Unix server

    B. The Windows NT server

    C. The primary DNS server

    D. The secondary DNS server

14. You are preparing to install Active Directory on the first domain controller in a forest. At present, there are no other servers installed, and therefore, no DNS servers. What will happen when you attempt to install Active Directory? (Choose all that apply.)

    A. An error message will occur, and installation will proceed. You will need to install DNS after installing Active Directory.

    B. You will be given the option to manually install DNS.

    C. You will be given the option to have DNS installed automatically.

    D. Installation will fail. You will need to install DNS before attempting to install Active Directory.

15. A company has a network consisting of two sites. Site A runs Windows NT Servers with Windows NT Workstations, and Site B runs Windows 2000 Server with Windows 2000 Professional Workstations. Site A has a third party DNS server that supports SRV RRs, dynamic updates, and incremental zone transfers. This is the only server running DNS server software on the network. A 128-Kbps link, which has the tendency to go down on occasion, connects these two sites. When this link goes down, how will it affect users in Site B?

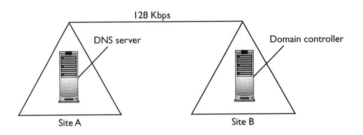

A. No effect. All Windows 2000 domain controllers provide DNS server services. Therefore, users in Site B will use the DNS server services provided by Site B's DC.

B. No effect. Since it is a third-party server, a Windows 2000 DNS Service must be present on the network. Because Site B is the only site running Windows 2000, this site already has a DNS server installed on the first domain controller.

C. Since users are separated from the DNS server, they will be unable to locate domain controllers. This means they will be unable to log on and access network resources.

D. If DNS is not available, clients will automatically use WINS for host name-to-IP address resolution. WINS is required to run on all Windows 2000 DCs.

16. **Current Situation:** A company has a Windows 2000 network consisting of two sites. Although you are planning to upgrade the link between the sites to a T1 line, the sites are currently connected with a 128-Kbps link. The link between the sites frequently goes down for periods of time. You have decided to use Active Directory integrated DNS and place domain controllers at each

of the two sites. Because of the time it takes to update DNS information, you do not want to manually enter new information regarding hosts.

Required Result: Implement a method that will allow hosts to dynamically update DNS information.

Optional Desired Results:

1. Determine what impact the link between the sites will have on users when it goes down.

2. Determine how changes to DNS will be replicated to other domain controllers.

Proposed Solution: Implement Dynamic DNS so that information is dynamically updated. IP address changes will be replicated from the primary DNS server to secondary DNS servers until all DNS servers have an upgraded copy of the database. Because domain controllers are located at each site, there will be minimal impact on DNS services when the link goes down.

What results are produced from the proposed solution?

A. The proposed solution produces the required result only.

B. The proposed solution produces the required result and only one of the optional results.

C. The proposed solution produces the required result and both of the optional results.

D. The proposed solution does not produce the required result.

LAB QUESTION

Objectives 12.01–12.04

You have just finished upgrading a network to Windows 2000 so that all servers are running Windows 2000 Server and all clients are running Windows 2000 Professional. The network consists of five domains and uses the minimum number of domain controllers. Three of the domains will be part of one site, and the other two domains will be part of another site.

1. How many domain controllers are used on this network?

2. By default, how many schema masters and domain-naming masters will be created for this network?

3. By default, how many RID masters, infrastructure masters, and PDC emulators will be created for this network?

4. By default, how many global catalog servers will be created for this network?

5. Which tools can be used to manage operation masters?

6. Since no BDCs or Windows NT clients exist on the network now, what should be done with the PDC emulator?

QUICK ANSWER KEY

Objective 12.01

1. A
2. D
3. D
4. C

Objective 12.02

5. D
6. B
7. B
8. A

Objective 12.03

9. B
10. B
11. D
12. D

Objective 12.04

13. C
14. B and C
15. C
16. B

IN-DEPTH ANSWERS

12.01: Designing the Placement of Operation Masters

1. ☑ **A.** There cannot be more than one domain-naming master in a forest. This is a forest-wide operation master role. There cannot be more than one domain-naming master, since changes to it affect the entire forest.

   ☒ **B** is incorrect because there cannot be more than one domain-naming master in a forest. **C** and **D** are incorrect because there is one RID master, infrastructure master, and PDC emulator per domain.

2. ☑ **D.** The proposed solution does not produce the required result. If the network uses both Windows 2000 and Windows NT domain controllers, only the Windows 2000 DCs can hold the operation master roles. The domain-naming master will be used to add the new domain after upgrading to Windows 2000 is complete.

   ☒ **A, B**, and **C** are incorrect because the proposed solution does not produce the required result. The proposed solution is also incorrect because there is only one schema master for the entire forest, and changes to the schema on this server will impact the entire network.

3. ☑ **D.** The infrastructure master and the other two domainwide roles are transferred or seized using Active Directory Users and Computers.

   ☒ **A** is incorrect because the schema master role is managed using the Active Directory Schema snap-in. **B** is incorrect because the domain-naming master is managed using the Active Directory Domains and Trusts snap-in. **C** is incorrect because NTDSUTIL is a command-line utility. Active Directory Sites and Services snap-in is not used for managing operation masters.

4. ☑ **C.** The domain-naming master is the only DC that can be used to add new domains to a forest. The domain-naming master can be used to add and remove domains or modify the domain namespace.

☒ **A, B**, and **D** are incorrect because none of these can be used to add a new domain. Only the domain-naming master can add new domains.

12.02: Designing the Placement of Global Catalog Servers

5. ☑ **D.** The GC is used to determine membership in the universal group. Since the link to the GC is down, membership in this group cannot be verified.

☒ **A** is incorrect because each domain does not need its own GC server. **B** is incorrect because if the user has a local account, the user can log on that machine. **C** is incorrect because if this were true, the user who did log on the network would not have been able to.

6. ☑ **B.** Microsoft Management Console with the Active Directory Sites and Services snap-in is used to create additional global catalog servers.

☒ **A** is incorrect because the Active Directory Users and Computers snap-in is not used. **C** is incorrect because although Windows 2000 designates additional GC servers when sites are created, this is not the only way to create a GC server. **D** is incorrect because additional GC servers can be created. However, it is true that when Active Directory is installed on the first DC in the forest root, the GC is created automatically and the DC becomes the global catalog server.

7. ☑ **B.** Schema master. Objects and attributes in the global catalog are modified through the schema. The only domain controller that can be used to modify the schema is the schema master.

☒ **A** is incorrect because the global catalog server stores a subset of objects and attributes found in Active Directory. It is not used to modify these objects or attributes. **C** is incorrect because the RID master is not used to modify the schema. **D** is incorrect because the only domain controller that can modify the schema is the schema master.

8. ☑ **A.** The proposed solution produces the required result only. GC servers are based on sites, and by default there is one GC server in each site. If multiple domains are in the same site, each domain does not need its own GC server because one GC server will have attributes of objects from all domains. Additional GC servers can be created.

☒ **B**, **C**, and **D** are incorrect because the proposed solution produces the required result only. The domain-naming master should be run on a global catalog server. When the domain-naming master creates a new domain, the name of that domain must be unique in the forest; therefore, running it on a GC server enables this operation master to ensure the uniqueness of domain names. The infrastructure master should not be run on a GC server because running these two on the same domain controller will inhibit the ability of the infrastructure master to resolve all cross-domain references.

12.03: Designing the Placement of Domain Controllers

9. ☑ **B.** Place additional domain controllers within Site B. A single DC is being used to process logons, authenticate users, and provide access to resources. Users in Site B have to access the DC across the link and wait for the DC to process their requests. Adding a DC to Site B will solve this problem. Since there is a fast connection between these sites, there should be few or no performance problems when domain controllers replicate information.

☒ **A** is incorrect because the problem is not the number of users using the DC in Site A who are logging on the network and accessing resources at the same time. **C** is incorrect because there are no distinct user limitations on Windows 2000. **D** is incorrect because there is already a fast link between the sites.

10. ☑ **B.** New York, Atlanta, and Redmond require one DC each. One domain controller is required for each domain. There are no set restrictions on the number of users for each DC because Windows 2000 can support thousands of users.

☒ **A**, **C**, and **D** are incorrect because a minimum of one domain controller is required for each domain.

11. ☑ **D.** The proposed solution does not produce the required result. Because the domain has the minimum number of DCs, there is only one domain. This means that the only domain controller is lost, and users will not be able to log on or use network resources. All domain information will be lost because the only DC in the domain has failed and is irrecoverable. It will need to be rebuilt from scratch.

☒   **A**, **B**, and **C** are incorrect because the proposed solution does not produce the required result. Multiple DCs in the domain will provide fault tolerance and prevent these problems in the future.

12. ☑   **D.** It will degrade performance because replication between Site A and Site B will use considerable bandwidth. Active Directory changes and a subset of AD (the global catalog) are replicated to other DCs. This replication traffic can also have a significant effect on network performance, especially when it has to occur over a slow WAN link.

☒   **A** is incorrect because replication will decrease performance. **B** is incorrect because replication will degrade performance and use up bandwidth, making access to resources slower. **C** is incorrect because replication within each site will not degrade the performance of accessing resources located across the WAN. Replication between the sites will, however, affect performance.

12.04: Designing the Placement of DNS Servers

13. ☑   **C.** The primary DNS server is authoritative for the zone because it is used to update the zone file. When a secondary DNS server starts on the network, it connects to the primary DNS server and requests a zone transfer. A zone transfer occurs when the DNS database is replicated to secondary DNS servers, which then load the DNS database into memory. Clients can then query either the primary or secondary DNS servers for name resolution. If a primary DNS server goes offline and cannot be recovered, a secondary DNS server can then be promoted.

☒   **A** and **B** are incorrect because neither the Unix-based server nor the Windows NT server support SRV RRs. Windows 2000 requires service resource records. Although existing DNS servers can be used by legacy machines and to provide name resolution, changes will need to be made on the Windows 2000 primary DNS server and then replicated to secondary DNS servers. **D** is incorrect because changes are made on the primary DNS server and replicated to secondary DNS servers.

14. ☑   **B** and **C** are correct. To install Active Directory on the first Windows 2000 server in a forest, a DNS server that supports SRV RRs must already be running on the network. If it is not installed, then the Active Directory Installation

Wizard will give the options of manually installing Windows 2000 DNS or having it automatically installed for you.

☒ **A** is incorrect because DNS must be installed before Active Directory can be installed. **D** is incorrect because installation will not fail. You will be given the options of manually or automatically installing DNS.

15. ☑ **C.** Since users are separated from the DNS server, they will be unable to locate domain controllers. DNS servers provide name resolution and allow clients to locate Windows 2000 DCs. Since this service is not available, they will be unable to log on and access network resources.

☒ **A** is incorrect because all Windows 2000 domain controllers do not provide DNS services. They will act as DNS servers if DNS is AD integrated, which is not the case here. **B** is also incorrect because a Windows 2000 DNS server does not need to be present on the network. Since the third-party DNS server supports SRV RRs, dynamic updates, and incremental zone transfers, there is no need for separate Windows 2000 DNS servers. **D** is incorrect because WINS is not required to run on all Windows 2000 DCs. Also, WINS provides name resolution for NetBIOS names and thus does not provide the same service as DNS.

16. ☑ **B.** The proposed solution produces the required result and only one of the optional results. Dynamic DNS allows hosts to provide information to dynamically update DNS records. A DHCP server, which dynamically assigns IP addresses, or the client receiving the IP address can update DNS records when IP address changes occur. There will be minimal impact on users because DNS information is stored within AD. Since zone files are stored in the Active Directory on each DC, DCs can perform name resolution.

☒ **A, C**, and **D** are incorrect because the proposed solution produces the required result and only one of the optional results. Since AD integration is used, all zone information is stored within Active Directory, and therefore, replication is not performed between primary and secondary DNS servers. Zone information will be replicated with AD.

LAB ANSWER

Objectives 12.01–12.04

1. Five. Each domain requires a minimum of one domain controller.

2. There will be one schema master and one domain-naming master for the forest.

3. Five of each. By default, there will be one RID master, one infrastructure master, and one PDC emulator per domain.

4. Two. By default, one global catalog server is created for each site in a network.

5. Microsoft Management Console and NTDSUTIL. MMC runs in Windows 2000 and has a GUI interface, whereas NTDSUTIL is a command-line utility that allows you to manage FSMO roles.

6. Nothing should be done with the PDC emulator. In Native mode, the PDC emulator acts as the final authority for authentication. When a password change is made, the change will take time to replicate to every DC in a domain, but will be replicated immediately to the PDC emulator. If a DC cannot authenticate a user because of an invalid password, authentication is referred to the PDC emulator.

MICROSOFT CERTIFIED SYSTEMS ENGINEER

13

Migrating to Active Directory

This chapter summarizes the processes of consolidating and upgrading existing Windows domains and discusses the impact of keeping any existing Windows NT 4.0 domain controllers. A domain upgrade is a process of upgrading an existing Windows NT 4.0 domain to a Windows 2000 domain. During an upgrade, most of the current environment is retained, unlike with domain consolidation. Domain consolidation deals with redesigning a domain structure so that it better suits the needs of an organization. Generally, this involves taking a number of smaller domains and consolidating them into fewer, larger domains.

When migrating to Active Directory, knowledge of DCPROMO is required, as are a number of other tools discussed in this chapter. DCPROMO is used to add or remove Active Directory from a Windows 2000 server. As we will see, these are important concepts when dealing with existing Windows NT environments.

TEST YOURSELF OBJECTIVE 13.01

Consolidating Existing Domains

There are two main consolidation techniques used to collapse domains: horizontal and vertical. A horizontal collapse involves moving all user accounts from multiple domains into another larger domain. A vertical collapse is performed after upgrading to Windows 2000 and involves moving servers from resource domains into an organizational unit (OU) or another domain. One or both of these techniques can be used to consolidate domains.

Microsoft provides a number of tools for domain consolidation or restructuring. Active Directory Migration Tool (ADMT) is a Microsoft Management Console (MMC) tool that takes you step by step through the process of migrating to Active Directory. It allows you to clone and move groups, user accounts, and computer accounts between domains. When user accounts are moved, passwords are not retained. ADMT gives the option of assigning a new password to each migrated account or setting the password to be the same as the username. In addition to these abilities, ADMT also merges groups, translates security information, and allows you to run Windows NT 4.0 and Windows 2000 domains in parallel with rollback capabilities. ADMT also enables you to test migration scenarios before they are carried out. When you are ready to consolidate domains, you can use ADMT's pruning and grafting technologies to decrease the number of domains you have.

ADMT provides reports that allow you to evaluate your migration process and analyze the potential impact of migration before making any changes. It provides reports about expired name conflicts, impact analysis, expired computer accounts, and users, groups, and computers that have been migrated. This tool can be run from any workstation with appropriate permissions and connectivity, but it should be run from a DC because ADMT must store migration information in a secure database, and the DC is the most secure computer on the network.

In addition to ADMT, there are several other tools that are useful in domain consolidation. These include Ldp, ClonePrincipal, MoveTree, and Netdom. Ldp is a graphical AD administrative utility for displaying object attributes, and it is used to determine whether security migrations have been completed correctly. Each of the other tools is a command-line utility. ClonePrincipal is used for interforest restructuring. Interforest restructuring occurs when you restructure instead of upgrade, and it is referred to as pruning and grafting or cutting and pasting. ClonePrincipal is a collection of VBScripts that can copy global groups, shared local groups, and users from a Windows NT or Windows 2000 domain to a Windows 2000 Native-mode domain. It does not disturb the source domain or require reassigning access control list (ACL) resources to maintain group membership. MoveTree is used for intraforest restructuring, which is when a whole forest must be restructured due to a widespread organizational adjustment. MoveTree allows you to move AD security principal objects between domains in a single forest. Because it supports the SIDHistory attribute, there is no need to reassign permissions to resources. Netdom, used for managing Windows domains and trusts, is useful for interforest and intraforest restructuring. It is used for adding and moving computer accounts between domains. It allows you to view current trusts and can also create new trusts automatically, based on the trusts that are already established.

When existing domains are manually consolidated, there are three main restructuring methods that can be used. The first method involves restructuring domains immediately after upgrading to Windows 2000. In such a post-upgrade restructuring, the account domain is upgraded to access Windows 2000 scalability and other features. An interforest restructuring is performed to consolidate resource domains into the new Windows 2000 domain. Alternatively, all Windows NT domains can be upgraded, and intraforest restructuring can then be performed. The second restructuring method that can be used involves restructuring at a later date. This method consists of performing an upgrade and later performing interforest or intraforest restructuring based on the original forest structure.

The final restructuring method involves restructuring instead of upgrading. In this method, the entire domain model is redesigned so that restructuring is planned in advance, rather than upgrading domains that will be eliminated afterward. A newly designed forest is called a pristine forest. This is a Windows 2000 forest that is completely isolated from the current environment, and in which domains operate as usual during the migration. This protects the current, stable domain from risk and allows a single-step migration. Once the pristine forest is created, groups, users, and resources can be migrated from the existing domain. The Windows 2000 domain operates parallel to the current Windows NT environment and is tested to confirm that the migration occurred properly. After testing, the Windows NT domain structure is decommissioned, and the remaining resources are redistributed.

When consolidating existing domains, it is important to consider the following points:

- You can use Microsoft's Active Directory Migration Tool (ADMT) to aid in domain consolidation.

- Domain consolidation is also known as domain restructuring.

- When you create a domain and a forest from scratch, it is referred to as a pristine forest.

exam
Watch

In Windows NT 4.0, there was an administrative limitation on how big the Security Account Manager (SAM) account database could get. The SAM is the security database used in Windows NT, which contains groups, users, and permissions for a domain. The primary domain controller (PDC) stores a read-write copy of the SAM, whereas a read-only copy is replicated to the backup domain controllers (BDCs) within the domain. The SAM was limited to a size of 40MB, which equates to about 40,000 users. If the number of users or the size of the SAM grew to this limit, additional domains needed to be created.

With the introduction of Active Directory (AD), this administrative limitation disappeared. Theoretically, a domain's Active Directory can contain ten million objects, one million objects being a more practical number. This means that extra domains are not needed if there are more than 40,000 user, group, or computer accounts. Previous domains that are upgraded to Windows 2000 can be collapsed into one or a few domains to simplify administration, which decreases the total cost of ownership (TCO).

QUESTIONS

13.01: Consolidating Existing Domains

1. As shown in the following illustration, a company's existing Windows NT environment consists of two domains. Based on the information in this illustration, determine whether you should consolidate them into one domain when upgrading and, if so, why this should be done.

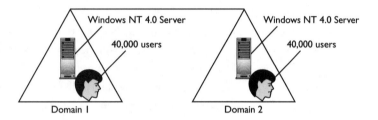

A. The domains should be consolidated into one domain because the Windows NT 4.0 requirement of one domain per Windows NT server is no longer applicable. Each Windows NT server acts as a primary domain controller for the domain.

B. The domains should be consolidated into one domain because Windows NT 4.0 had a limitation of 40,000 users per domain, but this limitation does not exist in Windows 2000.

C. The domains cannot be consolidated because there must be three or more domains before they can be consolidated into fewer domains.

D. The domains cannot be consolidated because domains cannot contain more than 40,000 users, groups, and computers.

2. You have recently consolidated two Windows NT domains into a single Windows 2000 domain and migrated to Active Directory. You use ADMT to clone and move groups, user accounts, and computer accounts between the

domains. When users attempt logging on to the new Windows 2000 Active Directory domain, the logons fail. What is the reason for this?

A. ADMT does not move user accounts. Since all user accounts had to be recreated, there was no way of knowing the user's previous password so that it could be added to the account.

B. Windows 2000 does not support the same type of passwords that are used in Windows NT because of changes in the way logons occur.

C. ADMT does not retain passwords when user accounts are moved.

D. ADMT does not move user accounts. ClonePrincipal needs to be run to migrate user accounts.

3. **Current Situation:** You are a member of the IT staff for a large company. Upon returning from vacation, you find that a project has been commenced to upgrade the current Windows NT environment to Windows 2000. The current Windows NT environment consists of two domains with approximately 30,000 users in each domain. It has been decided that migration will occur after upgrading to Windows 2000. Servers from resource domains will be moved into another larger domain. There is some concern about how well the migration plan will work, and the company would like to test migration before it actually takes place.

Required Result: Determine what Windows 2000 tool will be used to perform the domain consolidation.

Optional Desired Results:

1. Decide what technique will be used to collapse the domains.

2. Determine what tool will be used to test migration before it actually takes place.

Proposed Solution: Use Active Directory Migration Tool (ADMT) to consolidate the domains and test migration before it actually takes place. Based on the information given in this situation, a horizontal collapse will be used.

What results are produced from the proposed solution?

A. The proposed solution produces the required result only.

B. The proposed solution produces the required result and only one of the optional results.

C. The proposed solution produces the required result and both of the optional results.

D. The proposed solution does not produce the required result.

Migrating to Active Directory

There are two types of migration available when migrating to Active Directory. The first is performing a domain upgrade, wherein the PDC and some or all of the BDCs are upgraded to Windows 2000. The second is a domain restructure or consolidation, in which objects are moved to a Windows 2000 domain from other domains. A combination of these methods can be used when migrating to Active Directory.

When restructuring as opposed to upgrading, the infrastructure of Active Directory is designed from the ground up, and accounts are migrated after the design is complete. The new AD infrastructure runs alongside the current Windows NT domain model, using as much of the AD domain structure as can possibly be created, including the root domain, child domains, OUs, and other objects. The number of domains is minimized, even to the point of using a single domain, and one-way trusts are established between each Windows NT domain and the AD structure. Once this is done, accounts are migrated. After the accounts are migrated, the trusts between the Windows NT domains and AD are dissolved and the Windows NT domains are retired.

When upgrading from Windows NT to Active Directory, certain objects are automatically migrated into AD containers. User accounts migrate into the Users container. Local groups as domain local groups, and global groups as global groups, also migrate into the Users container. Built-in groups migrate into the Built-in container; computer accounts migrate into the Computers container. As we saw in the previous section, a number of tools, such as ADMT, can be used to aid in this migration.

To ensure a safe migration to AD, a backout BDC can be used. This is a BDC that is already in place or newly installed in the Windows NT domain. The BDC is replicated with the PDC and then removed from the domain. If any problems occur during the AD migration, you can back out of the migration by using the backout BDC.

When migrating to Active Directory, it is important to remember the following points:

- Domain consolidation is the combination of several domains into fewer, larger domains.

- Domain upgrading is upgrading your Windows NT 4.0 domain to Windows 2000.

e x a m

ⓌⓐⓉⓒⓗ

Applications should be tested to ensure there are no compatibility problems with Windows 2000. To test compatibility, use the Windows 2000 Compatibility tool. This tool can be started by running WINNT32.EXE /checkupgradeonly from the Windows 2000 installation CD. This produces a report that flags potential problems that might be encountered during the actual upgrade, such as hardware compatibility issues or software that might otherwise not be migrated during the upgrade.

QUESTIONS

13.02: Migrating to Active Directory

4. The following diagram shows your plan for restructuring an existing Windows NT domain to a newly designed Windows 2000 Active Directory structure. Another member of your IT staff has some concerns about the number of trusts appearing in this diagram. What will you tell him?

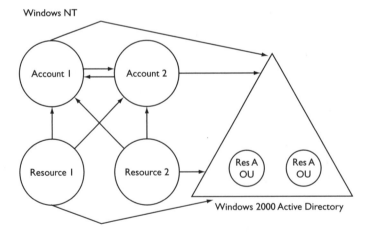

A. All trusts will be eliminated and the Windows NT domains will be removed once migration is completed.

B. After migration to Windows 2000 is complete, all one-way trusts will automatically become two-way, transitive trusts.

C. All trusts will continue after the Windows 2000 Active Directory network is completed, allowing AD to use existing accounts and resources.

D. There is no reason for the trusts since Windows NT domains with existing accounts and resources should only be upgraded.

5. After migrating accounts to Active Directory, a member of your IT staff says that he is unable to find certain accounts and groups, particularly the local groups. What will you tell him so he knows where to find the local group for the former PDC?

A. Local groups are migrated as domain local groups to the Users container.

B. Local groups are migrated as local groups to the Local Groups container.

C. Local groups are migrated as global groups to the Users container.

D. Local groups are migrated as domain local groups to the Computers container.

6. **Current Situation:** A company currently has a network running Windows NT 4.0, and you are planning to upgrade the PDCs and BDCs to Windows 2000. Members of the IT staff remember problems that occurred when upgrading from Windows NT 3.51 to Windows NT 4.0 and would like a fallback plan in case there are problems during the upgrade. There is also some concern about whether existing Windows NT applications will function properly on the Windows 2000 Server.

Required Result: Devise a recovery plan in case there is a problem when upgrading to Windows 2000 so that you can go back to using Windows NT if necessary.

Optional Desired Results:

1. Devise a method of migrating existing groups and user and computer accounts to Active Directory.

2. Determine how to test existing applications to ensure they will work with Windows 2000.

Proposed Solution: Use a backout BDC so that the upgrade can be rolled back in case of a problem. During an upgrade, the groups, user accounts, and computer accounts will automatically migrate to Active Directory. Although

Windows NT applications will function properly on Windows 2000 Professional machines, they will not work on Windows 2000 Server.

What results are produced from the proposed solution?

A. The proposed solution produces the required result only.

B. The proposed solution produces the required result and only one of the optional results.

C. The proposed solution produces the required result and both of the optional results.

D. The proposed solution does not produce the required result.

TEST YOURSELF OBJECTIVE 13.03

Developing a Migration Plan

A migration plan should be created as early as possible. It includes many elements of migration, but starts with an analysis of business objectives and an understanding of the technology being migrated. The business requirements focus on the needs of the company and why it is migrating to Windows 2000 Active Directory. This includes design, naming scheme, domain architecture, forest design, site planning, and policies that you want created. An understanding of technologies involves analyzing the current network architecture, including creating an inventory of all services users will require. The inventory should look at file and print services, as well as shared data required by users. Lastly, you should document the wide area network (WAN) to understand the overall structure, and plan the domain architecture that will be used.

By designing your domain early, you will avoid having to make sudden decisions as to how your domain will be laid out and where servers will be placed. Domain design involves assessing the current environment, including operational and physical environments, and requires an assessment of administrative needs. These needs are what drive the design. Once you determine the number of domains required, you then divide them into trees and forests and establish naming conventions. It is necessary to establish a naming convention in order to name the root domain and any subdomains. Finally, an organizational unit structure is designed to arrange company resources into a functional hierarchy.

In developing a migration plan, you need an awareness of Windows 2000 features and requirements. If servers do not meet the minimal requirements, then hardware, software, or both will need to be upgraded. In upgrading hardware, you will need to ensure that new and existing hardware is compatible with Windows 2000. To ensure hardware and software compatibility, the Windows 2000 Compatibility Wizard can be used. The Hardware Compatibility List (HCL) that is found on Microsoft's Web site is another useful tool in determining hardware compatibility.

As mentioned in the previous section, a recovery plan should also be created. This is a plan that details what will be done in the event problems arise during migration. It may include using a backout BDC to recover from a failed Windows 2000 Active Directory installation, and backing up all data on servers before the upgrade begins. The goal of this plan is to provide solutions to possible problems that may arise.

When developing a migration plan, you should remember the following points:

■ Be sure to check the HCL to verify that your hardware can support Active Directory before you migrate.

■ You should create a recovery plan in case things go wrong during the migration.

exam
ⓦatch

A migration path from Windows NT 3.51 to Windows 2000 is supported. Although Microsoft recommends upgrading from Windows 3.51 to Windows NT 4.0 before migrating to Windows 2000, it is not required. It is important to remember that versions of Windows NT before Windows 3.51 must be upgraded to a higher version before upgrading to Windows 2000.

QUESTIONS

13.03: Developing a Migration Plan

Questions 7–9   The following three questions are based on the scenario that follows. You may refer to this scenario as often as necessary.

A company has an existing Windows NT environment. One server is running Windows NT 3.5, another is running Windows NT 3.51, and the remaining two servers are running Windows NT 4.0. Each of these servers has run well for a number of years with a minimal number of problems. Because some of these servers are old, you are concerned that some hardware and software will not be compatible with Windows 2000.

7. In creating a migration plan, you need to determine which of the servers currently on the network can be migrated directly to Windows 2000. (Choose all that apply.)

    A. Windows NT 3.5.

    B. Windows NT 3.51.

    C. Windows NT 4.0.

    D. None. Because a mixture of Windows NT versions is used on the network, a complete restructuring is needed with a Windows 2000 clean install on all servers.

8. What steps should be taken to ensure the existing network is protected, even if upgrades to Windows 2000 fail? (Choose all that apply.)

    A. Restructure the network rather than upgrade. This will prevent problems from upgrading.

    B. Force replication and take a BDC offline before migration begins.

    C. Perform a complete backup of each server before upgrading to Windows 2000.

    D. Since each of these servers has had few problems in the past, there is no need to create a recovery plan.

9. Which of the following can be used to determine whether hardware is compatible with Windows 2000? (Choose all that apply.)

    A. Hardware Compatibility List

    B. Active Directory Migration Tool

    C. Windows 2000 Compatibility Wizard

    D. MoveTree

Understanding the Domain Upgrade Process

Upgrading a domain without consolidating the existing structure is an easier, low-risk method of having Windows 2000 domains on your network. If the current domain structure suits a company's needs, if a fast migration solution is required, or if there is a need to upgrade without impacting the current production environment, then a domain upgrade is a good option. With an in-place upgrade, the PDC and BDCs are upgraded from Windows NT to Windows 2000. An in-place upgrade retains most system settings, program installations, and preferences, and also retains user accounts, passwords, and existing trust relationships with Windows NT domains.

The first PDC that is upgraded establishes the root domain. This DC automatically takes on the roles of domain-naming master and schema operations master for the forest, and takes on the PDC emulator role, infrastructure master role, and relative identifier role for the domain. BDCs cannot be upgraded until the PDC is upgraded. If the PDC for a domain cannot be upgraded, the BDC can be promoted to a PDC and then upgraded to Windows 2000.

When the first PDC is upgraded to a Windows 2000 DC, Windows 2000 will run in Mixed mode. This is a mode used when there is a mixture of Windows NT 4.0 BDCs and Windows 2000 DCs. You may wish to use Mixed mode if some BDCs cannot be upgraded. This may be necessary when hardware is not supported or when you wish to fall back to Windows NT 4.0. BDCs can still be added to the network in this mode and are still replicated. It does not matter what clients are running. In Mixed mode, NTLM authentication is available for down-level clients, and objects are copied from the SAM database to AD.

In Mixed mode, transitive trusts become available using Kerberos or NTLM. However, it is advisable to keep existing Windows NT trusts as long as there are BDCs. If a Windows 2000 DC goes offline when the network is running in Mixed mode, then a BDC can be promoted to a PDC, and users will be able to access network resources. It also provides the option of rolling back to a Windows NT environment.

After the PDC is upgraded to Windows 2000, the rest of the network can be upgraded. It is recommended that at least one BDC be upgraded as a second

Windows 2000 DC so that it can replicate Active Directory. If this is done, the second DC can act as a backup if the first one fails. If you do not wish BDCs to function as domain controllers, they can be upgraded to Windows 2000 member servers. If all BDCs are upgraded to Windows 2000, then Native mode can be used, allowing you to take full advantage of Active Directory features. These features include universal domain local groups and nesting. You will also have full access to Kerberos logon, PKI, smart cards, application deployment, and security policies. It is important to realize that once the switch is made to Native mode, it cannot be undone, so you will not be able to return to Mixed mode. Windows NT 4.0 BDCs cannot be added to the domain, netlogon replication ceases, and the DC acting as PDC emulator will be unable to synchronize data with BDCs.

In understanding the domain upgrade process, the following points should be kept in mind:

- You must upgrade your PDC first.
- The first PDC that is upgraded to Windows 2000 will take on the PDC emulator role.

When planning an in-place upgrade, it is recommended that the latest service packs be applied to Windows NT 3.51 and Windows NT 4.0 Servers before the upgrade takes place. Computers can be upgraded before, during, or after the domain controllers are upgraded. After an in-place upgrade is performed, users will have transparent access. They will not be able to tell that the server operating system has changed or that AD has been implemented.

QUESTIONS

13.04: Understanding the Domain Upgrade Process

10. A company's network consists of two domains, as shown in the following illustration. You are trying to determine what mode should be used in these

domains so that the maximum number of Active Directory features is available. What options are available to you?

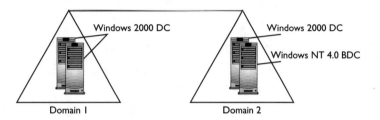

A. Domain 1 can use only Native mode because it consists entirely of Windows 2000 DCs.

B. Both domains must use Mixed mode because there is a Windows NT 4.0 BDC in Domain 2.

C. Domain 1 and Domain 2 can use either Mixed or Native mode.

D. Domain 1 can use either Native or Mixed mode, but Domain 2 can use only Mixed mode.

11. You are about to upgrade a Windows NT 4.0 BDC to Windows 2000. This will be the first server on the network that will be upgraded. When you attempt to do the upgrade, it fails. Why?

A. The PDC must be upgraded before the BDC.

B. Active Directory must be installed on the BDC before Windows 2000 can be installed.

C. DNS must be installed before the BDC can be upgraded to Windows 2000.

D. BDCs cannot be upgraded to Windows 2000.

12. **Current Situation:** You are planning to upgrade a Windows NT 4.0 domain to Windows 2000 Active Directory. You attempt upgrading the PDC for the domain to Windows 2000 but find that each time you try, the upgrade fails. There are three BDCs in the domain. You would prefer not using BDCs as domain controllers but would like to upgrade them to Windows 2000. These BDCs will remain for a short time on the new network before being upgraded,

but you need to determine whether Windows 2000 will be able to communicate and function with them.

Required Result: Devise a way to install Windows 2000 on a PDC for this network.

Optional Desired Results:

1. Determine how to upgrade BDCs to Windows 2000 without making them domain controllers.

2. Determine whether the Windows 2000 DC and BDCs will be able to function together.

Proposed Solution: Promote a BDC to a PDC, and then upgrade it to Windows 2000. Upgrade the BDCs to Windows 2000, but make them member servers. Communication between Windows 2000 and the BDCs will not be available until all servers are upgraded to Windows 2000.

What results are produced from the proposed solution?

A. The proposed solution produces the required result only.

B. The proposed solution produces the required result and only one of the optional results.

C. The proposed solution produces the required result and both of the optional results.

D. The proposed solution does not produce the required result.

TEST YOURSELF OBJECTIVE 13.05

Keeping Windows NT 4.0 DCs

Windows NT 4.0 DCs consist of primary domain controllers and backup domain controllers. The PDC must be upgraded to a Windows 2000 DC for Active Directory to be used in a particular domain. BDCs can be kept on the network after upgrading, but the Windows 2000 DC will have to run in Mixed mode. When in Mixed mode, the Windows 2000 DC acts as a PDC emulator, running Flexible Single-Master Operations (FSMO) that allows it to communicate with the BDCs.

If all servers are upgraded to Windows 2000 and switched to Native mode, then BDCs cannot be used. The PDC emulator continues to be used in Native mode because it receives preferential replication of password changes and acts as the final authority on authentication. Once switched to Native mode, it cannot be switched back to Mixed mode.

In Mixed mode, Windows 2000 has the capability of showing objects stored in Active Directory to downlevel clients. The objects are displayed to them in a flat Windows NT 4.0 style. In order to do this, the FSMO server, acting as a PDC emulator, creates security principles in Mixed mode that downlevel clients can use. Downlevel domain controllers rely on consecutively numbered relative IDs (RIDs) within security IDs (SIDs). RIDs in Windows 2000 are not consecutive because of multimaster replication. To communicate this information to Windows NT 4.0 DCs, the NTLM replication protocol is used. This same information is communicated to Windows 2000 DCs using the new replication protocol Kerberos.

Windows NT and Windows 9*x* workstations can run in a Mixed mode or Native mode environment. Windows NT 4.0 servers can also run in either mode, but they cannot operate as domain controllers. Active Directory aware clients can also be used on the network and can perform functions like global catalog queries and other AD functions. They will be able to use transitive trust relationships and access resources throughout the forest. AD aware clients are clients running Active Directory software, including machines running Windows 2000 Professional, Windows 9*x*, or Windows NT Workstation.

Windows 2000 requires DNS because it is used by Active Directory as its domain naming convention and location service. Names used in Windows 2000 are DNS names, and the DNS service allows clients to find Windows 2000 DCs on the network. DNS must be installed prior to Active Directory. If it is not, when you upgrade a Windows NT 4.0 DC to Windows 2000, you will be given the option of installing DNS. Dynamic DNS (DDNS) can also be used on the network. DDNS allows clients to update the DNS server when changes to their information occur. This saves administrators having to manually update the information stored on the DNS server.

DNS can be used with DHCP as a replacement for the Windows Internet Name Service (WINS). Windows 2000 DNS supports SRV RRs, which can authenticate client lookups for a DC. SRV RRs (service location resource records) are DNS records used to map a service name to the IP address of a server offering a particular service.

Domain controllers publish their IP addresses with SRV RRs in DNS so clients can find the DC through the SRV RR names.

Broadcasts or WINS previously handled such lookups. WINS is the Windows Internet Name Service, used to map NetBIOS names to IP addresses. WINS can be kept in service on a Windows 2000 network for downlevel clients when there are clients or applications that need to use NetBIOS for naming services. If this is not the case and there are no plans to add Windows NT 4.0 servers to a pure Windows 2000 network, then WINS can be removed.

In determining whether to keep Windows NT 4.0 domain controllers, it is important to remember the following points:

■ You can stay in Mixed mode with Windows NT 4.0 BDCs as long as you wish.

■ Client operating systems do not affect whether you can switch to Native mode.

■ You should keep WINS and NetBIOS for backward compatibility.

■ Keep in mind that DNS is required for Windows 2000.

exam
ⓦatch

You can switch from Mixed mode to Native mode only once. You cannot switch from Native mode back to Mixed mode. After switching to Native mode on a Windows 2000 DC, the change will be replicated to other DCs in the domain within 15 minutes. For immediate replication, you would need to reboot the DC on which the change was made, and then reboot all other DCs in the domain. It is also important to remember that when a DHCP server is upgraded to Windows 2000, a member of the Enterprise Admins group must authorize the DHCP server in Active Directory for DHCP to initialize and function properly.

QUESTIONS

13.05: Keeping Windows NT 4.0 DCs

13. As shown in the following diagram, a company's network consists of two domains. Domain 1 runs in Native mode, and Domain 2 runs in Mixed mode.

The IT staff programmers need to run software on a Windows NT 4.0 server and have asked that a BDC be put back on the network. What will you do?

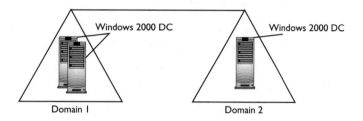

A. Add the BDC to Domain 1.

B. Add the BDC to Domain 2.

C. BDCs could be used in either domain.

D. BDCs cannot be used in either domain.

14. A company has just upgraded from Windows NT 4.0 to Windows 2000. The network is running Windows 2000 Server on all servers and Windows 2000 Professional on all machines. No applications on these computers need NetBIOS name resolution, and all are Active Directory aware. Which of the following is no longer required?

A. WINS

B. DNS

C. DHCP

D. None of the above

15. **Current Situation:** A company has two domains running Windows 2000 Servers in Native mode. Programming staff has discussed the need for Windows NT 4.0 Workstations and Windows 98 clients in their department, located in Domain 2. These will be used for programming and testing legacy applications they create for the company to sell to other businesses. This situation has raised an interesting point. Since some applications designed for Windows NT 4.0 will not run on Windows 2000, the IT staff has suggested putting a Windows NT 4.0 server on Domain 1. When these downlevel clients are added to the network, you want IP addresses dynamically assigned to them.

Required Result: Determine whether the Windows NT 4.0 server can be put back on the domain and, if so, how this can be done.

Optional Desired Results:

1. Determine whether Windows NT 4.0 Workstations and Windows 9*x* clients can be installed on Domain 2.

2. Devise a method of dynamically assigning IP addresses to downlevel clients.

Proposed Solution: Switch the Windows 2000 domain controller from Native mode to Mixed mode. Once the switch has been replicated to other DCs in the domain, the Windows NT 4.0 member server can then be added. Windows NT 4.0 Workstations and Windows 9*x* clients can be installed on the network without having to switch modes. WINS should be implemented to dynamically assign IP addresses to downlevel clients, since these clients will use NetBIOS names.

What results are produced from the proposed solution?

A. The proposed solution produces the required result only.

B. The proposed solution produces the required result and only one of the optional results.

C. The proposed solution produces the required result and both of the optional results.

D. The proposed solution does not produce the required result.

TEST YOURSELF OBJECTIVE 13.06

Using DCPROMO

DCPROMO is a program that is better known as the Active Directory Installation Wizard. It used to promote member servers to domain controllers, and demote DCs to being member servers. The capability to demote a Windows 2000 domain controller to a member server without having to reinstall the operating system is a new feature of Windows 2000. DCPROMO does this by installing Active Directory to a member server, thereby promoting it to a DC, or removing AD to demote the DC. DCPROMO.EXE runs automatically when upgrading a Windows NT 4.0 PDC or

BDC, but it can also be run on a Windows 2000 server that has already been set up on the network.

Active Directory can be installed either by using the Active Directory Installation Wizard or as a silent installation with a pre-made text file. The Active Directory Installation Wizard is started by selecting the Active Directory option in the Configure Your Server dialog box, or by selecting Run from the Start command and typing DCPROMO. To perform a silent installation, you would type DCPROMO/ answer:*answerfile* at the command prompt, using the name of your pre-made text file in place of *answerfile*. The answer file contains responses to the wizard and can be created by following the instructions found in the \support\tools\unattend.doc file on the Windows 2000 CD. Log files created during the installation of AD are stored in the <systemroot>\debug folder. In addition to these methods of installing Active Directory, Kerberos software is installed to allow the authentication service and ticket granting services to function in AD.

To install Active Directory, several requirements must be met. First, NTFS v5 is required. This is the new version of the New Technology File System used on previous versions of Windows NT. If this is not already installed, you will need to convert your existing file system. A DNS server must also be present on the network. If one is not present, then you will have the option of installing Windows 2000 DNS on the server when DCPROMO is run. Finally, you will need to decide where the AD database, logging files, and system volume will be stored.

In using DCPROMO, you will need to remember the following points:

- You must decide whether you will be joining an existing forest or creating a new one.

- You can run DCPROMO.EXE on a domain controller to demote it to a member server.

exam
ⓦatch

DCPROMO is generally associated with installing Active Directory, but it can also be used to install DNS. Using DCPROMO to install DNS should be done only on a server that is to be promoted to a DC. Installing DNS on a member server should be done manually. There are advantages to using DCPROMO to install DNS. When DNS is installed through DCPROMO, a number of DNS settings, such as the creation of zones, are automatically configured. These configuration settings are made based on information entered during the upgrade process, installation of Active Directory, or both. If DCPROMO is used to install Active Directory on the first DC in a domain, it specifies this server as the primary DNS server and creates forward and reverse lookup zones.

QUESTIONS

13.06: Using DCPROMO

16. You are promoting a Windows 2000 member server to a domain controller. This member server was upgraded from a Windows NT 4.0 member server. The server has 128MB of RAM, a 20GB hard drive that was formatted with NTFS v4 when it was running Windows NT 4.0, and a Pentium III processor. DNS is already running on a DC in this domain. When you attempt to promote this server, it fails. Why?

    A. Additional RAM is needed.

    B. DNS must be running on the server.

    C. The file format must be converted.

    D. A member server cannot be promoted.

17. You are preparing to install DNS on a member server running Windows 2000. You do not want this server to be promoted to a DC. How should DNS be installed?

    A. DNS should be installed using DCPROMO since it will make configuration easier.

    B. DNS should not be installed. DNS can run only on a DC.

    C. DNS should be installed using the Configure Your Server dialog box and choosing the Active Directory option.

    D. DNS should be installed manually.

18. You have decided to use DCPROMO to promote a member server to a domain controller. The member server is new to the network and has a clean install of Windows 2000. What options are available to you to start this process? (Choose all that apply.)

    A. DCPROMO will start automatically when the Windows 2000 installation CD is started and the member server is upgraded.

B. Type **DCPROMO/ANSWER:*answerfile*** and follow the instructions to create a response file and start the process.

C. Type **DCPROMO/ANSWER:*answerfile***, where *answerfile* is the name of a pre-made text file containing responses to wizard questions.

D. Select the Active Directory option from the Configure Your Server dialog box.

LAB QUESTION

Objectives 13.01–13.06

A company has three Windows NT domains on a network that spans a large city. There are numerous employees in each domain, which is why the additional domains were created. You design a new infrastructure that will run alongside the current Windows NT environment and into which accounts will be migrated as soon as the new AD infrastructure is implemented. Upon completion, all servers will be running Windows 2000.

1. What type of migration has occurred?

2. What tools are available with Windows 2000 for moving computer accounts between domains?

3. You want to use the full functionality of Active Directory on this network. In what mode will you run the servers?

4. What will occur if Windows NT 4.0 BDCs are added to the network in this mode?

A QUICK ANSWER KEY

Objective 13.01

1. **B**
2. **C**
3. **B**

Objective 13.02

4. **A**
5. **A**
6. **B**

Objective 13.03

7. **B** and **C**
8. **B** and **C**
9. **A** and **C**

Objective 13.04

10. **D**
11. **A**
12. **B**

Objective 13.05

13. **B**
14. **A**
15. **D**

Objective 13.06

16. **C**
17. **D**
18. **C** and **D**

IN-DEPTH ANSWERS

13.01: Consolidating Existing Domains

1. ☑ **B.** The domains should be consolidated into one domain because the Windows NT 4.0 limitation of 40,000 users per domain no longer applies. In Windows NT 4.0, there was an administrative limitation on how big the Security Account Manager (SAM) account database could get. The SAM was limited to a size of 40MB, which equates to about 40,000 users. If the number of users or the size of the SAM grew to this limit, additional domains needed to be created. This limitation does not exist in Windows 2000.

   ☒ **A** is incorrect because Windows NT 4.0 did not require one domain per Windows NT Server. **C** is incorrect because two or more domains can be consolidated into one or a few domains. **D** is incorrect because Windows 2000 Active Directory can support millions of objects.

2. ☑ **C.** ADMT does not retain passwords when user accounts are moved. ADMT gives the option of assigning a new password to each migrated account or setting the password to be the same as the username.

   ☒ **A** is incorrect because ADMT does move user accounts. **B** is incorrect because Windows 2000 does support the passwords that a user may have used in Windows NT. **D** is incorrect because ADMT does move user accounts.

3. ☑ **B.** The proposed solution produces the required result and only one of the optional results. ADMT can be used to test migration before it actually takes place and to consolidate domains.

   ☒ **A**, **C**, and **D** are incorrect because the proposed solution produces the required result and only one of the optional results. The technique suggested to collapse the domains is incorrect because a horizontal collapse involves moving all user accounts from multiple domains into another larger domain. This situation describes a vertical collapse, which is performed after upgrading to Windows 2000 and involves moving servers from resource domains into another domain.

13.02: Migrating to Active Directory

4. ☑ **A.** All trusts will be eliminated and the Windows NT domains will be removed once migration is complete. One-way trusts are established between each Windows NT domain and the AD structure during migration. These domains run parallel to one another. After the accounts are migrated, the trusts between the Windows NT domains and AD are dissolved, and the Windows NT domains are retired.

☒ **B** is incorrect because after accounts are migrated, the trusts between the Windows NT domains and AD are dissolved, and the Windows NT domains are retired. **C** is incorrect because accounts and resources are migrated to the AD domain, and the Windows NT domain is then retired. **D** is incorrect because accounts and resources can be migrated to AD.

5. ☑ **A.** Local groups are migrated as domain local groups to the Users container. This container contains user accounts, domain local groups, and global groups.

☒ **B** is incorrect because there is no Local Groups container in Active Directory. **C** is incorrect because global groups are migrated as global groups. **D** is incorrect because the Computers container contains computer accounts.

6. ☑ **B.** The proposed solution produces the required result and only one of the optional results. To ensure a safe migration to AD, a backout BDC can be used. This is a BDC that is already in place or newly installed in the Windows NT domain. The BDC is replicated with the PDC and then removed from the domain. If any problems occur during the AD migration, you can then back out of the migration by using the backout BDC. User, group, and computer objects will automatically migrate to Active Directory.

☒ **A, C**, and **D** are incorrect because the proposed solution produces the required result and only one of the optional results. The compatibility of Windows NT applications with Windows 2000 can be tested using the Windows 2000 Compatibility tool. This tool can be started by running WINNT32.EXE /checkupgradeonly from the Windows 2000 installation CD.

13.03: Developing a Migration Plan

7. ☑ **B** and **C** are correct. Windows NT 3.51 and Windows NT 4.0. Windows 2000 has a migration path from Windows NT 3.51 and Windows NT 4.0.

Versions before this must be upgraded to a higher version of Windows NT before they can be upgraded to Windows 2000.

☒ **A** is incorrect because this version is too early to be upgraded directly to Windows 2000. **D** is incorrect because it does not matter whether mixtures of operating system versions are being used on the network.

8. ☑ **B** and **C** are correct. By forcing replication and taking a BDC offline before migration begins, you will be able to roll back to a previous state if necessary. Performing a complete backup of each server before upgrading to Windows 2000 will ensure data is safe in case the upgrade fails.

☒ **A** is incorrect because problems can occur whether you are upgrading or restructuring. A recovery plan should be created regardless of which method is used. **D** is incorrect because problems may still occur during migration, even though the servers have been stable for years.

9. ☑ **A** and **C** are correct. The Hardware Compatibility List (HCL) is a list of hardware that is compatible with Windows 2000. It is available on Microsoft's Web site. The Windows 2000 Compatibility Wizard is a tool used to determine the compatibility of software and hardware with Windows 2000.

☒ **B** is incorrect because Active Directory Migration Tool (ADMT) is not used to determine hardware compatibility. **D** is incorrect for the same reason, because MoveTree is used to move AD security principal objects between domains in a single forest.

13.04: Understanding the Domain Upgrade Process

10. ☑ **D.** Domain 1 can use either Native or Mixed mode, but Domain 2 can use only Mixed mode. If the network consists entirely of Windows 2000 DCs, Native mode can be used. It can also use Mixed mode if the addition of Windows NT 4.0 BDCs is planned.

☒ **A** is incorrect because Domain 1 can use either Native or Mixed mode. **B** is incorrect because a domain can run in Native mode despite the modes of the other domains in your forest. **C** is incorrect because Native mode cannot be used in a domain running Windows NT 4.0 BDCs.

11. ☑ **A.** The PDC must be upgraded before the BDC. BDCs cannot be upgraded until the PDC is upgraded.

    ☒ **B** is incorrect because Active Directory cannot be installed until after Windows 2000 is installed. **C** is incorrect because the BDC cannot be upgraded until after the PDC is upgraded. **D** is incorrect because BDCs can be upgraded to Windows 2000.

12. ☑ **B.** The proposed solution produces the required result and only one of the optional results. Since the PDC cannot be upgraded, you can promote a BDC and then upgrade it to Windows 2000. Because you do not want all BDCs to be Windows 2000 DCs, the remaining BDCs can be made into member servers.

    ☒ **A, C**, and **D** are incorrect because the proposed solution produces the required result and only one of the optional results. The Windows 2000 DC and BDCs will be able to work together through the PDC emulator.

13.05: Keeping Windows NT 4.0 DCs

13. ☑ **B.** Add the BDC to Domain 2. BDCs can be added to a domain running in Mixed mode. In Mixed mode, Windows 2000 DCs and Windows NT 4.0 BDCs can coexist with no problems.

    ☒ **A** is incorrect because Domain 1 is running in Native mode in which Windows NT 4.0 BDCs cannot be used. **C** is incorrect for this same reason: Domain 1's Windows 2000 DCs are running in Native mode. **D** is incorrect because BDCs can be added to Domain 2.

14. ☑ **A.** WINS. WINS is the Windows Internet Naming Service used to resolve NetBIOS names to IP addresses. Since there are no downlevel clients on the network and no applications requiring NetBIOS name resolution, WINS can be removed from the network.

    ☒ **B** is incorrect because Windows 2000 uses DNS for name resolution. **C** is incorrect because DHCP continues to be used in Windows 2000 to dynamically assign IP addresses to computers. **D** is incorrect because WINS is no longer needed.

15. ☑ **D.** The proposed solution does not produce the required result. Although a Windows NT 4.0 member server can be added to a domain running in either Mixed mode or Native mode, you cannot switch from Native mode to Mixed mode.

☒ **A**, **B**, and **C** are incorrect because the proposed solution does not produce the required result. Windows 9*x* and Windows NT 4.0 clients can run in either a Native or Mixed mode environment. The use of WINS for assigning IP addresses is incorrect because WINS is used for NetBIOS name resolution. It is not used for assigning IP addresses.

13.06: Using DCPROMO

16. ☑ **C.** The file format must be converted. NTFS v5 must be used for Active Directory to be installed and the member server to be promoted to a DC.

☒ **A** is incorrect because a Windows 2000 DC requires a minimum of 128MB of RAM. **B** is incorrect because a DNS server must be running in the domain. It does not need to run on the server that AD is being installed on. **D** is incorrect because a member server can be promoted to a DC.

17. ☑ **D.** DNS should be installed manually. Although DNS can be installed using DCPROMO, it will be part of the process of installing Active Directory. If AD is installed, this will make the member server a DC.

☒ **A** is incorrect because using DCPROMO to install DNS means Active Directory will be installed as part of the process. This will make the member server a DC. **B** is incorrect because DNS can run on a member server. **C** is incorrect because this will start the Active Directory Installation Wizard, which will give the option of installing DNS as part of the process of installing AD.

18. ☑ **C** and **D** are correct. DCPROMO can be used to promote a member server to a DC. This can be started in several ways. You can type DCPROMO/ANSWER:*answerfile*, where *answerfile* is the name of a pre-made text file containing responses to wizard questions. This will perform a silent install. You can also select the Active Directory option from the Configure Your Server dialog box.

☒ **A** is incorrect because although DCPROMO starts when a Windows NT 4.0 PDC or BDC is upgraded, this server is already running Windows 2000. Therefore, it cannot be upgraded to Windows 2000. **B** is incorrect because to run DCPROMO with an answer file, the text file must be pre-made.

LAB ANSWER

Objectives 13.01–13.06

1. This migration uses domain restructuring. A domain restructure or consolidation involves designing the AD structure from the ground up, parallel to the current Windows NT environment. When the design is implemented, objects are moved to a Windows 2000 domain from other domains.

2. Tools that can be used to move computer accounts are Active Directory Migration Tool (ADMT) and Netdom. ADMT allows you to clone and move groups, user accounts, and computer accounts between domains. Netdom is used for managing Windows domains and trusts and for adding and moving computer accounts between domains.

3. To use the full functionality of Active Directory, Windows 2000 Servers should be running in Native mode.

4. If Windows 2000 Servers are running in Native mode, Windows NT 4.0 BDCs cannot be added to the network.

This practice exam is made up of two testlets. These testlets are scenarios that provide background on a specific company and pose a unique set of circumstances. Please read and review each testlet carefully; 20 multiple-choice questions, based on the information provided, will follow each testlet.

TESTLET I: URK MEDICAL PRODUCTS CASE STUDY

Company Profile and History

Urk Medical Products has been in operation for 14 years. It is a pharmaceutical company that also manufactures medical technologies. They have slowly moved into manufacturing of various medical products but continue to develop and produce various medications. The main office of this company is in San Diego, but it also has offices in New York and Atlanta.

Interview with Chief Executive Officer (CEO): Dianne Stevenson

"We've grown to be one of the major pharmaceutical companies over the last few years. We started as a company selling Carpal Tunnel Syndrome pain relief tablets to computer professionals, but we have grown into a company that makes various medical technologies and medications. In the future, we hope to be moving into the vitamin market. This will increase the number of employees we have and help us move into new areas."

Interview with Chief Operating Officer (COO): Jennifer Carruthers

"Our focus is on teamwork. Although we have offices across the country, each of which focuses on developing and producing different medical products, all of the offices work together as a single entity.

I do not know if this will affect the network, but there is some discussion about purchasing a vitamin company. This company's major product is a memory enhancement vitamin that no one can remember the name of. They seem to be doing well, but their major problem is marketing, which is our strong point."

Interview with Human Resources Manager: Sue Smith

"We have a number of co-op students from local colleges working during the summer in various company departments. We also have a number of temporary employees who are hired for approximately six months at a time. The students and temps will move from one department to another, doing various jobs. This happens at all offices. Over the last few years, we have been finding it difficult to keep track of who is a full-time employee, part-time employee, temporary employee, or co-op student."

Systems Infrastructure

The systems infrastructure consists of three domains. San Diego is Domain 1 and consists of three Windows NT 4.0 servers: a PDC, a BDC, and a member server. There are 38,000 users in this domain. The New York office is Domain 2, has a single Windows NT 3.5 server, and there are 7,000 users in this domain. The Atlanta office is Domain 3, and it has two Windows NT 4.0 servers. One of these is a PDC, and the other is a BDC. There are 14,000 users in this domain. San Diego and New York are connected through a T1 line, whereas San Diego and Atlanta are connected with an ISDN line.

TCP/IP is used as a protocol for this network, and each server runs an older, third-party DNS server. Several years ago, the network used Novell NetWare but migrated to Windows NT Server. In the old network infrastructure, NWLink was used to communicate with NetWare servers that used only IPX/SPX. Although NetWare is not used anymore, NWLink has continued to be used as a protocol. Some workstations use only NWLink as a protocol because of a limited number of IP addresses in each domain. There are no WINS servers presently in use on the network for name resolution. See the following illustration:

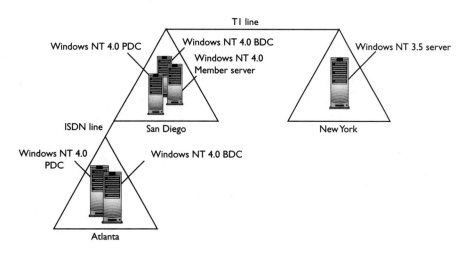

Interview with Sales Manager: Anne Legge

"Our sales reps are on the road quite a bit, and each of them has a laptop computer. To use files on the network and keep in touch with me, they use dial-up networking. Recently, we set up Internet accounts for them so that they can check information on different Web sites, including our own.

Despite having their own laptops, they do use workstations around the various offices of our company. A problem that our sales staff has complained about is that the programs they commonly use are not installed on all machines. This makes them have to either run for their laptops or find a computer with a particular application installed on it."

Interview with Information Technology Manager: Michael Williams

"Few people in our organization need Internet access, and those who do use dial-up accounts. Our e-commerce site is doing well, and we have recently hired an Internet Specialist who will be the Webmaster of our site. We are excited about the new Intranet that we are building for people in our organization to use.

You should also be aware that we have done some analysis on programs being used on our network. A number of major applications are used on the network but have varying importance. The Application 1 is mission critical, and no Windows 2000 version is available. Application 2 is not mission critical, and no Windows 2000 version is available. Application 3 was commonly used until a year ago but has not been used since then. We are not looking forward to installing new software on machines because of the time it takes for our sales staff to make these installations and upgrades of applications on each machine."

Technical Challenges and Considerations

The T1 line between San Diego and New York has a reliable link, but the one between San Diego and Atlanta has gone down several times over the last month. This is a regular occurrence. Each domain contains its own user accounts, and these domains have a complete trust relationship.

The PDC and BDC in San Diego have 20GB hard disks, with over 4GB of free space on each server. Each of these has Pentium III processors and 256MB of RAM. The member server in this domain has a Pentium III processor, 128MB of RAM, and a 10GB hard disk with 850MB of free space. The New York server has 128MB of

RAM, a Pentium 2 processor, and a 2GB hard disk with 1GB of free space. The Atlanta PDC and BDC have 10GB hard disks, with 1GB of free space on the PDC and 1.5GB of free space on the BDC. Each has Pentium 133MHz processing power, with 128MB of RAM.

Upon completion, all servers will be running Windows 2000 Server. There will be no servers running legacy versions of Windows NT. Also, all workstations will be upgraded to Windows 2000 Professional.

Considerable time and expenses have gone into installing software on each workstation. It is desired that the costs involved in sending out IT staff to install applications be lowered by implementing methods that will allow users to install applications themselves safely. The IT Manager would prefer that applications be installed only as users need them.

Growth and Expansion Plans

Urk Medical Products has recognized the value of having an Internet presence and recently has implemented an e-commerce site. The site is located on the server of the ISP that is providing Internet access to sales reps and some other company employees. They have registered the domain name urkmed.com for this site. There is also some discussion about acquiring a small pharmaceutical company called "Dr. Feelgood's Snakeoil, Inc." The vitamin industry is a health-related area that Urk Medical Products would like to develop and manufacture products for.

TESTLET 1: QUESTIONS

1. How will you design the domain structure of this company to best suit the needs of users and network administrators?

    A. Design the domain structure to use multiple forests within a single domain.

    B. Design the domain structure to use a single forest with multiple domains.

    C. Design a single domain structure within a forest. Create a hierarchy of organizational units to organize users and resources.

    D. Design a multiple domain structure. Create a hierarchy of organizational units to organize users and resources.

2. Using the design from the above question, where should domain controllers be placed?

    A. A domain controller should be placed at each site. At least one DC should be placed in San Diego, New York, and Atlanta.

    B. A domain controller should be placed in San Diego and New York.

    C. A domain controller should be placed in San Diego and Atlanta.

    D. A domain controller should be placed in New York and Atlanta.

3. How many FSMO servers will be needed in each domain? (Choose all that apply.)

    A. There will need to be one domain-naming master per domain.

    B. There will need to be one infrastructure master per forest.

    C. There will need to be one RID master per domain.

    D. There will need to be one PDC emulator per domain.

4. As the company experiences growth, which of the following will impact your design? (Choose all that apply.)

    A. Internet access for users

    B. Intranet

C. E-commerce site

D. Increased number of users

5. You are concerned about name resolution on the network and whether current systems can be kept or should be replaced. Which of the following will need to be considered when upgrading to Windows 2000 Server?

A. WINS will need to be used on the network for name resolution.

B. Third-party or older DNS servers are not supported by Windows 2000, unless they are Windows 2000 DNS servers.

C. The current DNS server must use service resource records.

D. The current DNS server must support WINS.

6. Based on the information provided by the Information Technology Manager, determine what should be done with the following applications.

A. Application 1 should be retired.

B. Application 1 should be replaced with a similar application that is Windows 2000 compatible.

C. Application 2 should be retired.

D. Application 3 should be replaced with a similar application that is Windows 2000 compatible.

7. What issues will affect the upgrade of servers to Windows 2000 Server, and what will you need to do to make the upgrades successful? (Choose all that apply.)

A. The New York server is running Windows NT 3.5 Server. It will need to be upgraded to Windows NT 4.0 before it can be upgraded to Windows 2000.

B. The member server in San Diego has insufficient hard disk space. It will need a larger hard disk.

C. The Atlanta PDC has insufficient hard disk space. It will need a larger hard disk.

D. The servers in Atlanta have insufficient processing power. Their processors need to be upgraded.

8. If a single domain structure is used, what is the minimum number of global catalog servers that will be needed on the network?

   A. Two

   B. Three

   C. Four

   D. None

9. You are preparing to upgrade the first Windows NT 4.0 server in the San Diego domain to Windows 2000. Which of these servers will you upgrade first?

   A. The PDC.

   B. The BDC.

   C. The member server.

   D. Any of these servers can be upgraded first.

10. Based on information provided by the company and your own knowledge of Windows 2000, which of the following protocols must be present in your installation of Windows 2000? (Choose all that apply.)

    A. TCP/IP

    B. NWLink

    C. NetBEUI

    D. AppleTalk

11. You need to decide in what mode Windows 2000 will run when performing the upgrade. Which of the following will you choose for this network?

    A. Only Mixed mode can be used on this network because of the types of servers running on the network.

    B. Only Native mode can be used on this network since all servers are running Windows 2000.

    C. Either Mixed or Native mode can be used since all servers are running Windows 2000 Server.

    D. You can switch back and forth between modes because of the types of servers running on this network.

12. After you explain to users in Human Resources that they will be able to make queries and view attributes of user objects, they readdress the issue of tracking employment status. Which of the following will you suggest?

    A. The schema can be modified from the schema master for the domain. Each domain has its own schema and can be modified so that the needed field is added to user objects.

    B. The schema can be modified from any domain controller so that the needed field can be added to user objects.

    C. The schema can be modified from the schema master so that the needed field can be added to user objects.

    D. The schema can be modified from any operation master so that the needed field can be added to the user objects.

13. You assign the task of modifying the schema for Human Resources to a member of your project team. When this person attempts to modify the schema, he cannot. You check and find that he is using the correct computer to modify the schema. You assume that the problem lies in his group membership. Which of the following groups does this person need to be a member of?

    A. The user must be a member of the Schema Admins group.

    B. The user must be a member of the Schema Master group.

    C. The user must be a member of the Enterprise Admins group.

    D. The user must be a member of the Domain Admins group.

14. Once upgrades are completed, you are told that Urk Medical Products has purchased the Dr. Feelgood's Snakeoil, Inc., company. Because of its high sales volume in vitamins, this company will operate as a subsidiary. You have decided to make this company a child domain of the urk.com domain. What will its fully qualified domain name (FQDN) be?

    A. drfeel.urkmed.com

    B. urkmed.drfeel.com

    C. drfeel.com

    D. drfeel.urkmed

15. When implementing Group Policy, you want to specify scripts that will run when a user's computer first boots up. Where will you specify these scripts and configure settings for them?

    A. Scripts and Security Settings, found in Software Settings

    B. Scripts and Security Settings, found in Windows Settings

    C. Scripts and Security Settings, found in Administrative Templates

    D. Administrative Templates will be used, found in Administrative Settings

16. You have decided to use Group Policy to assign and publish packages to users and computers. This will address the problems encountered by users needing updated software or particular programs on machines. What methods will you use to meet the needs of these users? (Choose all that apply.)

    A. Publish applications to the computer so that the sales staff will be able to install the software, regardless of which machine they log on to.

    B. Assign applications to sales staff users so that they will be able to install the software, regardless of which machine they log on to.

    C. Publish applications to users who use a single workstation.

    D. Publish applications to the computer of users who use a single workstation.

17. After upgrading the member server in San Diego to Windows 2000, you decide to make it a domain controller. In doing so, you do not want to lose any data. Which of the following must be present for this server to be promoted? (Choose all that apply.)

    A. The server's hard disk must be formatted as NTFS v5.

    B. Active Directory must be installed on the server.

    C. WINS must be installed on the server.

    D. DNS must be installed on the server.

18. The Information Technology Manager has mentioned he is concerned about the amount of administration the network administrator is required to perform for Human Resources. He would like to delegate administration of the Human Resources organizational unit (OU) to users in this container. This OU resides

below the Admin OU in the hierarchy. He would also like these users to administer the Recruiting OU below this container, and the Training OU below the Recruiting container. How will you delegate administration of OUs so that the Human Resources users control only the OUs they are supposed to control?

A. Delegate administration at the Admin OU level.

B. Delegate administration at the Human Resources OU level.

C. Delegate administration at the Recruiting OU level.

D. Delegate administration at the Training OU level.

19. You are considering modifying your initial design by creating sites so that each of the former domains will be a site. Which of the following will influence your decision and possibly prevent you from implementing sites?

A. The link connecting San Diego and Atlanta.

B. The link connecting San Diego and New York.

C. The lack of a link between New York and Atlanta.

D. Sites can be created only at the time when Windows 2000 is first installed on the first server on the network.

20. You have decided to run the network in Native mode. Upon doing so, what purpose will the PDC emulator serve on the network?

A. The PDC emulator will continue to be available, in case you decide to switch back to Mixed mode and add BDCs to the network.

B. The PDC emulator will be removed from all Windows 2000 servers serving this role.

C. The PDC emulator will become dormant until a downlevel client is added to the network.

D. The PDC emulator will become the final authority for authentication.

TESTLET 2: HADES HOTELS AND RESORTS CASE STUDY

Company Profile and History

Hades Hotels and Resorts is a major company that owns a number of hotels and motels. Its main office is in New York, but it has a Canadian office in Toronto. It also owns a subsidiary chain of popular restaurants called Planet Blech. The restaurant chain is autonomous of the hotel chain and has offices in Atlanta. Recently, Planet Blech has gone global and opened restaurants in Japan. Because of this, it has opened an office in Tokyo to manage these restaurants.

Interview with Chief Executive Officer (CEO): Cathy Hunt

"Just like our logo of a child in an elephant suit, we are a young company that has grown big. If you include administrative, hotel, and restaurant employees, we have almost 70,000 staff members. I expect that number will double in the next few years. We are always looking for new ventures to invest in."

Interview with Restaurant Chain Divisional Manager: Mike Brenton

"Information is commonly exchanged between the Tokyo and Atlanta offices. Not only does this include financial and marketing plans and projections, but it also includes recipes that are exclusive to our chain. We exchange information on a quarterly basis with the hotel chain, since it is the parent company. Security is important to our needs because we cannot risk the secret behind our secret sauce getting out."

Interview with Human Resources Manager: Julie Carruthers

"Because of differences in legislation among the countries, the American, Canadian, and Japanese locations are largely autonomous. There are too many differences in laws dealing with employees, including income taxes, workman's compensation, benefits and so forth. Our hiring practices also differ from country to country. Because of this, the different locations work independently of one another."

Interview with Information Technology Manager: Joe Fragomeni

"Despite the number of users that have accounts in the current domains, only a third of these users are regularly on the network. Many of the accounts are for hotel and restaurant staff so that they can look at their work schedules and access work-related information, such as our employee manual. These users also log on to workstations to input information regarding restaurant orders and hotel bills. The restaurant workers use an application to input orders, which calculates the bill and adds the order to the tally of how much was sold that day. The Divisional Manager of the restaurant chain uses this information to see how much each restaurant is making and what menu items are being ordered. A similar application is used in the hotels to calculate guest bills and track what extra services are being used. Like the restaurant software, the information from the hotel software is used by finance."

Systems Infrastructure

The systems infrastructure consists of four domains. Domain A is located in New York, Domain B is located in Toronto, Domain C is located in Atlanta, and Domain D is located in Tokyo. All of these domains use Windows NT 4.0 Servers and Workstations. The New York office has two servers for its 22,000 users. One is a PDC, and the other is a BDC. The Toronto office also has two servers, but one is a PDC and the other is a member server. This domain has 18,000 users. The Atlanta office has one server that is PDC for that domain. It has 16,000 users. The Japanese office has the same setup as the Toronto office and has one PDC and a member server. It has 13,000 users. The New York and Toronto offices are connected with a 128-Kbps connection. The New York and Atlanta offices are connected with a T1 line. The Atlanta and Tokyo offices use a dial-up connection to exchange data.

There are no DNS servers on the network because WINS is currently used for name resolution. This has worked well for the network, and they have experienced few problems with WINS. WINS is installed on each PDC and BDC on the network. See the illustration on the following page.

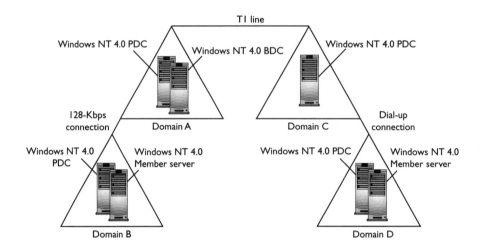

Interview with Information Technology Manager: Joe Fragomeni

"The restaurant chain and hotel chain have differing security needs, so they will need separate security policies. Although links between New York and Toronto, and between Atlanta and Tokyo are slow, it has not been a major concern because of the types of data being transferred. Graphics or large files are rarely transferred between locations. This may change in the future, however, which is why we put in the T1 line between the restaurant and hotel chains. Additional T1 lines have been budgeted for so that all of the domains will be connected with these fast links. These links should be in place before the server upgrade begins."

Interview with Human Resources Manager: Julie Carruthers

"We have concerns about other people accessing resources in our department. We cannot allow users outside of our department access to personnel files. Also, each department is responsible for its own budget, and we have an expensive color laser printer that is hooked up to the network. We do not want people outside of our department printing to it, because it is expensive to maintain."

Technical Challenges and Considerations

Domain A contains the user accounts for Domain B. Domain C and Domain D contain user accounts for their own domains. Domain B trusts Domain A. Domain A and Domain C trust each other. Domain C and Domain D trust each other.

It is important that users are prevented from being able to make changes to their computers. The CEO wants an image of the company logo as the desktop background on all Windows 2000 Professional workstations. The Information Systems Manager wants these users to be prevented from making modifications to system settings on their workstations, and he has expressed concern about users installing programs on their machines.

Interview with Information Technology Manager: Joe Fragomeni

"It is important that you realize that the Japanese domain will continue to use applications that are designed for Windows NT and that this software probably will not run on Windows 2000. Therefore, we want this site to have a Windows NT server running as a BDC. For this same reason, we would also like the member server at the Toronto office running Windows NT Server."

Growth and Expansion Plans

When analyzing current growth trends, a modest estimate of corporate growth is 50 percent over the next three years. The company is growing, but currently there are no plans to acquire or merge with any companies, as current efforts are focused on the success of the new restaurant chain. Because many users are accessing the network for scheduling and informational purposes, an Intranet is expected to be implemented in the next year. The company would like internal email services to be available now but is concerned about the level of administrative tasks that will be added once email servers are in place.

TESTLET 2: QUESTIONS

1. Which of the following is the best design for the new network?

   A. A single domain.

   B. A single domain with each location in a different site.

   C. Two domains with multiple sites. New York and Atlanta would be in one domain but in separate sites. Toronto and Tokyo would be in another domain but in separate sites.

   D. Two domains with multiple sites. New York and Toronto would be in one domain but in separate sites. Atlanta and Tokyo would be in another domain but in separate sites.

2. Which of the following services must be available when the first PDC is upgraded to Windows 2000?

   A. WINS

   B. DNS

   C. IPSec

   D. Active Directory Connector

3. Since the company has offices in several countries, you are concerned about breaking laws regarding data encryption. You want to use the strongest encryption possible that adheres to the laws of each country. You realize that there are different methods used by Windows 2000, and members of your project team offer the following advice. (Choose all that apply.)

   A. The Toronto office can use 56-bit DES IPSec.

   B. The Tokyo office can use 3DES IPSec.

   C. The Atlanta office can use MPPE Standard security.

   D. The New York office can use MPPE Strong security.

4. If left to continue as four domains, which of the domains will need to run in Mixed mode? (Choose all that apply.)

    A. Domain A

    B. Domain B

    C. Domain C

    D. Domain D

5. The Information Technology Manager stresses that the hotel chain and restaurant chain will need different security policies. What limitations do you have in determining the number of security policies that can be maintained after upgrading to Windows 2000?

    A. You can have an unlimited number of security policies in a forest.

    B. There is one security policy per forest.

    C. There is one security policy per domain.

    D. There is no limit to the number of security policies that can be used.

6. Based on the information available to you through analysis and interviews, what impact will the company's growth have on the network design? (Choose all that apply.)

    A. New York will need to be split into two domains because the number of users may double in the next few years.

    B. Since there are no acquisitions or mergers, there is no need to make the design flexible.

    C. The increase in users may be as high as 200 percent over the next few years. Increases in user accounts will increase network traffic.

    D. The proposed Intranet will create additional network traffic.

7. Which of the following is true of the domain models used in the existing Windows NT environment?

    A. Domain A and Domain B follow a master domain model.

    B. Domain C and Domain D follow a master domain model.

    C. All domains follow a single domain model.

    D. All domains follow a multiple-master domain model.

8. Assuming the current domain structure and trust relationships are kept, after Windows 2000 Active Directory has been implemented on this network, what changes will occur in the trust relationships among these domains? (Choose all that apply.)

    A. Domain A and Domain B will trust each other.

    B. Domain B will trust Domain A, but Domain A will not trust Domain B.

    C. Because Domain C and Domain D trust each other, and Domain C and Domain A trust each other, Domain D and Domain A will trust each other.

    D. All trusts will be removed, since they are not used in Windows 2000.

9. When preparing to upgrade the first server in Domain A, you force replication to the BDC. You then remove the BDC from the network. During the upgrade to Windows 2000, problems occur and the upgrade fails. You are unable to restart the server properly after this. What will you do?

    A. Put the BDC back on the network. Upgrade the BDC, because it has the information that was replicated from the PDC.

    B. Keep the failed PDC on the network and perform a clean install of Windows 2000 on it.

    C. Remove the failed PDC from the network and put the BDC on the network. Demote the BDC to a member server, and then upgrade it to Windows 2000.

    D. Remove the failed PDC from the network and put the BDC on the network. Promote the BDC to a PDC, and then upgrade it to Windows 2000.

10. When naming the first domain of your Windows 2000 network, you decide to use the name hadeshotel&resorts.com and to name the first domain controller fs-hades. In attempting to do this, you receive an error message. Which of the following is the problem?

    A. The domain name contains too many characters.

    B. The domain name contains invalid characters.

    C. The fully qualified domain name of the server contains too many characters.

    D. The server name contains invalid characters.

11. After upgrading to Windows 2000, the member server in Domain B will continue to function as a member server. The Information Technology Manager has some knowledge of Windows 2000 and asks where user accounts will be stored on this server. What will you say?

    A. All Windows 2000 servers store user account information in Active Directory.

    B. Only domain controllers store user account information in Active Directory. Member servers will store user account information in the Security Account Manager (SAM) database.

    C. Only PDCs store user account information in Active Directory. BDCs and member servers will store user account information in the SAM database.

    D. Since Domain B is a member server, it will not store user account information.

12. How will you address the concerns of the Human Resources Manager, who does not want users outside of her department accessing resources? (Choose the best answer.)

    A. Create organizational units (OUs) and place Human Resources users and resources in this OU. This will allow them to manage their own resources.

    B. Subnet the network so that this department is on a different IP address. Create a site for this subnet, and assign members of Human Resources to this group. This will allow them to manage their own resources.

    C. Make the Human Resources Manager a member of the Domain Admins group so that she can manage users and resources.

    D. Do nothing. Each user has the ability to take ownership of objects in Active Directory and control access to them.

13. Once migration to Windows 2000 is complete, the Information Technology Manager says that he would like to be able to manage the network from his home computer, which is a 486-computer running Windows 95. What will you do?

    A. Install Windows 2000 Professional on the home machine, and use dial-up networking so that it can connect to the network.

    B. Use Terminal Services. Install Terminal Services Client software on the Windows 95 machine and Terminal Services on the Windows 2000 server.

C. Use Terminal Services. Install Terminal Services on the Windows 2000 server.

D. There is no way to access the Windows 2000 server remotely because this would be a security risk.

14. The CEO and Information Technology Manager have expressed concerns about users changing desktop settings and installing their own applications. What will you do to address these concerns?

A. Use Group Policy to lock down the workstations.

B. Use roaming profiles to control user displays and prevent users from installing software.

C. Publish applications to users.

D. Use organizational units to lock down the workstations.

15. When using Active Directory, the network administrator accidentally deletes an object. In designing and implementing the Windows 2000 Active Directory network, you have not configured a specific amount of time before purges take place. You need to determine what happened to the object and if the object can be restored.

A. Since the default has not been changed, the object cannot be restored because it is purged automatically.

B. Since it is unconfigured, the object can be restored because it will never be purged. Until it is configured, purges will not occur.

C. Since the default has not been changed, objects can be restored within 12 hours. After that, they are purged.

D. Since the default has not been changed, objects can be restored within 24 hours. After that, they are purged.

16. You install Microsoft Exchange Server 5.5 on a domain controller. What issues regarding administrative tasks will be involved that the network administrator should be aware of in using Windows 2000 Server with Exchange?

A. Microsoft Exchange Server 5.5 has the native ability to communicate and synchronize information with Active Directory. This means that any new data will need to be input in only one of the two directories.

B. Microsoft Exchange Server 5.5 does not have the ability to communicate and synchronize information with Active Directory. There is no way either of these directories can communicate with each other or synchronize information. This means that any new data will need to be input into both Active Directory and Exchange.

C. Microsoft Exchange Server 5.5 does not have the ability to communicate and synchronize information with Active Directory. Active Directory Connector is used to provide this capability and uses LDAP to automatically keep information consistent.

D. Microsoft Exchange Server 5.5 does not have the ability to communicate and synchronize information with Active Directory. LDAP is used to provide this ability and uses Active Directory Connector to automatically keep information consistent.

17. Julie is the Human Resources Manager and a member of the HR group and the HRAdmin group. She asks Joe, the Information Technology Manager, to create a new printer object for her in the HR organizational unit so that she can administer it. Joe creates the object and then denies permissions to the HR group so members of this group cannot modify the settings, thereby causing more work for Julie. He gives Julie's user account permissions to change object attributes for the printer. When Julie attempts making modifications, she finds she cannot. Choose all of the following possibilities as to why this might be.

A. Julie does not have ownership of the object.

B. Julie is not a member of the Schema Admins group.

C. Julie is restricted by settings on the HR group.

D. Julie is restricted by settings on the HRAdmin group.

18. You decide to check permissions that have been given to a new printer object. Which of the following is the minimum permission that must be present for a user to make changes to the object and take ownership of it?

A. Full Control

B. Write

C. Read

D. Change All Child Objects

19. You have decided that there are more domain controllers than necessary in a domain, and you want to make one of the domain controllers into a member server. You want to use the fastest, safest possible method. How will you do this?

    A. Run Active Directory Installation Wizard, and remove Active Directory.

    B. Reinstall Windows 2000 without Active Directory on the member server.

    C. Reinstall Windows 2000 and Active Directory on the member server.

    D. You cannot demote a domain controller to a member server.

20. Replication of Active Directory and DNS information is bogging down the network at peak hours when users are logging on the network. The network uses Active Directory–integrated DNS. Which of the following will have an impact on this situation?

    A. The links between each city are too slow, causing replication data to bog down the network at these points.

    B. Replication should be scheduled so that it does not occur during peak hours.

    C. Incremental replication should be implemented so that only changes to DNS are replicated when Active Directory is copied in full to other domain controllers.

    D. Compression should be used so that the replication data is smaller when it is being replicated within a site.

TESTLET I: ANSWERS

1. ☑ **C.** Design a single domain structure within a forest and create a hierarchy of organizational units to organize users and resources. It will be easier to move objects between organizational units (OUs) than it will be to move them between domains. Since some users move often from one department to another, administration will be easier if an OU hierarchy is used in a single domain structure.

    ☒ **A** is incorrect because the various company offices operate as a single entity. Consequently, only one forest or domain is necessary. **B** and **D** are incorrect because multiple domains are again suggested. The design of your domain structure should be kept as simple as possible because this will make the network easier to build and administer.

2. ☑ **C.** A domain controller should be placed in San Diego and Atlanta. Currently, the ISDN line between them is unreliable, so when it goes down, users in Atlanta are unable to log on the network and use network resources. Since the line between San Diego and New York is stable, users in New York are able to log on the DC in San Diego and thus do not necessarily need a DC.

    ☒ **A** is incorrect because the line between San Diego and New York is reliable. Since they will be in the same domain, there is no need for a DC at each site. **B** is incorrect because the T1 line between San Diego and New York is reliable. **D** is incorrect because there is no link between New York and Atlanta. Therefore, any traffic between them would need to go through the unreliable ISDN line between San Diego and Atlanta.

3. ☑ **C** and **D** are correct. There will need to be one RID master and one PDC emulator per domain. These are operation master roles that need to be on each domain. This means that in a forest with more than one domain, there is more than one of each of these FSMO servers.

    ☒ **A** is incorrect because there is only one domain-naming master in a forest. The domain-naming master takes care of all domains in the forest. **B** is incorrect because there is one infrastructure master in each domain.

4. ☑ **B** and **D** are correct. Intranet and an increased number of users. As the company experiences growth, more users will use the network and access the Intranet. More users will mean increased administration because more user accounts will be created and added to groups, and more resources will be consumed. The growth will increase network traffic because the HTML files, graphics, and any applications such as Java applets will be transferred across the network from the Web server to the user's browser. Such increases will affect the design of your network infrastructure.

   ☒ **A** is incorrect because users access the Internet through dial-up access, not through the network. **C** is incorrect because the e-commerce site is hosted on the ISP's server.

5. ☑ **C.** The current DNS server must use service resource records (SRV RRs). Windows 2000 uses SRV RRs to locate services on a network using DNS.

   ☒ **A** is incorrect because the network does not currently use WINS, and Windows 2000 does not require it. Therefore, there is no need to implement it. **B** is incorrect because Windows 2000 can use other DNS servers if they meet the standards required, such as supporting SRV RRs. **D** is incorrect because DNS is separate from WINS, which makes this an invalid requirement.

6. ☑ **B.** Because Application 1 is mission critical but not compatible with Windows 2000, it should be replaced with a similar application. This will allow users to continue doing their jobs, as well as make the application run on a Windows 2000 machine.

   ☒ **A** is incorrect because without this application, some users will be unable to do their jobs. **C** is incorrect because Application 2 is not mission critical. Thus, there should be no problem retiring it. **D** is incorrect because this application has not been used for a year. Since it is not being used, it should be retired.

7. ☑ **A** and **B** are correct. The Windows NT 3.5 server in New York will need to be upgraded to Windows NT 4.0 before it can be upgraded to Windows 2000. There is no upgrade path for versions of Windows NT previous to Windows NT 3.51. Therefore, this server would need to be upgraded to Windows NT 3.51 or migrated to Windows NT 4.0 before upgrading to Windows 2000. The San Diego member server has only 850MB of free disk space, so additional hard disk space is required. Windows 2000 requires a 133MHz or higher Pentium compatible processor, 128MB of RAM, and a 2GB hard disk with 1GB of free space.

☒ **C** and **D** are incorrect because these servers meet the minimum requirements for upgrading to Windows 2000.

8. ☑ **D.** None. The global catalog (GC) is a subset of the objects and attributes making up Active Directory. Since each domain controller will contain a full replica of Active Directory, no GC server is required.

☒ **A, B,** and **C** are incorrect since a GC server is not needed in a single domain network. In a network with more than one domain, a minimum of one GC server is needed for each domain.

9. ☑ **A.** The PDC. The first Windows NT server to be upgraded to Windows 2000 must be the PDC. The PDC holds information used by the domain, including user account information that is replicated to all BDCs. This information is used in an upgrade to build Active Directory.

☒ **B, C,** and **D** are incorrect because the PDC is the first server in a Windows NT domain that must be upgraded to Windows 2000.

10. ☑ **A** and **B** are correct. TCP/IP is heavily used by Windows 2000 and must be present for Windows 2000 to function properly. Since a number of machines still use NWLink, it is important that this protocol also be present in your installation of Windows 2000 so that the Windows 2000 server can communicate with these computers.

☒ **C** is incorrect because NetBEUI is not required by Windows 2000 and is not used on the current network. **D** is incorrect because there are no Apple Macintosh machines on the network, so AppleTalk is not required by the current network or Windows 2000 after upgrades are completed.

11. ☑ **C.** Either Mixed or Native mode can be used since all servers are running Windows 2000 Server. In a pure Windows 2000 environment, either of these modes can be used.

☒ **A** is incorrect because Mixed mode is not the only mode that can be used. Since no Windows NT BDCs are present on the network, Windows 2000 can support either mode. **B** is incorrect because Native or Mixed mode can be used. **D** is incorrect because you cannot switch back and forth between Mixed and Native mode. Once Native mode is in use, you cannot switch back to Mixed mode.

12. ☑ **C.** The schema can be modified from the schema master so that the needed field can be added to user objects. The schema master is the only server that can modify the schema. Because the schema is shared by a forest, there can be only one schema master in a forest.

    ☒   **A** is incorrect because there is only one schema for the entire forest. Therefore, there is one schema master per forest, not per domain. **B** is incorrect because modifications to the schema cannot be made from any domain controller. **D** is incorrect because modifications cannot be made to the schema from any operation master. The schema must be modified on the schema master.

13.   ☑   **A.** The user must be a member of the Schema Admins group. If only users who are members of the Schema Admins group are able to modify the schema, this prevents excessive modification of the schema.

    ☒   **B** is incorrect because there is no Schema Master group in Windows 2000. **C** and **D** are incorrect because only members of the Schema Admins group can modify the schema.

14.   ☑   **A.** FQDNs are hierarchical, with child domains being beneath parent domains. This relationship is read from left to right, with the child domain as the leftmost name, and the parent domain to its right.

    ☒   **B** is incorrect because this name would make urkmed the child domain of drfeel.com. **C** is incorrect because this name removes the new domain from the urkmed namespace. **D** is incorrect because it is missing the .com designation.

15.   ☑   **B.** Windows Settings contains Scripts and Security Settings, which is used to specify one of two types of scripts: startup/shutdown, which runs the script when the computer starts or shuts down, and logon/logoff, which runs when a user logs on or off.

    ☒   **A** and **C** are incorrect because neither Software Settings nor Administrative Templates offers Scripts and Security Settings. **D** is incorrect because there is no Administrative Settings container used for Administrative Templates. Both computer configuration settings and user configuration settings are broken into three sections: Software Settings, Windows Settings, and Administrative Templates.

16.   ☑   **B** and **C** are correct. Assign applications so that sales staff will be able to install the software, regardless of which machine they log on to, and publish applications to users who use a single machine. When an application is assigned to a user, it is advertised when the user logs on. This advertisement follows the user, regardless of what computer this person is using. The first time the user starts the application or opens a file associated with the software, the application is installed. When an application is published to a user, users can install the application through the Add/Remove Programs applet in Control Panel.

    ☒   **A** and **D** are incorrect because an application cannot be published to a computer.

17.   ☑   **A** and **B** are correct. The server's hard disk must be formatted as NTFS v5, and Active Directory must be installed on the server. The installation of Active Directory on a Windows 2000 server makes the server a DC. For AD to be installed, the hard disk must be formatted as NTFS v5, and DNS must be present on the network.

    ☒   **C** is incorrect because Windows 2000 does not require WINS. **D** is incorrect because DNS is already present on the network.

18.   ☑   **B.** Delegate administration at the Human Resources OU level. This will allow the Human Resources users to control that container and the ones below it in the hierarchy. Inheritance will allow lower organizational units to be administered by this group of users.

    ☒   **A** is incorrect because the Admin OU is too high in the hierarchy. Delegation at this level will allow users to control the Admin OU. **C** and **D** are incorrect because they are too low in the hierarchy, so users would be unable to control the Human Resources OU.

19.   ☑   **A.** The link connecting San Diego and Atlanta, which is an ISDN line. Sites need to be connected using fast connections. Because ISDN operates at speeds up to 128 Kbps, and the minimum recommended by Microsoft is 512 Kbps, the connection between the offices is not suitable.

    ☒   **B** is incorrect because this is a T1 line, which is more than fast enough for sites. **C** is incorrect because New York will be able to connect to other sites using its link with San Diego. **D** is incorrect because sites can be created at any time using Active Directory Sites and Services.

20.   ☑   **D.** The PDC emulator will become the final authority for authentication. In Native mode, when a password change is made, the change will take time to replicate to every DC in a domain but will be replicated immediately to the PDC emulator. If a DC cannot authenticate a user because of an invalid password, the password may be invalid because it has not been replicated to the originating DC yet. In such a case, authentication is referred to the PDC emulator, which checks whether the password is valid or not.

    ☒   **A** is incorrect because you cannot switch from Native mode to Mixed mode. Switching modes is a one-time act. **B** and **C** are incorrect because the PDC emulator will not become dormant on the Windows 2000 network after switching to Native mode.

TESTLET 2: ANSWERS

1. ☑ **D.** Two domains with multiple sites. New York and Toronto would be in one domain but in separate sites. Atlanta and Tokyo would be in another domain but in separate sites. These locations need to be separate from one another but still have the ability to exchange information. The restaurant chain and hotel chain exchange information at least quarterly and should be part of the same forest. Because they require different security policies, and since there can be only one security policy per domain, they will need to be separated into two domains. Putting them in different domains would retain their autonomy but make it easier to administer them and allow them to exchange data more easily. Although they are in different countries, placing them in different sites would put the New York and Toronto offices, and the Atlanta and Tokyo offices on different subnets. This would allow them to exchange information easily but keep them separated.

   ☒ **A, B,** and **C** are incorrect because they each place restaurant and hotel locations in the same domain. The restaurant chain and hotel chain are autonomous of one another. Consequently, they should be in different domains.

2. ☑ **B.** DNS is the Domain Name System and is a service that provides name resolution of host names to IP addresses. Windows 2000 uses DNS to locate other domain controllers on the network, and DNS is heavily used by Active Directory. A DNS server must be either available before installing Windows 2000 or installed as part of the Windows 2000 upgrade process.

   ☒ **A** is incorrect because Windows 2000 does not require the Windows Internet Name Service (WINS). Since WINS is installed on each PDC and BDC throughout the network, not having WINS available on the first PDC you upgrade will not disrupt users who use WINS for name resolution. **C** is incorrect because encryption such as IPSec is not essential to the functioning of Windows 2000 Active Directory. **D** is incorrect because Active Directory Connector (ADC) is used to share information with Microsoft Exchange Server.

3. ☑ **A** and **C** are correct. The Toronto office can use 56-bit DES IPSec, and the Atlanta office can use MPPE Standard security. Since information is commonly exchanged among the offices making up the restaurant chain, data will be exchanged between the North American offices and the Japanese office. MPPE Standard security is 40 bit or 56 bit and adheres to U.S. export encryption legislation, as does the 56-bit DES standard of IPSec.

   ☒ **B** and **D** are incorrect because each of these uses a level of encryption that makes it illegal to export data outside of North America. MPPE Strong security uses 128-bit encryption. The 3DES standard of IPSec uses two 56-bit keys and is designed for use in high-security environments located in North America. Neither of these can be used when exporting data outside of the United States and Canada.

4. ☑ **D.** Domain D. Since a BDC will continue to run in this domain, the Windows 2000 network for this domain will run in Mixed mode. Windows 2000 must run in Mixed mode if there are Windows NT 4.0 BDCs running in the domain.

   ☒ **A** and **C** are incorrect because Domain A and Domain C will be running Windows 2000 servers, and no BDCs will be present in either of these domains. Therefore, Windows 2000 could run in either Mixed or Native mode. **B** is incorrect because this domain will run a Windows NT member server, but no BDC will be present in the domain.

5. ☑ **C.** There is one security policy per domain. Windows 2000 allows you to implement one security policy in each domain. If additional security policies are needed, additional domains must be created.

   ☒ **A** and **B** are incorrect because the number of security policies that can be implemented is not determined by the forest. **D** is incorrect because there can be only one security policy per domain.

6. ☑ **C** and **D** are correct. Increases in user accounts will increase network traffic. The CEO expects the number of employees to double in the next few years. Although the modest estimate is 50 percent, you should use the higher number for your design. Even though all users are not constantly using the network, they do access the network to input data or access information. A new Intranet is being planned for the company, which these users will probably access to view scheduling and other information. Since there will be more users accessing information, this will mean higher traffic. The content being accessed

through the Intranet indicates that HTML documents, graphics, and other data will be transferred from the Web server to a user's computer, thus adding to traffic.

☒ **A** is incorrect because there is no 40,000 user limit in Windows 2000. This was a limitation of Windows NT domains. It has been removed in Windows 2000 because Active Directory can support millions of objects. **B** is incorrect because any design should be flexible.

7. ☑ **A.** Domain A and Domain B follow a Master Domain model. This model has a single master domain with additional domains containing network resources. The master domain (Domain A) contains user accounts and can contain network resources, whereas the resource domain (Domain B) contains network resources. The resource domain trusts the master domain, allowing user accounts in the master to be granted permissions to resources in the resource domain. Accounts created in the resource domain cannot be granted permissions to resources.

☒ **B** is incorrect because both Domain C and Domain D contain user accounts for their own domains, and no resource domains are used. Therefore, these domains use a Single Domain model. **C** is incorrect because Domain A contains the user accounts for Domain B, and trust relationships do not exist between all domains. **D** is incorrect because a multiple master domain has two or more domains containing user accounts that act as master domains. These domains have trust relationships with resource domains below them.

8. ☑ **A** and **C** are correct. Trust relationships in Windows 2000 are bi-directional and transitive. Being bi-directional means that both domains trust each other. Thus, Domain A and Domain B will trust each other. Being transitive means that the trust relationship passes from one domain to another. Therefore, because Domain C and Domain D trust each other, and Domain C and Domain A trust each other, Domain D and Domain A will trust each other.

☒ **B** is incorrect because trusts in Windows 2000 are two-way trusts. This means that, because a trust relationship exists between Domain A and Domain B, both Domain A and Domain B will trust each other. **D** is incorrect because trust relationships are used in Windows 2000.

9. ☑ **D.** Promote the BDC to a PDC, and then upgrade it to Windows 2000. Since the BDC has the replicated information from the PDC, upgrading it to a PDC will provide you with a server that is the same as the one you initially

attempted the upgrade on. This will allow you to roll back the upgrade. You can use the BDC you promoted to PDC to upgrade to Windows 2000, and use the existing domain information on the new PDC.

☒ **A** is incorrect because the first server upgraded in the domain must be a PDC. **B** is incorrect because this will require you to rebuild any domain information, including all user accounts. **C** is incorrect because the first server to be upgraded in the domain must be a PDC.

10. ☑ **B.** The domain name contains invalid characters. Windows 2000 supports the DNS characters A to Z, a to z, 0 to 9, and the hyphen (-). The ampersand (&) cannot be used as part of the domain name.

☒ **A** is incorrect because domain names can be up to 63 characters in length, including periods. **C** is incorrect because the total length of the fully qualified domain name (FQDN) can be 155 characters for domain controllers. **D** is incorrect because the server name contains valid characters.

11. ☑ **B.** Only domain controllers store user account information in Active Directory. Member servers will store user account information in the Security Account Manager (SAM) database. Although the SAM database is associated with Windows NT 4.0, Windows 2000 still uses the SAM to store user accounts on a member server.

☒ **A** is incorrect because member servers do not use AD to store user account information. Only domain controllers use Active Directory for storing user accounts, which are replicated among all domain controllers. **C** is incorrect because a Windows 2000 server can be a domain controller or a member server. Windows 2000 servers do not use the PDC and BDC roles. **D** is incorrect because member servers do have the ability to store user account information in the SAM database.

12. ☑ **A.** Create organizational units (OUs) and place Human Resources users and resources in this OU. Organizational units are used to organize users, groups, computers, and other resources, and they allow members of the OU to manage their own resources.

☒ **B** is incorrect because this will not give users the ability to control their own resources. Although members of this department will be on a different site, they will not have the ability to manage their own resources. **C** is incorrect because although this would give the Human Resources Manager the ability to control users and resources, it would give the user more security access than is necessary. **D** is incorrect because users do not have the ability to take ownership of AD objects or control access to them.

13. ☑ **B.** Use Terminal Services. Install Terminal Services Client software on the Windows 95 machine and Terminal Services on the Windows 2000 Server. Terminal Services Client software provides terminal emulation, allowing applications to be accessed from a Windows-based terminal, a remote PC, or even a non-Windows device. Terminal Services is a service that allows users to access Windows 2000 software.

☒ **A** is incorrect because Windows 2000 Professional cannot be installed on this machine. It does not meet the minimum requirements for this computer. **C** is incorrect because Terminal Services Client software needs to be running on the Windows 95 computer. **D** is incorrect because Terminal Services is available to access Windows 2000 software remotely.

14. ☑ **A.** Use Group Policy to lock down the workstations. Group Policies allow you to control the display settings of users, keeping them from making the modifications that the CEO of this company does not want them to make. It also allows you to keep users from installing software or changing settings, which is the concern of the Information Technology Manager.

☒ **B** is incorrect because although roaming profiles can be used to control the display, they cannot be used to lock down a computer so that users are unable to install their own software. **C** is incorrect because when an application is published, the user must still install it through the Add/Remove Programs applet in Control Panel. **D** is incorrect because OUs are not used to lock down workstations.

15. ☑ **C.** Since the default has not been changed, objects can be restored within 12 hours of the last purge. When objects are marked for deletion, they are not deleted automatically but are marked as a "tombstone." A tombstone is similar to a file that is deleted and sent to the Recycle Bin. It is marked for deletion but is not actually gone from Active Directory. These purges are called garbage collections and occur by default every 12 hours.

☒ **A** is incorrect because the object can be restored and is not purged automatically. **B** is incorrect because the default for garbage collection is every 12 hours. **D** is incorrect because the default interval between garbage collections is 12 hours.

16. ☑ **C.** Microsoft Exchange Server 5.5 does not have the ability to communicate and synchronize information with Active Directory. Active Directory Connector (ADC) provides the ability to automate administrative tasks such as creating a new mailbox when a new user is created, tracking its changes, and removing the mailbox if the user is ever removed from the system. It uses the Lightweight Directory Access Protocol (LDAP) to automatically keep information consistent between the Exchange Server and Active Directory. When changes are made to either directory, the information is synchronized with the other directory.

☒ **A** is incorrect because Microsoft Exchange Server 5.5 does not have the native ability to communicate and synchronize with AD. **B** is incorrect because ADC can be used to provide the capability for AD and Exchange to communicate and synchronize information. **D** is incorrect because the purposes of ADC and LDAP are reversed in this choice.

17. ☑ **A** and **C** are correct. Julie does not have ownership of the object and is restricted by settings on the HR group. By default, the user who creates the object is made its owner, giving him or her full control over it. If you do not have access to a particular object you created, then ownership allows you to grant yourself access. Since Julie is also a member of the HR group, which has been denied permissions to change the object, these permissions will take precedence over any permissions assigned to Julie's user account.

☒ **B** is incorrect because the Schema Admins group is used to modify the schema but is not necessary to manage object attributes. **D** is incorrect because restrictions have not been placed on this group.

18. ☑ **A.** Full Control. Full Control is a permission that allows you to take ownership and change permissions on an object. When this permission is selected, all other standard permissions are also allowed.

☒ **B** is incorrect because the Write permission will give the user only the ability to change the object's permissions. It will not allow the user to take ownership of the object. **C** is incorrect because the Read permission allows users to view permissions, ownership, objects, and their attributes. **D** is incorrect because Change All Child Objects allows a user to add any type of child object to an OU.

19. ☑ **A.** Run Active Directory Installation Wizard. This will allow you to remove Active Directory from the server and demote it from a domain controller (DC) to a member server.

☒ **B** is incorrect because it is not the fastest, safest possible method. This will make the DC a member server, but it will take longer because it requires reinstalling the entire operating system. **C** is incorrect because reinstalling Active Directory will make the server a DC again. **D** is incorrect because DCs can be demoted to member servers.

20. ☑ **B.** Replication should be scheduled so that it does not occur during peak hours. This will prevent replication from taking place during times when there is the greatest activity, such as when users are logging on the network.

☒ **A** is incorrect because the Information Technology Manager stated that T1 connections would be in place before server upgrades began. Since these should be in place after the servers are upgraded, link speed would not be impacting this situation. **C** is incorrect because incremental replication copies just the changes, whether these are changes to DNS information or to AD itself. **D** is incorrect because compression is available for replication between sites, but it is not available for replication within a site.